Managing Innovation and Change

D0424736

This critical introduction discusses the origins of creativity, group approaches to innovation, managing innovative teams and how to manage organizations. By understanding the psychological principles, theories and techniques applied in these areas, managers can improve organizational strategies and their responses to change. This book:

- explores how organizations can enhance the creativity of their staff and the psychological reasons for resistance to change;
- describes case histories of innovation and change to illustrate theory in practice;
- considers the individual, group and organizational contexts;
- discusses the controversial topic of organization development and the competencies needed to be effective.

In addition to managers and HR professionals, students of management and occupational psychology at undergraduate and MBA level will benefit from the clear and concise coverage of this importance topic.

NIGEL KING is Reader in Psychology in the Department of Behavioural Sciences, and Director of the Primary Care Research Group, University of Huddersfield. A Chartered Psychologist and active researcher in the areas of creativity, innovation and change in organizations, he has contributed to a number of books.

NEIL ANDERSON is Professor of Work Psychology in the Department of Psychology, Goldsmiths' College, University of London. He is a Chartered Occupational Psychologist and a Fellow of the American Psychological Association. He is an active researcher in the area of innovation and creativity at work. He has contributed to a number of books and is co-editor of the *Handbook of Industrial, Work and Organizational Psychology*.

Psychology at Work

Series editor: Clive Fletcher

This series interprets and examines people's work behaviour from the perspective of occupational psychology. Each title focuses on a central issue in management, emphasizing the role of the individual's workplace experience.

Books in the series include:

Creating the Healthy Organization
Well-being, Diversity and Ethics at Work
Sue Newell

Impression Management
Building and Enhancing Reputations at Work
*Paul Rosenfeld, Robert A. Giacalone
and Catherine A. Riordan*

Managing Employee Performance
Design and Implementation in Organizations
Richard S. Williams

Managing Innovation and Change
A Critical Guide for Organizations
Nigel King and Neil Anderson

Managing Teams
A Strategy for Success
Nicky Hayes

Recruitment and Selection
A Framework for Success
Dominic Cooper, Ivan Robertson and Gordon Tinline

Psychology
at Work

Managing Innovation and Change

A Critical Guide for Organizations

Nigel King and Neil Anderson

THOMSON

TM

Australia • Canada • Mexico • Singapore • Spain • United Kingdom • United States

Managing Innovation and Change: A Critical Guide for Organizations – 2nd edition

Copyright © Nigel King and Neil Anderson 2002

The Thomson logo is a registered trademark used herein under licence.

For more information, contact Thomson, Berkshire House,
168–173 High Holborn, London, WC1V 7AA or visit us on the World Wide Web at:
http://www.thomsonlearning.co.uk

British Library Cataloguing-in-Publication Data
A catalogue record for this book is available from the British Library

ISBN 1-86152-783-7

First edition published 1995 by Routledge, under the title
Innovation and Change in Organizations

This edition 2002 by Thomson

Typeset by LaserScript, Mitcham, Surrey
Printed in Great Britain by TJ International, Padstow, Cornwall
Cover design by Metamorphosis
Text design by Malcolm Harvey Young

Contents

Figures

Every effort has been made to obtain permission for the reproduction of these figures. If you have any queries, please contact the publisher.

Tables

Boxes

Series editor's preface

Understanding the psychology of individuals and teams is of prime importance in work settings as rapid and far-reaching changes continue to occur. Organizational structures are shifting radically to the point where individual managers and professionals have far greater autonomy, responsibility and accountability. Organizations are seeking to reduce central control and to 'empower' individual employees. These employees combine in teams that are frequently cross-functional and project based rather than hierarchical in their construction. The traditional notion of careers has changed; increasingly, an individual's career is less likely to be within a single organization, which has implications for how organizations command loyalty and commitment. The full impact of information technology has now been felt, with all the consequences this has for the nature of work and the reactions of those doing it.

The capacity of people to cope with the scale and speed of change has become a major issue and the literature on work stress only increases. The belief in the importance of individuals' cognitive abilities and personality make-up in determining what they achieve and how they contribute to teamwork has been demonstrated in the explosive growth in organizations' use of psychometric tests and related procedures. Perhaps more than ever before, analysing and understanding the experience of work from a psychological perspective is necessary to achieve the twin goals of effective performance and quality of life. Unfortunately, it is the latter of these that all too often seems to be overlooked in the concern to create competitive, performance driven, or customer focused cultures within companies.

It is no coincidence that the rise in the study of business ethics and increasing concern over issues or fairness paralleled many of the organizational changes of the late twentieth century. Ultimately, an imbalance between the aims and needs of the employees and the aims and needs of the organization is self-defeating. One of the widely recognized needs for the twenty-first century is for a greater emphasis on innovation rather than on simply reacting to pressures. However, psychological research and theory indicate that innovation is much more likely to take place where individuals feel secure enough to take the risks involved, and where organizational reward systems encourage experimentation and exploration which they have signally failed to do in the last century. Seeking to help organizations realize the potential of their workforce in a mutually enhancing way is the business challenge psychology has to meet.

The central theme of the *Psychology at Work* series is to interpret and explain people's work behaviour in the context of a continually evolving pattern of change, and to do so from the perspective of occupational and organizational psychology. Each of the books draws together academic research and practitioner experience, relying on empirical studies, practical examples, and case studies to communicate their ideas. The reader, whether a student, manager or psychologist, will find that they provide a succinct summary of accumulated knowledge and a guide to how to apply it in business. The themes of some of the books cover traditional areas of occupation psychology, while others focus on topics that cut across such boundaries, tackling subjects that are of growing interest and prominence. They are directly relevant for practitioners, consultants and students of HR and occupational psychology but much of what they deal with is of great value to managers, and students of management, more generally. This broad appeal is demonstrated by the fact that an earlier version of the series, the *Essential Business Psychology* series, was highly commended by the Management Consultancies Association book award. The *Psychology at Work* series shares the aims, and some of the titles, as the original series but the individual books have been substantially updated and the range of titles is expanded. Although the books share a common aim and series heading, they have not been forced into a rigid stylistic format. In keeping with the times, the authors have had a good deal of autonomy in deciding how to organize and present their work. I think all of them have done an excellent job; I hope you will find that too.

Clive Fletcher

1 Introduction

After reading this chapter you should be able to

- define 'innovation'
- define 'organizational change'
- identify innovation research questions at three levels of analysis
  (a) individual
  (b) group
  (c) organization
- overview the structure of this book.

This book provides a critical introduction to the psychology of innovation and change at work. It is a broad, complex subject, and one which crosses many of the traditional boundaries within psychology – thus as well as occupational psychology, we will be looking at relevant work from social, cognitive, personality and lifespan developmental psychology. We will also be drawing on material from other related disciplines – particularly from organizational behaviour and the sociology of organizations. Nevertheless, our central focus is a psychological one, examining the way that people (individually and collectively) are involved in and affected by processes of change in organizations. In this introductory chapter we will examine how innovation and organizational change have been defined and outline how these topics have been studied by occupational psychologists, before describing the structure of the rest of the book.

Innovation and organizational change: defining the fields

The terms 'innovation' and 'organizational change' have become management buzz-words over the last twenty years. Business leaders and politicians have constantly urged upon industry the need to respond to competition by becoming more innovative, whilst management gurus have achieved best-seller status by offering recipes for how to enact such change successfully. At the same time, occupational health specialists have blamed rapid organizational change for increases in stress-related illnesses, an issue considered important enough to be the subject of a European Community directive. Yet despite the familiarity of the terms, defining them with any precision has proved problematic.

Innovation

If we take the narrower concept of innovation first, the main definitional issue which has occupied academic writers is how to distinguish it from organizational change generally. After all, if this cannot be done then the use of two separate terms does little more than muddy the waters. Probably the most widely cited formulation of this distinction is that developed by Michael West and colleagues (West and Farr, 1990; King and West, 1987). They characterize organizational innovation as follows.

- An innovation is a tangible product, process or procedure within an organization. A new idea may be the starting point for an innovation, but cannot be called an innovation in itself.
- An innovation must be new to the social setting within which it is introduced (e.g. work group, department or whole organization) although not necessarily new to the individual(s) introducing it.
- An innovation must be intentional rather than accidental. If a factory reduced its production because of the effects of a heatwave on staff and equipment, this would not be an innovative action. If, however, the factory took the same action in order to improve product quality or decrease staff sickness, we could describe it as innovative (so long as it also met the above criterion of novelty).

- An innovation must not be a routine change. The appointment of a new member of staff to replace one who had retired or resigned would not be considered an innovative change. The creation of an entirely new post would.
- An innovation must be aimed at producing benefit to the organization, some subsection of it, and/or the wider society (whether it succeeds in so doing is another matter). Intentionally destructive actions such as sabotage or purely whimsical changes are excluded from the definition.
- An innovation must be public in its effects. If an individual introduces a change to his or her work which has no discernible impact on, or implications for, other people in the organization, it would not be considered an innovation.

This approach is not without its weaknesses. As Nigel Nicholson (1990) has argued, it can be seen as simply pushing the definitional problems back a step, so that we face the difficulty of defining what is meant by terms such as 'intentional', 'beneficial' and even 'new'. Nicholson suggests that instead of trying to impose their definitions of innovation on the organizations they study, researchers should focus their investigations on the way that the term is defined and used by people in organizations. Another criticism that can be made of West's definition is that it does not take into account the scale or scope of the products, processes or procedures to which it is applied. By implication, any change meeting the above criteria – no matter how trivial – could be called an innovation. Writers such as Kimberly (1981) have argued that it only makes sense to define as innovations those changes which have a substantial impact upon the organization (or subdivision of an organization) into which they are introduced. This makes sense in that the changes which concern managers are those which may significantly influence organizational performance, but setting criteria for what is or is not a substantial change is extremely difficult – especially as this may not be apparent when a new idea is first adopted.

As a conceptual basis for theorizing about innovation, West's definition has limitations, but as a pragmatic working definition it remains valuable. It fits well with common usage of the term amongst academics and managers, and provides boundaries to the field to which most researchers and practitioners would not strongly object.

Organizational change

If it is hard to identify innovation as a distinct area within organizational change research, it is harder still to characterize the wider field of organizational change more generally. The term 'change' is so broad that it could be taken to embrace almost every topic in organizational psychological research. But if we look at the contents of texts on organizational change we see that they tend to focus predominantly on the management of formally planned changes, especially changes to the ways in which the organization relates to its environment and different parts of the organization relate to each other. Routine, maturational, evolutionary or accidental changes to organizations receive less attention, as do changes emerging from levels of the organization below senior management.

From this it appears that the types of change predominantly addressed by writers on organizational change do not differ greatly from those encompassed by the innovation field. Where there is a difference is in the perspective taken. The label 'organizational change' generally indicates a macro-level approach, which is more concerned with the organization as a whole and its major subsystems than with the experiences of small work groups and individuals. Similarly, the focus is very much on large-scale changes, whereas innovation research sometimes concerns itself with changes which are quite localized in their impact within an organization. For this reason it has mostly been the case that innovation research has been conducted over recent years by organizational psychologists, whilst organizational change and development has remained largely in the domain of management scientists and organizational sociologists. Finally, innovation research tends to be at least as much concerned with the origination and initiation of changes as with their implementation, whilst organizational change research places its emphasis firmly on implementation. Nevertheless, in many cases either of the terms could be validly applied to a piece of research, particularly on topics such as management styles and individual or group resistance to change.

Studying innovation and organizational change

Who is 'the innovator'?

A brief scan through managerial and professional job advertisements reveals the different ways in which 'the innovator' can be defined. Commonly it is the individual, where a company states that it is looking for 'an innovative person' to fill a particular post. Sometimes the emphasis is on the work group where the request is for someone to join 'an innovative team'. On other occasions the organization describes itself as 'innovative'. These distinctions neatly illustrate the fact that innovation can be studied at several different levels of analysis: the individual, the group or the organization. (A wider societal level of analysis also exists, but is beyond the scope of this book.) The research questions addressed by occupational psychologists vary according to the level which is the main focus of interest. Table 1.1 presents some of the key research questions that have been addressed at each of the three levels.

Table 1.1	Research questions at different levels of analysis		
	Individual level	Group level	Organizational level
	How should organizations select for creativity?	What are the characteristics of innovative work groups?	What are the causes and consequences of resistance to change?
	Can training enhance creative performance at work?	What implications have social psychological theories of group processes for understanding organizational innovation and change?	Is there an ideal structure, climate and culture for innovation?
	How is individual creativity related to organizational innovation?		Does the innovation process develop in clearly defined stages?
		How effective are team-building initiatives for promoting innovation?	How manageable is organizational change?
			What are the pros and cons of using internal and external change agents?

Of course, an important point to note is that although these three levels of analysis provide a convenient way of organizing the literature, they also impose something of a false boundary between each of the levels. Indeed, one of the most significant contributions which innovation research can offer to the understanding of organizational behaviour is the possibility of integrating different levels of analysis (Staw, 1984). For instance, to obtain an accurate picture of the effects upon innovative performance of differing management styles, we can look at their impact on individual subordinates, on work groups and on the entire organization. Another reason for not treating the boundaries between levels of analysis as rigid and impermeable is that some of the most interesting research questions are concerned with the interfaces between levels. To take one example: when examining the effectiveness of innovation project teams, it is crucial to look at the way they interact with the wider organizational structure, climate and culture as well as processes such as leadership and communication within the teams.

Approaches to research

As with other topics in work and organizational psychology, most research into innovation and change has taken a positivist stance; that is to say, it has been concerned with establishing causal relationships between variables and producing general theories applicable across many – if not all – organizational settings. Most of this research is quantitative in nature, producing numerical data (for example, ratings on standardized survey measures) which are subject to statistical analysis. Over the last decade, however, there has been a growing interest in non-positivist perspectives in this area, including social constructionist, phenomenological and grounded theory approaches (e.g. Steyaert, Bouwen and van Looy, 1996; Meston and King, 1996; Symon, 2000; Carrero, Peiró and Salanova, 2000). Whilst there are important differences amongst these approaches, they share an emphasis on attempting to understand innovation and change in particular contexts, a suspicion of individualistic explanations, and the utilization of qualitative methods such as depth or semi-structured interviews, participant observation and analysis of documentary materials. (See Williams and May, 1996, for a good account of the philosophical issues associated with the choice of research approach and method.)

In terms of specific research designs, five broad types can be identified. We will come across many examples of these later in the book, and critically consider their strengths and weaknesses. Here we will confine ourselves to a brief description of each.

- *Experimental designs* involve the manipulation of one or more variables in order to determine their causal relationship to a further variable (or variables). In a true experiment, a comparison is made with a control condition in which the experimental manipulation is not made. Most experimental studies are conducted in laboratory settings, though sometimes field experiments are possible. In the areas covered in the present volume, experimental designs are most commonly used in studies of creativity (see Chapters 2 and 3) and of group processes (see Chapter 4).

- *Cross-sectional studies* involve measuring a range of variables in one or more organization(s) at a single point in time, in order to examine their association with some aspect of innovation/change. Often this has meant comparing individuals, groups or organizations to test predictions that the presence or absence of certain characteristics is associated with differences in attitudes or behaviour towards changes. For instance, organizations in the same sector with flat structures might be compared with those with more stratified structures in terms of members' attitudes towards innovation.

- *Repeated measures* (or *before-and-after* designs) require the researcher to measure the selected variables at two or more points in time: perhaps immediately prior to the introduction of a major innovation, immediately after its implementation and one year later. This type of study provides the researcher with a better opportunity to examine cause and effect in innovation/change processes than does the cross-sectional design. For example, if a cross-sectional study found a significant positive correlation between office staff's attitudes towards new technology and reactions to computerization, we could not tell whether their attitudes caused their hostility or whether the computerization had caused them to form negative attitudes towards new technology generally. With a before-and-after design, if attitudes to new technology before computerization were found to predict subsequent reactions, we could feel some confidence in saying that the former played a role in causing the latter. (Of course, it is essential that the researcher is aware of other factors which might have affected the outcome variable he or she is looking at.)

- *Longitudinal designs*, like repeated measures, involve collecting data over a period of time. The difference is that a true longitudinal study requires many more data collection points than the two or three usually seen in repeated measures studies, because the aim is to produce as full a description as possible of the way in which the innovation/change process unfolds. Longitudinal studies therefore often need to continue for long periods, perhaps several years. A good example of this approach is the Minnesota Innovation Research Program (Van de Ven, Angle and Poole, 1989; Van de Ven, Polley, Garad and Venkataraman, 1999), in which a large team of researchers followed the development of 14 diverse major innovations over a period of seven years, using a variety of methods including interviews, questionnaires, observations and analysis of documents such as the minutes of meetings.

- *Retrospective designs* aim to reconstruct the histories of innovations/ changes in one or more organization(s). For researchers working from a positivist perspective, such studies always face the problem of potentially unreliable and incomplete data, so they typically strive to use as many sources as possible. Interviews or questionnaires may be used to gather information from organizational members, clients or customers, suppliers and other business associates. These may be supplemented by analysis of formal and informal documentation such as minutes of meetings and various kinds of reports. Non-positivist researchers are not generally concerned with the accuracy of retrospective accounts. Rather, their interest is in the uses to which organizational members put their stories about innovations; to justify or challenge different responses to change, for example, or to make sense of their own reactions in terms of professional and organizational cultures and identities.

Structure of the book

Although this book is not explicitly divided into sections covering the three levels of analysis noted earlier, the next seven chapters may be seen as moving from a largely individualistic focus (Chapters 2 and 3), through the group level (Chapter 4) to an organizational focus (Chapters 5 to 8). We would reiterate our earlier point that these distinctions are ones of convenience and disguise considerable overlap; for instance, in examining how individuals generate new ideas we must inevitably consider the kind of organizational structure, climate and culture within which they are working.

The *Psychology at Work* series, of which this text is a part, aims to provide relevant, usable psychological knowledge. We thus begin in Chapter 2 by addressing the practical question of how organizations may attempt to enhance the creativity of their staff members. Starting with a critical discussion of issues in the definition and measurement of creativity, we go on to examine the various creativity enhancement strategies available to organizations. These include idea generation techniques such as 'brainstorming' (with special reference to recent developments in electronic brainstorming), creativity training, selecting and assessing for creativity, and developing creative climates. We note that despite the widespread use of such strategies, evaluations of their effectiveness within real organizations remain rare.

Chapter 3 continues on the theme of individual creativity, but here we present an overview of psychological research on the subject, not restricting ourselves to that which is particularly focused on workplace creativity. This chapter serves to put the more applied work covered in Chapter 2 into a broader theoretical context. It also lays foundations for subsequent chapters, as much of the work on innovation at the group and organizational levels draws on an understanding of the nature of individual creativity – for instance, in predicting which leadership styles will encourage or discourage innovation. We stress that creativity is not just the concern of cognitive psychologists and personality theorists, but that developmental and especially social psychological understandings are of great importance.

Chapter 4 is concerned with the impact of group processes on innovation in organizations. The first part of the chapter examines the relevance of social psychological research into group processes for understanding organizational innovation. Three areas are considered: social influence, group decision making and social identity. We will also look at the potential contribution of social constructionist approaches which have risen to prominence in European Social Psychology in recent years. The latter part of this chapter goes on to evaluate studies conducted by organizational psychologists into work group innovation.

Five main factors are identified as influencing innovativeness in groups: leadership style, group composition, group structure, group climate, and group longevity and development. The chapter concludes by examining the increasingly popular use of team-building techniques in organizations.

Chapters 5 and 6 set out to overview the mass of research over the last twenty years or so into innovation at the organizational level. In Chapter 5 the focus is on research which has sought to identify factors that facilitate or inhibit organizational innovation, the underlying aim being to explain why some organizations (or parts of organizations) are more innovative than others. Four main groups of factors are considered: people, structure, climate and culture, and environment. Chapter 6 moves on to discuss the literature devoted to describing and explaining the nature of the innovation process, using longitudinal or retrospective research designs. An important issue here is whether there is any value in trying to devise a general model of the innovation process which is applicable to all types of innovation in all organizations.

From a broad coverage of the organizational innovation literature, we proceed in Chapter 7 to consider specifically the sometimes controversial topic of organization development (OD). OD can best be described as a series of planned intervention techniques designed to improve organizational functioning and employee psychological well-being, including innovation and creativity, these techniques being based upon well-established behavioural scientific principles and research. This chapter contrasts the proliferation of OD practice, particularly by independent consultants, with the paucity of applied evaluative research over recent years. It also considers the range of popular OD techniques used by change agents and the evidence to support their efficacy. The chapter concludes with a discussion of the competencies required to be an effective OD consultant and, by implication, those sought by managers when buying-in OD expertise to their organizations.

The penultimate chapter in this text, Chapter 8, turns to an issue which has received undiminished attention in the management literature over the last five decades – resistance to change. In this chapter, however, resistance is viewed from an essentially *psychological* vantage point. We consider some of the classical writings on resistance, the common theme binding all of them being, we argue, a naïve and managerialist assumption that resistance is counter-productive – even irrational – behaviour which 'needs to be overcome'. We show that resistance is rarely, if ever, irrational to those engaging in it, and can sometimes be constructive for the organization as a whole. The review discusses the multitude of reasons why individuals may resist change at work and how resistance can be manifest both as a covert, hidden response and as overt behaviour varying in severity from minor grumbling to acts of sabotage.

In our concluding chapter we draw together some of the main themes emerging from the rest of the book and highlight the issues that we believe will be at the forefront of concerns for both managers and researchers in the near future.

Using this book

Naturally we would not want to discourage anyone from reading this book from cover to cover, and the structure described above progresses logically towards a rounded picture of innovation and change research at its different levels of analysis. Nevertheless, we recognize that for some readers certain topics are likely to be of paramount interest, and they will want to turn straight to the chapters relating to them – OD in Chapter 8, perhaps, or creativity in Chapters 2 and 3. We have borne this in mind when writing the book, and it is therefore possible to 'dip into' individual chapters without having to read preceding chapters first. We hope, though, that such readers will be tempted to turn to the remaining chapters, as there is much to learn from the overlaps and interconnections between topics within this area. We have included case histories of innovation and change throughout the book which provide detailed illustrations of points made in the text. To give credence to the claim that organizational change and innovation are processes which touch most people's working lives, many of these are based upon real-life examples, including first-hand experiences of the authors.

Change and innovation remain ever-present aspects of the experiences of people in virtually all industrial, commercial and service organizations in public and private sectors of the economy. An understanding of the application in these areas of psychological principles, theories and techniques holds out the promise of improving organizational strategies and responses to change and of maximizing the benefits and minimizing the costs of innovation to people in the workplace.

2   Enhancing creativity at work

After reading this chapter you should be able to

- define 'creativity'
- identify different types of measures of creativity
- describe different creativity enhancement and idea generation techniques
- discuss the advantages and disadvantages in selecting for creativity.

It is conventional to view the innovation process as starting with the spark of individual creativity; a clever and original idea adopted by organizational decision makers and implemented as a significant change to products, practices or procedures. This rather simple picture has been increasingly challenged in recent years, both in terms of the limitations of an individualistic account of creativity (Montuori and Purser, 1999) and the inaccuracy of linear 'stage' models of innovation (King, 1992). Nevertheless, few writers would disagree that creativity plays an important part in organizational innovation, even if its role is less straightforward than is often envisaged. Because of the practical and applied bias of this book we will turn immediately to issues concerning how a psychological understanding of creativity can be used to enhance creative performance at work. In Chapter 3 we will provide an overview of the broader academic literature on creativity.

There is no problem for managers in obtaining advice and assistance with creativity enhancement – consultants offer numerous training programmes, idea elicitation packages, selection instruments and the like, and popular texts on the subject abound. The difficulty rather is in assessing the effectiveness of such services and materials, as all too often they have not been properly evaluated. Fortunately a number of good reviews exist in the area, including Stein's (1974, 1975) classic two-volume work *Stimulating Creativity*, Hocevar and Bachelor's (1989) review of creativity measures, and Kabanoff and Rossiter's (1994) overview of 'Recent developments in applied creativity'. However, before we look at the evidence concerning effective creativity enhancement, we need to consider what we mean by creativity and how it can be measured.

Defining creativity

Defining concepts in psychology is never a simple matter, and creativity is one of the most difficult. As early as 1960, an unpublished report to the Dow Chemical Company identified between fifty and sixty different definitions in the psychological literature (Taylor, 1988), and undoubtedly the present total is many times higher than this. Parkhurst (1999), in a detailed discussion of the issue of definition, argues that this lack of consensus is a serious impediment to achieving the goal of increasing societal creativity through education. A useful distinction can be drawn between three types of definition, focusing on:

1 the creative person
2 the creative product
3 the creative process.

According to the first of these approaches, people are seen as creative to the extent that they demonstrate certain abilities, achievements and/or personality traits. In some cases, particular types of person are judged as creative by virtue of their field of activity: for instance, artists, research and development (R&D) scientists, and architects. This allows comparisons with a general population, but there still remains the question of how to account for variations in creativity within 'creative' groups – after all, no one would argue that all artists or architects are equally creative. In any case, the choice of which groups to label 'creative' is inevitably highly contentious, and there is a great danger that it will just reflect popular stereotypes. A more flexible approach to defining the creative person is in terms of their possession of particular attributes. Barron (1955), for example, sees the creative person as someone who shows a strong disposition towards originality. The notion that we can identify levels of creativity in individuals underlies the strong tradition of personality research in the creativity literature, which we discuss below.

There is a considerable degree of consensus in definitions of the creative product. Its key characteristic is *novelty*; the product must differ significantly from that which has gone before. The *degree* of novelty required varies. Some only stipulate that it should be novel to the person producing it (e.g. Johnson-Laird, 1988), some that it should also be new to the individual's social group (e.g. Amabile, 1983), and some that it should be unique (e.g. Reber, 1985). However, if we accept the requirement of uniqueness, we would have to say that should two scientists working entirely independently make the same discovery, only the one who made it first could be called creative. Novelty to the creator is therefore favoured as the criterion by most writers in the field.

Definitions commonly require that the product should be appropriate to the situation it was created to address. If Rover were to design a car with square wheels it would be a novel, but not an appropriate, response to the challenge of competition. By many definitions it therefore could not be called a creative product. A third criterion sometimes proposed for the creative product is that it should evoke a particular kind of response from those exposed to it. Bruner (1962) says that creative products cause a 'shock of recognition' that they are the correct or appropriate response to the problem addressed. The difficulty with focusing on the nature of responses to a product is that these may vary widely from person to person. Equally, individual responses may change over time; what at first may have seemed a brilliant idea may after a short period of reflection appear flawed or inappropriate.

Most commonly, creativity is conceived of as a mental process. The *Penguin Dictionary of Psychology* (Reber, 1985) defines creativity as 'mental processes that lead to solutions, ideas, conceptualizations, artistic forms, theories or products that are unique and novel'. While there is debate over whether the creative process can be said to occur in the absence of a creative product, in most cases the process is defined in relation to its product. (Of course the phrase 'creative product' does not necessarily mean a physical object; it could be a verbally expressed idea or a new pattern of behaviour. What it *must* be is something that is perceptible to people other than its creator.) Some definitions are very broad and say no more about the process than that it results in a creative product. Reber's (1985), quoted above, is one such; others include Harmon's (1955) which states that creativity is 'any process by which something new is produced – an idea or an object, including a new form or arrangement of old elements'. Others are quite precise in specifying the mental activities involved in the creative process. Torrance (1988), for example, gives the following process definition of creativity: 'the process of sensing difficulties, problems, gaps in information, missing elements, something askew; making guesses and formulating hypotheses about these deficiencies; evaluating and testing these guesses and hypotheses; possibly revising and retesting them; and finally communicating the results' (page 47).

The problem for process definitions such as Torrance's is that they locate creativity entirely within the individual creator. There is a growing body of work that insists we take a more social understanding of creativity; that the social context in which people exist fundamentally shapes the production and recognition of creative products and constructs our understanding of what counts as 'creative'. We discuss this perspective in Chapter 3, but in terms of definition, the implication of such an approach is that we should not define creativity in terms of specific mental processes. Freeman (1993) argues for a definition of creativity which is both social and developmental – the latter because creativity is always manifest within the life-history and experiences of the person.

> Framed another way, the study of creativity, to the extent that it is situated in the concrete lives of individual creators . . . is at the same time about the study of development; it is about how human beings move forward to what can arguably be considered more ideal modes of experiencing the world, thinking about it, and acting in it. (pages 1–2)

Personal initiative: a complementary construct

Before progressing with our discussion of defining and measuring creativity, it is important to note the complementary and overlapping construct of '*personal initiate*' (PI). Recent seminal work into PI has been undertaken by Michael Frese and Dorris Fay at Giessen University, Germany. They define PI and distinguish it from innovation as follows:

15

> Personal initiative is a behaviour syndrome resulting in an individual's taking an active and self-starting approach to work and going beyond what is formally required in a given job.
>
> *(Frese* et al., *1996, p. 38)*

In a series of studies, Frese and his co-workers have examined the personality and motivational correlates of PI (Fay and Frese, 2001), how PI can be an important component of 'dynamic self-reliance', itself an increasingly important aspect of surviving modern business organizations (Frese, 2001), and various behavioural and job performance outcomes associated with PI (Frese *et al.* 1997). The Giessen group have produced some particularly interesting findings in comparisons between the former West and East Germany, suggesting that the nature of state control in the latter had a suppressing effect on personal initiative.

There are clear overlaps between the PI concept and individual creativity and innovation, but there are also important distinctions, as Fay *et al* (1998) point out. First, personal initiative is not always related to the introduction of an element novel to a particular context, a key aspect of most definitions of creativity and innovation. Second, they argue that:

> ... a crucial characteristic of personal initiative is that it is self-started and that it goes beyond the formal requirements of the job. This does not necessarily apply to innovation: innovation can be both self-started or part of an assigned task.
>
> *(Fay* et al., *1998)*

PI therefore is a potentially useful complementary construct to individual innovativeness, especially when applied in areas such as selection and assessment. It should be noted, though, that the emphasis on personal agency in work on PI must be balanced by an understanding of the way the social context of the organization shapes the scope for action available for individuals.

Measuring creativity

Approaches to the measurement of creativity parallel the different approaches to its definition, focusing on characteristics of the *person*, the *process* or the *product*. Person-based measures can be further divided into three types: personality inventories, biographical inventories and creative ability tests. Let us consider each in turn.

Person-based measures

Personality measures

Many psychologists have attempted to identify and measure a normally distributed personality trait of creativity (e.g. Guilford, 1959; Torrance and Khatena, 1970; Harrington, 1975). Typically, the construction of such measures involves the selection of a sample of people whose level of creativity has been reliably assessed by 'expert' judges. They are then asked to select from a large list of descriptive terms those that most accurately describe themselves. The terms which best differentiate between the highly creative and the less creative are included in the final measure of creative personality. For example, Gough's (1979) creative personality scale includes 30 adjectives: 18 positively related to creativity and 12 negatively related. The former include: clever, confident, informal, original, egotistical and resourceful. The latter include: cautious, sincere, conventional and submissive.

There is a reasonable degree of consensus over the traits which tend to be typical of highly creative individuals, but the real challenge for measures of creative personality is to be able to distinguish levels of creativity amongst those who are not of exceptional ability. If creativity is a normally distributed trait, then those distinctive characteristics found to be significantly related to each other in eminent creative persons ought to be related in the same way amongst those of moderate or low creativity. Reviewing the large amount of literature on creative personality from the 1950s and 1960s, Nicholls (1972) found poor support for such relationships in studies of children, though somewhat better support in adult samples. However, the generalizability of the adult findings is questionable, as most studies had a highly restricted range – young, American college students. Nicholls therefore questioned the utility of personality measures for studying creativity in the general population.

Some personality theorists have argued for a distinction between level and style of creativity; the former referring to the propensity for creative production, the latter to the type of creative activity engaged in. Kirton (1976; 1989) distinguishes between 'adaptors' who are creative within an existing paradigm, and 'innovators' who enact their creativity through challenging the paradigm. He claims that these two aspects of creativity are independent of each other – innovators are not more creative than adaptors, they are just creative in a different way. Other writers have suggested that the widely used Myers-Briggs Type Indicator (MBTI: Myers and McCaully, 1985) may be used to distinguish styles of creativity (Teft, 1990, cited in Isaksen and Dorval, 1993). There remains debate as to whether style can be entirely separated from level of creativity, both conceptually and methodologically (Payne, 1987; Taylor, 1989). Nevertheless, this approach does allow greater subtlety in personality-based measures than a uni-dimensional one based simply on level.

Biographical inventories

In contrast to trait measures of creativity, biographical inventories focus not on personality but on the life events and experiences that shaped the testee's individual development (e.g. Schaeffer, 1969; Michael and Colson, 1979). These measures are based on the assumption that highly creative individuals are likely to share certain combinations of biographical features which differ from those of less creative people, such as family and educational histories, interests and hobbies, and personal relationships. Again, the initial construction of such inventories requires that individuals are reliably rated by appropriate judges as to their level of creativity. Biographical features consistently associated with high or low creativity can then be identified. The biographical inventory approach has the advantage of recognizing that an individual's creative ability at any point in time is inextricably bound up with his or her life history. However, the biographical features assessed in existing inventories sometimes appear to be based more on intuition and assumption than on the systematic study of how life events and experiences influence the development of creativity.

Tests of creative ability

Creative ability tests are the best-known type of creativity measure. They evolved from tests to measure intelligence, and generally resemble them in many ways. Most are 'paper-and-pencil' tests, presenting the test taker with a series of problems to solve, often in a fixed time period. J.P. Guilford's (1956) theory of the structure of intellect played a crucial role in highlighting the mental abilities which were involved in creative thought and which therefore should be measured in creativity tests. In particular the ability to engage in 'divergent thinking' has been a key criterion used in most tests (although it is important to note that Guilford did not see it as synonymous with creativity, which also involves sensitivity to problems and the ability to redefine problems). Divergent thinking can be defined as the ability to produce remote or unusual associations to a stimulus question. It contrasts with convergent thinking, which is logical, sequential and involves the narrowing of focus towards one 'correct' solution to a problem. A well-known test of divergent thinking is Torrance's (1974) 'Unusual Uses' test, in which the subject is asked to think of as many different ways of using an everyday object (e.g. a paper-clip) as possible.

E. P. Torrance constructed a series of creative ability tests in the early 1960s (the Torrance Tests of Creative Thinking, or TTCT) which have probably been used more widely than any others (Torrance, 1974). Originally devised for educational settings, they include both verbal and non-verbal tests. Subjects are instructed to produce as many clever and unusual responses as they can in a set period of time. These responses can then be scored in four different ways, reflecting four components of creative thinking: *fluency, flexibility, originality* and *elaboration*. Fluency is the ability to produce a large number of different responses within a set time, and is scored as the total number of different responses. Flexibility is the ability to produce different categories of response, and is scored by summing the number of categories. For example, on the Unusual Uses test, a subject might suggest four uses for the brick which involved hitting things with it and three which involved building things. This would result in a fluency score of seven, but a flexibility score of two. Originality is the ability to produce uncommon responses. It is scored by awarding points according to the rarity with which responses occur in a previously studied population. Elaboration is the ability to develop or embellish ideas. 'Smashing the window of a jeweller's shop in order to rob it' is a more elaborated response to the Unusual Uses test than just 'smashing a window'. Most of Torrance's tests are scored on all four components, as are many other creativity tests.

The question of the utility of tests like the TTCT continues to provoke contrasting opinions amongst researchers. They have been criticized for their predominant focus on general divergent thinking skills. Baer (1994) and Wallach (1985) argue that creativity is domain specific, and that this should be reflected in testing: visual tests for assessing potential artists, verbal tests for creative writing ability and so on. Weisberg (1993) argues on the basis of experimental evidence that creative problem-solving does not rely upon the use of divergent thinking skills. Traditional creative ability tests have also been attacked for underplaying the role of thinking skills other than divergence, especially convergent thinking (e.g. Hampden-Turner, 1999), and for neglecting the central importance of motivation (Amabile, 1987). Other criticisms have centred on the ability of tests to predict actual creative achievement (Hocevar and Bachelor, 1989) and the well-established effects on test performance of characteristics of the test environment, such as time pressure, formality of setting and the precise wording of instructions (e.g. Baer, 1994; Wallach, 1985).

The argument is not one sided, though. In recent years there have been several studies which have found quite good predictive validity for the TTCT in particular (Cramond *et al.*, 1999; Yamada and Wen, 1996) and have shown it to correlate well with creativity tests employing very different methodologies (Ferracuti *et al.*, 2000). Runco (1993) has argued that divergent thinking tests can play a useful role in assessing potential for creativity, although theoretical developments in under-standing the role of divergence in creativity have lagged behind technical developments in means of assessing it.

Common to all person-based approaches to the measurement of creativity are two assumptions, that:

1 they are assessing qualities or abilities of individuals, not of their products;
2 that measurements are objective, not subjective.

Both these assumptions are open to question. Although personality measures address personal characteristics such as originality and unconventionality, almost invariably the measures are initially constructed on the basis of qualities observed in people identified as highly creative. Selecting such people involves a subjective judgement, and that judgement will inevitably be made on the basis of their creative products. For instance, if one rated Lennon and McCartney as amongst the most creative popular music writers of the 20th century, one would cite as evidence not the personality traits they possessed, but their songs – their products. Researchers have generally attempted to reduce subjectivity by using agreed ratings from an appropriately expert group to identify creative eminence (e.g. MacKinnon, 1962). However, it is likely that such judgements would be swayed by factors other than creativity. Taking the example of scientists, eminence – which could easily be attributed to creativity – may owe as much or more to personal power and influence, communication skills, abilities to motivate a research team, or the reputation of the academic institution they work in.

Creative ability tests too can be seen to rely on subjective judgements of products in many of their scoring techniques. Dimensions such as flexibility and elaboration clearly require scorers to make subjective judgements. Even the dimension of originality, scored purely in terms of frequency of response, will require decisions to be made about whether a response is sufficiently different from previous ones to be counted towards the total score.

Product-based measures

The difficulty, perhaps impossibility, of escaping from subjective judgements of products in person-based measures has led many writers to recommend that creativity should be measured through characteristics of products (Nicholls, 1972; Getzels and Csikszentmihalyi, 1976; Amabile, 1983). Can we define features of creative products in such a way as to enable a procedure for the objective assessment of creativity to be devised? Ghiselin (1963) argues that such a goal is achievable, but does not specify how it could be achieved, and few subsequent researchers have attempted to do so. The most notable exception is Simonton (1980), who developed a method of quantifying the originality of musical themes in terms of the rarity of the combinations of their first six notes.

A difficulty with attempts to measure creativity purely in terms of objective features of the product is that the means by which the product was created cannot be taken into account. The product, and the product alone, is the unit of assessment, although the purpose of such assessment from a psychological viewpoint is to determine the creativity

21

of its creator. Taken to its extreme, the logic of such an approach can lead to some bizarre conclusions. For instance, if you were to photocopy the text of *King Lear*, this approach to assessment would judge you to be as creative as Shakespeare, since your product and his are identical.

Theresa Amabile (1983) supports a product-based strategy for measuring creativity but states that we should not waste our energies in striving for the unattainable goal of defining objective criteria for creative products. She proposes a consensual assessment procedure, based on the subjective judgements of experts in the field being investigated. Furthermore, she maintains that products created purely by following a known, straightforward set of instructions for problem solution cannot be considered creative; creativity must involve the individual in defining the problem for him- or herself. This consensual assessment procedure therefore requires that the judges have enough information about the creator and the way in which the product was created to determine whether problem definition was required. Amabile's support for this subjective approach to measurement is not solely an acknowledgement that objective judgements are impossible. She makes the important point that all judgements about creativity must be subjective because they are bound up with the cultural and historical context in which they are made.

Process-based measures

By far the least common strategy for assessing creativity is the direct measure of creative processes. This is hardly surprising as our knowledge of the process remains limited, with different writers taking substantially different views as to its nature. One of the few attempts to devise a measure of the creative process is Ghiselin *et al.*'s (1964) 'Creative process checklist'. Devised for use with scientists, it asks subjects to select adjectives which best describe their feelings and state of attention before, during and after the moment of insight or problem solution. By comparing scientists rated as high or low in creativity, process descriptions associated with differing levels of creativity can be identified. Once again, this raises the question of whether the initial global ratings of individuals as more or less creative are valid. The checklist method assumes that all the mental processes involved in creativity are accessible to the individual and easily verbalized. By no means all researchers (the present authors included) would agree with such a proposition. Additionally, it may be argued that the method does not measure differences between individuals in the actual creative process, but rather differences in what creative problem solving means to them. The checklist could not then claim to be a measure of creative process, though it could be a useful tool in understanding the personal meanings people attach to creativity – an issue that has received little attention.

Strategies for creativity enhancement

If an organization wants to increase the creative production of its members there are four broad strategies it can follow. First, it may introduce procedures to encourage the generation of new ideas – such as the well-known 'brainstorming' (Osborn, 1953) technique. Second, it may train people in the skills required for successful creative performance. Third, it may use selection and assessment processes to recruit creative individuals and allocate people to positions appropriate to their level of creativity. Fourth, it may change its own characteristics, such as structure, climate and culture, in ways which facilitate creativity. In the present chapter we will examine the evidence relating to each of these strategies in turn.

Idea elicitation techniques

Idea elicitation techniques seek to enable individuals in organizations to generate more and better new ideas to tackle particular problems or meet particular challenges. To the extent that they teach people creative thinking techniques they may be seen as a form of training. However, they differ from the training programmes discussed later in that their principal intention is not to make people generally more creative in all aspects of their work, but rather to provide them with a tool to be used in specific situations. Often, though not always, the techniques require people to interact with others as a group at some point in the procedure.

Idea elicitation techniques have a long history in the psychological study of creativity. Two of the best known – brainstorming and synectics – were first developed more than forty years ago, and the former in particular has been subject to numerous modifications and refinements. Many others have since been produced, some by academic psychologists, some by managers and consultants working in organizations, and some by popular writers such as Edward de Bono (1971) whose concept of 'lateral thinking' has entered common parlance. Their popularity notwithstanding, the effectiveness of such techniques is the subject of considerable debate, with some claiming conspicuous success for them (Brahm and Kleiner, 1996) whilst others maintain that they do not lead to any substantial increase in creative performance (Weisberg, 1986; Diehl and Stroebe, 1987). We will concentrate here on the evidence relating to brainstorming, followed by a brief description of synectics and other techniques.

Brainstorming

The technique of brainstorming was first described by Alex Osborn (1953) and has since been used in many types of organization around the world to tackle many types of task and problem. It is based on the observation that one of the main blocks to the emergence of creative ideas in organizations is 'evaluation apprehension' – the fear that a new idea will be met with derision or hostility by colleagues or superiors. Because of this, good ideas may simply never be voiced. Brainstorming aims to side-step this block by suppressing all evaluative comment at the initial idea-generation stage of creativity. The classic form of brainstorming, as propounded by Osborn, is based on two major principles: *deferment of judgement* and *quantity breeds quality.* The former recognizes the need to keep separate the production and the evaluation of ideas. The latter stems from the belief that as good-quality ideas are rare, the greater the total number of ideas produced the more likely it is that some at least will be good. In developing practice from these principles, four major rules for conducting brainstorming sessions are proposed.

1 *Criticism is ruled out* – at the idea generation stage group members are not allowed to voice criticisms of others' (or their own) ideas, no matter how daft they may sound.
2 *Freewheeling is welcomed* – people are encouraged to let their imaginations run as free as possible; no idea should be considered too wild or impractical to voice.

3 *Quantity is wanted* – group members are explicitly encouraged to come up with as many ideas as possible.

4 *Combination and improvement are sought* – people are encouraged to build upon ideas suggested by other group members, for example by combining elements of two or more previous ideas. They are not limited to suggesting ideas which are wholly novel to the session.

The typical brainstorming group, as used by Osborn and his co-workers, consists of approximately twelve people including the group leader and sometimes an associate leader, plus a recording secretary who notes down ideas as they are produced but otherwise does not take part in the session. The leader's role (assisted by the associate) is to explain the instructions for brainstorming, to present the problem to be tackled at the beginning of the session, to ensure that the rules presented above are adhered to during the session, and generally to act as a facilitator – for instance, if ideas are drying up towards the end of the session, by suggesting new angles from which participants might address the problem. An additional rule frequently enforced by group leaders is that only one person may speak at a time. Experts vary in the optimal length of session they recommend, but half an hour is a common duration.

Osborn's brainstorming technique does not stop at the generation of ideas by the group; once the list of ideas is compiled, they then have to be evaluated and a preferred solution adopted. Osborn recommends a five-person evaluation group, whose members should have a direct responsibility for the problem at hand and thus a real stake in the quality of the decision arrived at. A checklist of criteria is frequently used, against which each of the listed ideas can be assessed; for instance, the evaluators might consider cost, skills required to implement, time taken to implement, probable reactions of groups and individuals in the organization, and so on. If a consensus choice of idea is not attainable, a simple majority decision of the evaluation group is accepted (hence the need for an odd number of members).

Electronic brainstorming

The 1990s saw a rapid increase in the use of computer-based brainstorming (usually referred to as 'electronic brainstorming' or

'EBS'), and a parallel growth in research looking at this technique. This grew out of more broadly focused work looking at computerized decision-support systems (e.g. Gallupe, DeSanctis and Dickson, 1988). In part, these developments reflect technological changes, with an ever wider range of organizations utilizing networked computers, ensuring that the hardware and basic computer skills required for EBS are readily accessible. Many software packages for EBS are available, often at quite modest prices. Because some (though not all) EBS systems do not require participants to be in physical proximity, organizations can benefit from including individuals in sessions who work in different locations – even in different countries. EBS also has the potential to overcome some of the group process problems which researchers have identified in ordinary brainstorming groups (discussed below), for example by allowing anonymous interaction to overcome evaluation apprehension (Jessup, Connolly and Galegher, 1990). Clearly, EBS has many strengths, but it has limitations too, as Kay (1995) points out. It seems to work less well with smaller compared to larger groups, it necessitates more training for participants than conventional brainstorming, and the loss of social interaction may have a detrimental effect on participants' motivation.

Testing the principles of brainstorming

Brainstorming has been widely used in many kinds of organization, and the general principles of the technique have become so well known that the term has entered into the popular vocabulary. The technique has also been tested extensively in experimental settings (unlike other idea elicitation techniques). Studies have focused particularly on three areas: the effects of deferring judgement on idea quality and quantity; the idea productivity of groups in comparison to individuals working alone; and the impact of group structure and membership factors on group performance. On the first of these issues research generally indicates that there is a loss in idea productivity when ideas are evaluated at the same time as they are generated. A recent study by Basadur, Runco and Vega (2000), for instance, found that 'preference for avoiding premature evaluation of options' was the key attitudinal skill for creative thinking amongst managers participating in a creativity training course. However, it may not be strictly necessary for all thoughts of evaluation to be held over until after the idea generation phase is complete, as Osborn maintains. An experiment by Brilharte and Jochem (1964) introduced a condition in which the group decided upon evaluation criteria before commencing idea generation, though still deferring evaluation of the *individual* ideas produced. Osborn's rationale would suggest that thinking about evaluation criteria before the generation phase would inhibit productivity by interfering with the free flow of ideas. In fact, the 'reversed' condition did not produce any fewer or poorer-quality ideas than the conventional procedure. It seems that what is important is not that all consideration of evaluation is deferred, but that generation and evaluation of ideas are kept separate.

Regarding the comparison of group and individual performance, the bulk of the evidence contradicts Osborn's position. Numerous experimental studies have compared the quantity and quality of ideas produced by interacting groups of brainstormers with that of individuals working alone. The great majority have found that interacting groups produce fewer non-redundant ideas than same-size 'nominal' groups of individuals working on their own whose ideas are then summed for comparison. The findings relating to idea quality are more ambiguous, in part reflecting the difficulty in defining and measuring quality, but it is fair to say that groups do not consistently produce better-quality ideas than individuals.

This 'production loss' in interacting groups compared to nominal groups has been the focus of much research, pioneered by Michael Diehl and Wolfgang Stroebe. These authors considered three possible explanations for production loss.

1 *Free-riding* – because in a real brainstorming group ideas are not attributed to the individuals who suggested them but to the group as a whole, people in such groups may make less effort than they would if working individually, safe in the knowledge that they will not be held to account for their underperformance.
2 *Evaluation apprehension* – despite the injunction not to be critical and the encouragement to suggest any idea, however wild, people in a real, interacting group cannot wholly rid themselves of concerns that others will make judgements about them on the basis of their suggestions. This inevitably inhibits idea production.
3 *Production blocking* – the mechanics of running a real brainstorming group actually get in the way of maximum individual productivity.

Specifically, the fact that only one person can speak at a time is inhibitive, perhaps because people forget ideas whilst waiting their turn, or have second thoughts about making them public.

Diehl and Stroebe (1987) found that it was the third explanation, production blocking, that accounted for most of the productivity loss in real groups. Subsequent research reported by Stroebe (1994) found that regulating waiting time, so people knew in advance when their turn to speak would come up, and asking people to write down their ideas whilst waiting their turn, did not prevent production blocking. Gallupe, Bastianutti and Cooper (1991) developed a form of computerized brainstorming which did remove the production blocking effect for real groups. Group members entered their ideas at a terminal as they occurred and at the same time a random selection of ideas from other group members were displayed. Groups using 'electronic brainstorming' produced more ideas than face-to-face groups, and as many ideas as electronic nominal groups where there was no access to other group members' ideas. However, they did not produce *more* ideas than the nominal groups. In contrast, a field experiment by Jarvenpaa, Rao and Huber (1988) found that interacting computer-supported brainstorming groups actually produced more ideas per member than nominal groups.

Although Diehl and Stroebe found that evaluation apprehension was a less important cause of production loss than blocking, other research affirms that it can have a strong effect on how brainstorming groups perform. Studies of electronic brainstorming, where individual anonymity is possible in interacting groups, have generally shown that anonymous groups produce more controversial ideas and fewer redundant ideas (Cooper *et al.*, 1998), are more flexible in their idea production (Sosik, Kahai and Avolio, 1998) and make more contributions overall (Jessup, Connolly and Galegher 1990) than identified groups. However, a study by Valacich, Dennis and Nunamaker (1992) found that anonymous groups did not produce significantly more or better ideas than identified groups, although large groups (nine members) outperformed small groups (three members) on both idea quantity and quality, whether the groups were anonymous or not. They suggest that the non-controversial nature of the task combined with the random allocation of student participants to group may well have dissipated any evaluation apprehension. The positive relationship between group size and performance – the converse of what is generally found with traditional face-to-face groups – is probably a function of the technology. The EBS system used allowed participants to attend to others ideas or not as they wished; they therefore obtained the benefit of possible cross-fertilization of ideas in a relatively large group (as Osborn himself argued) without the production blocking that occurs in face-to-face groups.

Brown and Paulus (1996) suggest two other factors which might result in production loss in brainstorming groups. 'Output decay' simply refers to the fact that individuals within a group will in time run out of ideas. This of course will happen to individuals working on their own in nominal groups; however, in interacting groups Brown and Paulus claim that the impact of 'output decay' will be compounded by the tendency for 'matching' to occur. Matching is a social comparison process, whereby group members judge the appropriate level of output by examining the output of their colleagues. Matching may lead to either a decrease in performance (where groups match downwards towards the performance of the less productive members) or an increase (where their is upwards matching towards the most productive members' levels). However, given that group productivity may be depressed by the factors discussed above, and that at least in experimental studies task motivation may not be particularly high, negative impacts from matching may be more likely than positive.

Aspects of group structure and membership have not received as much attention from researchers as the group production loss phenomenon, although their importance has been recognized for many years (see, for example, Stein, 1975). A number of studies have examined whether the presence of a facilitator is necessary for effective performance in a brainstorming group, and whether the style of group leadership influences performance. On the former issue, evidence suggests that interacting groups employing a skilled facilitator may perform as well as, or better than, nominal groups (Oxley, Dzindolet and Paulus, 1997; Offner, Kramer and Winter, 1996). Regarding leadership, positive effects have been found for transformational/ inspirational leadership styles, and for leaders who engage in trans-actional goal setting with their groups (Sosik, Kahai and Avolio, 1998; Sosik, Avolio and Kahai, 1997).

Over twenty-five years ago, Morris Stein (1975) argued for the importance of group composition in brainstorming effectiveness, and since then writers in the area have commonly argued that diverse (or heterogeneous) groups are likely to perform better than groups whose members have very similar backgrounds and experiences (homogenous). Despite this, there have been relatively few studies which have directly examined the effects of group heterogeneity. Rather, in most cases, the participants in brainstorming groups are highly homogenous (e.g. all undergraduate students on the same year of the same degree course). Where experiments have manipulated heterogeneity, they tend to support the theoretical claims that it is positively related to brainstorming effectiveness. An experiment by Michael Diehl (1992) found that brainstorming groups whose members were selected for heterogeneity performed better than groups selected for homogeneity or randomly. Similarly, a study by McLeod, Lobel and Cox (1996) showed that ethnically diverse groups produce ideas rated higher on feasibility and effectiveness than ethnically homogenous groups.

A significant weakness in the brainstorming literature is the relative lack of attention to issues of how brainstorming might actually function in the real world. Most studies are laboratory based, and they are often designed specifically to exclude (in the name of experimental control) the influence of factors likely to be important in organizational settings. For example, the decisions made by experimental groups rarely, if ever, have any long-term consequences for participants, group members tend to be of equal status and power, and researchers are commonly more concerned with the number of ideas generated rather than the quality of the idea finally selected. Many studies neglect the idea selection stage entirely.

Studies which have attempted to take into account these kinds of real-world issues have often come to somewhat different conclusions about the effectiveness of brainstorming from the apparent consensus in more traditional studies. Kramer, Kuo and Dailey (1997) found that although brainstorming groups (using both face-to-face and nominal procedures) did not produce better-quality ideas than untrained groups, they were more satisfied with the experience, more positive about the decision process used, and communicated more effectively than untrained groups. The authors suggest that the real value of brainstorming in organizations may be the enhancement of teamwork through stronger decision participation and ownership, rather than an increase in the quantity or quality of creative ideas. In a field study of two prototype electronic decision-support systems, Jarvenpaa, Rao and Huber (1988) found partial support for their greater effectiveness in idea generation and evaluation compared to conventional meetings.

Perhaps their most striking finding, though, was that there were very marked differences between the teams involved in the study in how successfully they employed the technologies, suggesting the crucial role of team composition and dynamics. Gopal and Prasad (2000) have recently made a strong case for a shift in focus in EBS research, away from the technology and towards the nature of social interaction in such groups. To achieve this, they advocate the use of qualitative rather than experimental methods, within a symbolic interactionist theoretical framework. We will return to issues of how best to understand and study group creativity and innovation in Chapter 4.

The very substantial amount of research on brainstorming enables us to come to clearer informed judgements about its utility than that of any other idea elicitation technique. There is good evidence to support the claim that deferral of judgement facilitates idea generation, that face-to-face groups tend to suffer production losses compared to nominal groups (mainly due to production blocking, but also free-riding and evaluation apprehension), and that structural features of groups impact on performance. Nevertheless, writers come to very different conclusions from the research evidence, some arguing that it shows that brainstorming does not achieve what Osborn and his followers claim for it, while others insist that it is a highly effective technique. We would argue that whether one judges brainstorming to be effective depends on one's criteria for effectiveness. If the chief criterion is sheer quantity of ideas, then it is hard to disagree with the case that Osborn's model of brainstorming is inefficient, because of production losses in groups. If broader criteria are used, such as member participation, commitment to decisions made, and satisfaction with the process, brainstorming fares better. The rapid rise of electronic brainstorming adds an important new element to this debate, as research appears to be suggesting that EBS may be able to avoid some of the pitfalls of traditional brainstorming whilst retaining many of its advantages. As we noted earlier, what this field urgently needs is a much stronger emphasis on real-world issues and real-world settings.

Synectics and other idea generation techniques

The term synectics is derived from the Greek and means the joining together of apparently unassociated and irrelevant elements. Its originator, William Gordon, observed real problem-solving groups in the late 1940s and 1950s, and recognized that very often creative solutions were achieved when someone drew an analogy between elements of the problem they were tackling and similar problems in very different contexts. He also studied biographical accounts of eminent creators and again detected analogy as playing a key role in creative thought. Probably the most famous example is that of the chemist Kekulé, whose discovery of the ring structure of benzene molecules followed a dream in which he saw snakes biting their own tails. On the basis of this early work, Gordon developed the technique of synectics, first within a subgroup of the consulting firm Arthur D. Little, and subsequently in his own company, Synectics, Inc., which he set up in 1958 with George M. Prince.

At the heart of synectics is the notion of making the strange familiar, and the familiar strange. When faced with a problem the individual needs to make connections between the unfamiliar situation and his or her own experience, skills and knowledge ('making the strange familiar') in order to understand clearly the nature of the task facing him or her. However, this process alone, though an essential first step, will not yield creative solutions. What the problem solver must also do is look at the problem from as many different perspectives as possible, including those which might seem bizarre, so as to find a genuinely novel yet relevant viewpoint on which to base a solution ('making the familiar strange'). In synectics groups, the leader encourages participants to use various types of analogy and metaphor to identify the underlying concepts of a problem and to address the problem from new directions. Examples of analogies emerging from real synectics groups include:

- the Indian Rope Trick, in the development of a hydraulic jack (Gordon, 1961);
- a machine-gun belt, in the development of a soluble tape used to ensure seeds are evenly spaced across a field (Howard, 1987);
- the properties of wet leaves, in solving the problem of how to pack Pringle's crisps (Evans, 1991).

Synectics is a much more complex technique than brainstorming, and it is not possible in the space available to give details of the training of group leaders and members, or the running of sessions. For those interested, we would recommend the excellent chapter in Morris Stein's *Stimulating Creativity: Volume 2* (1975), as well as Gordon's original book, *Synectics* (1961).

Evaluating the effectiveness of synectics

There are many examples of positive testimonies from organizations which have used synectics groups in such diverse sectors as manufacturing, retailing and public services. One such is the Remington Arms Company, whose research and design manager initiated synectics groups in the 1960s. Amongst the problems they solved was how to hold gun stocks securely on a conveyor belt; an analogy with the way an earthworm grips the side of its hole to prevent itself being pulled out was used (Garcha, 1969). Much of this anecdotal evidence has been published in material produced by Synectics, Inc., or by people closely involved in the development of synectics. This is not to say that such testimonies are invalid, merely that questions need to be asked regarding the representativeness of the evidence. It may be that failed synectics groups are simply not reported; in fact, given the time and cost involved in training and running groups, organizations may be unwilling to admit to failures.

There have been far fewer academic research studies of synectics than of brainstorming, again largely because synectics groups are relatively time consuming and expensive to set up. Some studies have looked at elements of the technique. Bouchard (1972) examined the effect of adding the use of personal analogies (where the problem-solvers imagine themselves in the role of some aspect of the problem) to brainstorming sessions. He found that groups using the brainstorming plus personal analogy procedure were superior to those just using brainstorming. Gendrop (1996) found that a synectics-based intervention led to increased creativity test scores for nurses. Further research is needed to determine how synectics interventions compare with other forms of idea elicitation and creativity training.

Other techniques

In addition to brainstorming and synectics there are numerous other techniques which have been used to elicit creative ideas, though most are based on principles similar to those underlying one or other of the two techniques we have discussed. Some organizations have developed their own procedures (which may be quite elaborate) tailored to their particular needs, but many techniques are straightforward and easy to use in most contexts. We will discuss three of the most commonly used below.

Checklists

A simple but often effective way of eliciting ideas is to produce checklists which act as a spur to thinking about the problem and its potential solutions in as many ways as possible. (Note the similarity with the way analogies are used in synectics.) Different checklists may be used at different stages of the creative process. For instance, a checklist may be used to help generate diverse ideas which could then form the basis of a problem solution. One such list, originally proposed by Osborn, consists of the following questions, representing ways in which elements of the problem situation might be manipulated (Stein, 1975):

Put to other uses?
Adapt?
Modify?
Magnify?
Minify?
Substitute?
Rearrange?
Reverse?
Combine?

This list would be used to generate ideas. For example, if a manufacturing firm was concerned to speed up its communication with suppliers, the question 'substitute?' might suggest the use of a different medium – such as e-mail. A different checklist could be used later in the creative process to identify problems which possible solutions might face.

Attribute listing

This is in effect a specialized form of checklist in which the problem solver identifies as many attributes as possible of elements of the problem situation. The list of attributes then becomes the focus for devising new ideas towards a solution by considering as many possible modifications of each, deferring judgement at the generation stage as in brainstorming. James Evans (1991) gives the example of finding new uses for a paper-clip. Attributes of a paper-clip include that it is made of metal, thin, can be bent, has sharp ends. By considering other objects that have one or more of these characteristics, possible new uses may be identified. Focusing on the attribute 'sharpness' might lead to the proposed design of a paper-clip which doubles as a letter opener.

Forced relationships

In this technique, the problem solver attempts to generate ideas by finding ways in which normally unrelated ideas or objects may be connected with each other. Again, there is a connection with brainstorming as users are generally advised to produce relationships uncritically and evaluate them afterwards. For instance, forcing together the ideas of 'bed' and 'book' might lead to ideas such as a bed which folds open and shuts like a book, a device for holding a book whilst reading in bed, or a bed with storage compartments for books (and other small items) built into the headboard.

Creativity training

The second broad approach to enhancing creativity at work is to train organizational members in the skills associated with creative perform-ance. There is clearly an overlap here with the use of idea generation techniques. Most creativity training programmes include the learning of one or more such techniques, and the techniques can themselves be seen as a form of training. However, with brainstorming and the like, the focus is on improving people's performance within formally designated problem-solving sessions. The types of training programme we are considering in this section aim for a wider effect, intending to make organizational members more creative in their whole approach to work. A real-world example, the EQUIP programme run by Ford, is described later in Box 7.1.

The Parnes Creative Problem-Solving programme

A highly influential and commercially successful package is the Creative Problem-Solving (CPS) programme developed by Sidney Parnes. It grew out of Osborn's ideas on creativity enhancement, including the brainstorming technique, though it includes much more than just that one procedure. The original programme was first described in 1967, in the *Creative Behaviour Guidebook* and the *Creative Behaviour Workbook*, both authored by Parnes. Other creativity training initiatives have evolved from it, some under the direction of Parnes and colleagues at the Creative Education Foundation, and some by other workers. It is fair to say that most creativity training programmes in popular usage are based at least in part on the CPS.

Parnes describes the creative problem-solving process as occurring in five stages:

1 *Fact finding* – information about the problem at hand is gathered.
2 *Problem finding* – to begin with, problems tend to be messy and ill defined. They need to be clarified and restated in ways which encourage the production of ideas for solutions.
3 *Idea finding* – a range of ideas which might provide a solution to the problem are generated.
4 *Solution finding* – criteria for evaluating ideas are formulated and applied to ideas generated at the previous stage.
5 *Acceptance finding* – the chosen solution is presented to those concerned with its implementation in as persuasive a way as possible. Anticipating likely sources of resistance is a key part of this.

Participants in the CPS programme are taught a series of techniques for use at each of these stages, including elements of brainstorming, especially the principle of deferred judgement, checklists and forced relationships. The original training programme consists of 16 sessions which last about twenty-four hours, and are usually run over three days. Individuals may take themselves through the programme, using the material in the *Guidebook* and *Workbook*, but Parnes recommends instructor-led classes of up to twenty-five participants as more effective.

Evaluating creativity training

Evidence from experimental studies by Parnes and his colleagues (Parnes *et al.*, 1977) shows that participation in the programme does lead to improved creativity scores on some of the standard tests. However, most evaluations focus only on the brainstorming element of the programme, and the tests used are very similar to some of the material encountered in the course of the training. Again, this evidence originates from the programme inventors and one needs to remain somewhat sceptical of only positive results being published. Another question is whether the effects of the training are generalizable to other types of problem, and to real-life creative performance, outside of formal test settings. These issues – which do not only apply to the CPS programme – were highlighted by Morris Stein in 1975, and it is rather disheartening to find that the same weaknesses in the evaluation of training packages are identified in the much more recent review by Boris Kabanoff and John Rossiter (1994). It is not easy to assess the longer-term effectiveness of creativity training in the work context, but it is essential if we are to make sound judgements as to its worth.

One of the best-known current training programmes for creativity at work is the 'Simplex' system, developed by Min Basadur and colleagues (Basadur, 1995). It has the strength of having a foundation in research evidence directly testing its core principles. The programme takes a problem-solving approach to creativity and emphasizes the need to use a combination of divergent and convergent thinking skills at each stage of the process – problem finding, problem solving, and solution implementation. Like brainstorming, the programme also argues for the importance of deferral of judgement. In early work with engineers, Basadur and colleagues compared a group receiving creativity training with a placebo group who watched and discussed a film about creativity and a control group who received no creativity-related intervention (Basadur, Graen and Green, 1982). The effects of training were examined using a variety of measures taken immediately after the programme ended and two weeks later at work. These showed that there had been cognitive, attitudinal and behavioural changes which persisted into job performance, at least in the short term. A later study (Basadur, Graen and Scandura, 1986) found evidence of creativity training producing attitudinal changes which persisted quite strongly at five weeks though showed signs of fading at ten weeks.

Clapham (1997) has criticized research into the effectiveness of creativity training for its tendency to focus on overall outcomes to the exclusion of seeking an understanding of which aspects of training are most effective. In her own study she showed that a ten-minute introduction to ideational skills was as effective at improving creative performance as a 30-minute, more broadly based, creativity training programme. Caution is needed in generalizing from this to the effectiveness of real-world programmes, as her work was laboratory based, using a student sample, and was a much shorter creativity programme than those usually run for organizations. Also, she measured creativity only in terms of TTCT test scores, and several authors have argued that these disproportionately weight divergent thinking skills – a strong relationship between these scores and ideation may therefore be expected. Nevertheless, if similar findings were obtained in organizational settings there would be clear implications for managers, given the high cost of most creativity training programmes.

Until there have been more long-term evaluation studies which focus on the transfer of creativity skills to real work performance, the effectiveness of creativity training in organizations remains uncertain. As we will see in the next chapter, such areas as motivation, self-image and support from colleagues are as important to creative performance as thinking skills, and it therefore seems likely, as Kabanoff and Rossiter (1994) state, that training courses which cover these as well as equipping participants with idea generation and evaluation techniques will transfer most effectively. It is also probable that enduring effects would be better achieved by training which did not consist solely of a single intensive course but which included regular 'top-up' sessions to review how well people have been able to use what they have learnt in the initial course and to consider ways to overcome obstacles they have encountered to creative performance.

Selecting for creativity

So far we have concentrated on ways in which organizations may become more creative by improving the performance of their existing staff members. Another strategy is to use selection and assessment to try to ensure that new members of the organization are high in creative ability, and that existing members are placed in jobs which enable them to fulfil their creative potential. Approaches to selecting for creativity reflect the main ways of measuring creativity, discussed earlier. An organization may examine whether candidates' personality or biographical characteristics match those considered to be associated with creativity. It may measure candidates' creative thinking skills, using one or more of the many tests available. It may assess the quality of creative products produced by candidates. We will weigh up the strengths and weaknesses of each of these approaches below.

Personality and biographical measures

Personality tests

The use of personality measures of various types is one of the most common ways in which selection and assessment for creativity is carried out by organizations. Instruments employed include conventional trait measures, biographical inventories, and attitude and interest inventories, almost all in the form of paper-and-pencil tests. Many of the best-known personality measures such as Cattell's 16PF and the Occupational Personality Questionnaire, can be used to assess candidates for creativity. Table 2.1 describes the approach taken in four such tests. The ready availability and familiarity of these instruments makes them attractive to personnel managers, and the stability of most traits over time, including those associated with creativity, means that they can be taken as predictors of long-term creative potential as well as indicators of current and past creative performance.

Trait measures are not without problems, though. One is that candidates may 'fake' responses to appear more creative than they are. Faking has long been a problem in selection contexts (Anderson and Shackleton, 1993) and self-reported creativity is especially vulnerable to it, in part because on many tests the items relevant to creativity are rather transparent in intent. Consider the items designed to assess creativity taken from widely-used personality measures, shown in Figure 2.1. If applying for a job in which creativity was known to be a desirable characteristic, would you be unprepared to respond to items such as these in a way which cast you in a favourable light? To further

Table 2.1 Popular selection tests used to measure creativity

Measure	Kirton Adaption Innovation Inventory (KAI)	16PF	Occupational Personality Questionnaire (OPQ)	Belbin Team Roles Inventory (BTRI)	Patterson's Innovation Potential Indicator (PIPI)	Team Selection Inventory (TSI)
Structure	Single-dimension measure of creative cognitive style	Multidimension (16 personality factors: 16PF) measure of adult personality	Multidimension measure of occupationally relevant personality traits. Several versions available	Type measure of preferred team role	Multidimension innovation specific test measuring four dimensions of innovation-related behaviours	Multidimension test of individual preferences for team-working style and climate for innovation
Items	Thirty-three self-report items	Forms A and B: 187 items total; Forms C and D: 105 items total	Varies according to version Factor 5.2 version: 136 items loading onto 16 scales	Seven-section questionnaire, eight items per section, quasi-ipsative scoring	36 items rated on five-point scales (strongly disagree through strongly agree)	50 items rated on five-point scales (Non preferred through Absolutely essential)
Factors	Adaptors – individual scoring towards this end of the KAI are argued to accept problem parameters but try to 'do things better' within these constraints; Innovators – individual scoring towards this end of the KAI are argued to redefine problems by breaking established constraints, thus 'doing things differently'	Several 16PF dimensions are argued to predict creativity: • *Factor B: Abstract thinking* – more intelligent, bright; • *Factor G: Expedient* – disregards rules, self-indulgent; • *Factor M: Imaginative* – absent-minded, absorbed in thought, impractical • *Factor Q₁: Experimenting* – liberal, critical, open to change *Note:* The new 16PF5 version of this measure also includes a number of creativity-relevant dimensions	Several OPQ dimensions are argued to predict creativity: • *Outspoken* – prepared to argue, candid and critical, independent view, challenging • *Traditional* (negative loading) – prefers well-proven methods, orthodox, disciplined, following rules • *Conceptual* – theoretically, intellectually curious, enjoys complex and abstract problems • *Innovative* – likes to generate ideas, shows ingenuity, is creative, thinks up solutions	Nine team roles argued to be: plant, resource investigator, co-ordinator, shaper, monitor evaluator, teamworker, implementer, completer, specialist (1993 version) *Plant* argued as pre-eminently creative-type Strengths – creative, imaginative, unorthodox, solves difficult problems Allowable weaknesses – ignores detail, too preoccupied to communicate effectively	*Motivation to change* – 'intrinsic motivation to seek and adopt change' *Challenging behaviour* – 'an individual's propensity to challenge others' thinking and points of view in order to solve problems at work' *Adaptation* – 'whether an individual typically adopts an evolutionary or revolutionary perspective; (see also Chapter 5) *Consistency of work styles* – 'a preference for methodological, systematic and consistent approaches to work, and for conformance to organisational norms *Social Desirability* – Impression management check scale	*Participative safety* *Support for innovation* *Vision* *Task orientation* *Social desirability* See Chapter 4, especially Box 4.1, for a detailed description of these factors originally as the Team Climate Inventory (Anderson and West 1994, 1999)
Test supplier	Occupational Research Centre/ASE	ASE/NFER-Nelson	Saville & Holdsworth Ltd	Belbin Associates Ltd	Oxford Psychologists Press	ASE/NFER-Nelson

| Figure 2.1 | **Items assessing creativity from personality tests** |

- I like to 'dream up' new ways of doing things rather than to be a practical follower of well-tried ways.

  a. true
  b. uncertain
  c. false

- Creative ideas do not come easily to me

  strongly disagree
  disagree
  unsure
  agree
  strongly agree

- People come to me for creative ideas

  strongly disagree
  disagree
  unsure
  agree
  strongly agree

- I am not particularly inventive

  strongly disagree
  disagree
  unsure
  agree
  strongly agree

illustrate this dilemma, our case study, Box 2.1, below, provides a fictitious example of the issues inherent in selecting for creative individuals at work.

Another problem in using a trait approach to selection is the sheer number of different traits which have been associated with creativity. Added to this there is evidence that the importance of particular traits for creativity varies according to the area of activity concerned: creative engineers may well be rather different people from creative advertising copy-writers. Organizations need to think carefully about what *they* mean by creativity, and to ensure that the tests they employ are in

Box 2.1 **Selecting for innovation and change in Nixon Publishing**

The organization

Nixon Publishing PLC has grown throughout its sixty-year history into one of the three largest publishers in its particular field. Nixon specializes in commissioning and publishing management text-books, collections of case studies, edited texts, and manuscripts aimed primarily at the academic business studies market. The 1994 catalogue contains over 200 book titles, academic journals and professional magazines covering a diverse range of topics in management, including:

- organization behaviour
- human resource management
- finance and accounts
- information technology
- qualitative methods
- strategic management, and
- business legislation.

During the 1992/93 financial year the turnover for the whole group was just under £70 million, divided between two divisions, Textbooks and Journals, in the ratio of approximately 3:1. Nixon remains a profitable and competitive publishing house, but in the words of its chairman, Sir James Whittington-Smythe, 'certain sectors of our business have seen better times. We cannot afford to continue to live on past glories – it's one thing being a profitable publisher in the 1940s, totally another being so in the 1990s.'

The chairman's comments, made in the 1992/93 annual report of company accounts, did not go unnoticed within the organization, nor more widely within the publishing industry in Europe. Currently employing over 500 staff in the UK alone, with most being based at the group's East London headquarters, many informed staff began to see the Textbook Division as the one which was ripe for reorganization. Moreover, the HRM director, John Salesbury, has been under increasing pressure to introduce changes in personnel policies, especially those relating to the recruitment and selection of new staff into the organization. ▶

Selecting for change makers

Salesbury has risen rapidly throughout his career, attaining the status of personnel manager by the age of 32 in another competitor publishing house. He was appointed personnel director of Nixon PLC three years ago when he was only 38. Educated at Queen's College, Cambridge, gaining a second-class honours degree in modern languages, he then progressed directly onto a postgraduate MBA at Warwick University, where he gained a distinction-level pass. In more recent years he has consistently been tipped by managerial colleagues as a dedicated high flyer and someone who does not suffer incompetence at all gladly.

McKenzie and Took

Salesbury has, over the last few months, completed a detailed analysis of the recruitment and selection policies and procedures operated by the HRM department. Not entirely satisfied with the findings of his own research, Salesbury has recently commissioned a firm of independent personnel management consultants, McKenzie and Took, to generate ideas on how to improve existing selection methods. As a consultancy firm, McKenzie and Took was a well-known local family business which had been engaged in this type of highly lucrative consultancy for some years. Under the direction of its charismatic but egotistical founder, Ian Took, the consultancy had arranged a series of interviews with staff in Nixon. After several weeks of interviews and discussions with senior executives in the Textbook Division, McKenzie and Took last week presented their final feedback report (running to over ninety pages) to John Salesbury. The personnel director now feels that he has an obligation to act upon one of their main recommendations as a matter of urgency – to review selection procedures for textbook commissioning editors.

Behind the McKenzie and Took Report

Commissioning editors have long been treated as the elite of the Textbook Division by Nixon. Benefits have included salaries on the senior management scale, exceptional degrees of job autonomy and freedom to commission whomsoever the editors felt appropriate for any book, highly generous expense accounts (most ▶

commissioning editors meet with authors only at the Ritz or the Café Royale for discussions over lunch – a gesture which has been greatly appreciated by academic authors), and more significantly, personal access and accountability direct to the group chairman, Sir James Whittington-Smythe. As if to reciprocate this treatment, a few of the section of 12 commissioning editors have always behaved in a rather eccentric manner. To staff in less esteemed job functions in the organization (including copy-editors, marketing staff, typesetters and publishing assistants) the role of the commissioning editor can seem one long round of exclusive business lunches, late-night drinking sessions at academic conferences, and travel by first-class rail to hold informal tête-à-têtes with university academics.

Commissioning editors: performance monitoring

The issue of performance targets and financial rewards to commissioning editors has arisen over recent months. As Rose Watergate, a senior commissioning editor for HRM textbooks, commented during an interview with a consultant from McKenzie and Took:

> Part of the problem is a lack of creativity in Nixon generally, but especially in relation to the reward structure for us commissioning editors. Basically, our performance-related pay is determined by the sales of books that we each commission. So most of us tend to stick to tried-and-tested authors and topics, knowing that they will probably sell fairly well, if not set the cash registers alight. As you can imagine, to take the risk of commissioning a highly innovative text by an unknown author or editor is just not worth it because it may not sell. We stick to the Charles Handys, John Childs and Henry Minzbergs of the academic world because we know that we can literally cash-in upon their name. Certainly, creativity is not valued as highly as it should be and I know that many of us would like to break out of the ways we have tended to do things in Nixon ... but we simply cannot afford the chance of failure.

It is clear then that commissioning editors place considerable value upon achieving 'safe sales' on management textbooks but that their instincts tell them that more imaginative commissions may ▶

reap rewards in the longer term. Armed with these facts, McKenzie and Took have proposed that selection criteria and methods for commissioning editors be radically updated.

Selecting for creativity

In addition to modifying the application form and reference request form by including sections on creativity and innovations implemented, McKenzie and Took have designed an entirely novel group discussion technique for selecting editors. Short-listed applicants arrive at the offices of Nixon in groups of eight for a psychometric testing session, including ability and personality tests, and to undergo the group discussion exercise. Candidates are given the following written instructions:

Nixon Publishing PLC: commissioning strategy exercise

Instructions

As the Commissioning Board of eight editors for the Textbook Division, you have been asked by the group chairman, Sir James Whittington-Smythe, to agree an innovative commissioning strategy for the coming financial year. No one individual leads the group and you all hold the same positional status within Nixon. Discuss all types of future strategy, addressing the issues of author choice, marketing company image, contractual arrangements and choice of academic titles. In your discussion try to offer radically new and improved ways of managing the commissioning process. As a result of your discussion, agree a group strategy for all aspects of the commissioning process for presentation to the group chairman.

Concluding comments

This group discussion exercise has been well received by John Salesbury. He feels it adds a dynamic and realistic edge to the selection process for commissioning editors. To conclude, the only question that remains in his mind is how to recognize 'creative' or 'innovative' behaviour by particular candidates in this group exercise.

Questions

1 How would you advise John Salesbury to recognize, evaluate and interpret creative/innovative behaviour in this exercise? ▶

2 What might be the causes of this behaviour? (For instance, personality, group norms, motivational, or even intentional deception, etc.)

3 In the longer term, how can the personnel department check the veracity and reliability of this exercise in selecting highly creative commissioning editors? Suggest an ideal research study design for this validation check.

4 What barriers to creativity might newly appointed commissioning editors face in their job role? Is it therefore feasible to try to enhance innovation in organizations solely by selecting-in creative individuals? If not, why not?

5 How would you advise the personnel director to tackle the wider problem of a lack of creativity in the Textbook Division more generally? What organization development (OD) techniques seem *prima facie* to be possibilities in the case of Nixon Publishing?

keeping with their requirements. We would also suggest that using trait measures in conjunction with other approaches may provide a more reliable prediction of creative potential than a purely trait-based approach – especially if only a single trait measure is used.

Biographical inventories

Biographical inventories (or biodata inventories as they are sometimes called) have a number of advantages over trait measures. One is that many are domain specific, having been designed to identify biographical predictors of creativity in particular fields such as scientific research, engineering and design. Also, their validity in selection contexts has been found to be comparatively high (Anderson and Shackleton, 1993). If an organization cannot find an inventory that addresses its specific needs, there are a number of general inventories as well, such as Schaeffer's (1970) 'Biographical Inventory: Creativity'. These inventories embrace a wide range of life experiences and achievements, going back to childhood in most cases, and commonly include descriptive factual data such as parental educational levels. They may therefore be less transparent in their purpose than some trait measures, and less easily faked. A disadvantage of biographical inventories is that they may be of limited use in assessing school leavers and new graduates simply because they will only be able to provide data on pre-work experiences (except for mature student graduates). There are fewer biographical inventories than trait measures available, and correspondingly less information on norms and psychometric properties. Virtually all have been compiled and evaluated in the United States, which must raise questions as to their appropriateness for non-American organizations. It is entirely possible that there are different biographical predictors of creativity in different cultures; this is an area where further research is called for. Equally, it is open to question how appropriate it is to use biographical inventories which were devised several decades ago. There is no guarantee that life-event predictors of creativity have remained stable historically.

Many authors have pointed out that the personal qualities which best distinguish between creative and non-creative people are motivational ones. They work hard, prefer to set their own agendas, strive for originality and show flexibility in tackling problems. Similarly, Theresa Amabile (1983) has shown that greater creativity results from intrinsic motivation – enjoying a task for its own sake – than from extrinsic motivation (i.e. seeking reward and/or avoiding punishment). On the basis of this evidence, Kabanoff and Rossiter (1994) have suggested that the development of 'motivational inventories' which measure motivational state could constitute a valuable advance in selection for creativity.

Selection – specific tests of innovation

In keeping with Kabanoff and Rossiter's (1994) suggestion, quite recent advances in psychometric tests show promise to address this issue. The tests in particular have recently been published by different test suppliers, both of which were developed specifically for recruitment and selection contexts and specifically related to innovation potential as a multifaceted dimension in selecting for new organizational employees. Of these two measures, Fiona Patterson's Innovation Potential Indicator (IPI: Oxford Psychologist's Press, 1999) focuses specifically upon individual-level potential for innovation across numerous job types. One advantage of this measure is that it includes a social desirability scale which acts as a check against applicants who are attempting to 'face-good' or impression manage upwards their true levels of innovation potential – a longstanding problem noted previously in this section with older, non selection-specific measures of general personality which include an innovation scale. The second recently published test, Anderson and St John Birch's Team Selection Inventory (TSI: ASE/NFER-Nelson, 2001) similarly includes a social desirability check scale but is intended as a measure of an individual's preferences for team-working styles and climate for innovation. It thus to some extent bridges the individual and group levels of analysis in innovation (see Chapter 1 for an overview), but this measure is completed by individual applicants being selected by an organization interested in their person–team fit (see Chapter 4).

Creative thinking tests

There is a wide range of tests of creative thinking ability, many of which have been used extensively in research and organizational practice. When considering the use of such a test for selection and assessment there are two issues over which special care must be taken. First, how has the test constructor conceptualized (explicitly or implicitly) creativity? Many tests which purport to be of creative thinking are in fact purely measures of divergent thinking ability. As discussed earlier, divergent ability is only one aspect of creative thinking – and its importance has almost certainly been exaggerated. Tests which only measure divergent thinking are therefore unreliable predictors of creative performance. Second, research evidence over many years has suggested a considerable degree of domain-specificity in creative thinking skills. Regarding divergent thinking (DT) abilities, Frank Barron and David Harrington (1981), in their review of research into creativity, intelligence and personality, state that: 'Because the DT abilities presumably underlying creative achievements probably vary from field to field, there is little reason to expect any randomly selected DT test to correlate with creative achievement in any randomly selected domain' (page 448). They argue for the development of creative thinking tests which index the skills required in individual fields, as does Michael Wallach (1985). Kabanoff and Rossiter's (1994) more recent review does see value in the use of general creative thinking tests, in combination with domain-specific tests. However, the use of general tests alone is now widely seen as inadvisable in selection and assessment as well as in research.

Assessing creative products

There are practical and theoretical advantages in measuring creativity through evaluation of creative products, as we saw earlier, because we can only ever say that creativity has occurred when there is a creative product to judge – be it a physical object or an idea expressed in written or spoken language. Hocevar and Bachelor (1989) conclude in their review of the whole range of creativity measures that assessing creative products is the most valid and reliable method, largely because 'past behaviour is generally the best predictor of future behaviour' (page 58). While their main concern was with research usage, a product-based approach can also be useful in selection and assessment; it can be seen in the very common practice of asking candidates to provide some kind of sample of their creative work as part of the assessment process. Graphic designers and photographers will usually be asked to provide a portfolio of their work; academic researchers might be asked for samples of recent papers as well as a full list of publications; actors will often show reviews of their performances to casting directors. Of course, this method of assessment is easiest to use where work involves the creation of some kind of tangible product. Where the main creative products are ideas – as is often the case in management – the task of the assessors is more difficult, although it may still be useful to ask candidates for examples of instances in which they have solved problems creatively.

This approach shares a limitation with the use of biographical inventories in that relatively inexperienced candidates (especially school leavers and new graduates) will have had fewer – if any – relevant examples of products than those who have been working in an area for some time. Also there are times when past creative behaviour *does not* predict potential well. Most of us can think of examples of organizational members who were promoted on the basis of a highly creative track record but, having reached their desired position of seniority, very soon became anything but creative. Again, this underlines the importance of examining creative motivation as part of the selection and assessment process.

Creativity and organizational characteristics

So far we have looked at how organizations can enhance their creativity by stimulating the creative performance of their members (using idea generation techniques and creativity training packages) and by utilizing selection and assessment procedures to recruit creative individuals and place them in appropriate work roles. However, no matter how well such strategies are implemented, they may fail to have any substantial effect if features of the organization itself act to inhibit creativity. There is a substantial research literature examining factors which help or hinder organizational innovation, much of which is also applicable to individual creativity. We discuss this in detail in subsequent chapters in relation to group processes (Chapter 4), antecedents to innovation (Chapter 5), the innovation process (Chapter 6), and resistance to change (Chapter 8). Table 2.2 summarizes organizational characteristics commonly found to impact on creative performance. Although we would strongly caution against the assumption that these will generalize to all types of creativity in all organizations, they do indicate areas where there are clear trends in the research literature.

If we consider the processes by which the above characteristics impact upon creativity, two stand out as being of central importance: motivation and communication. Many of the factors considered to be inhibitors of innovation operate by restricting people's freedom to work

Table 2.2	Organizational characteristics influencing creativity

Leadership
Democratic, participative styles facilitate creativity; authoritarian styles inhibit it

Job characteristics
Discretion is positively associated with creativity

Structure
Strongly hierarchical structures inhibit creativity; flat structures with permeable boundaries between subdivisions facilitate it

Climate
Creativity is encouraged by climates which are playful about ideas, supportive of risk taking, challenging and tolerant of vigorous debate

Culture
Creativity is impeded by cultures which emphasize formal rules, respect for traditional ways of doing things and clearly demarcated roles

in the way that best suits them (i.e. authoritarian leadership, routinized low discretion jobs, hierarchical structures and bureaucratic cultures). By so doing they make it less likely that people will be motivated by enjoyment of the job itself and more likely that they will find motivation in material rewards. As we have seen, Theresa Amabile's (1983) research has demonstrated that an extrinsically motivated state is less conducive to creativity than an intrinsically motivated state. These same factors also tend to inhibit the free flow of ideas within and between organizations. Without effective intra- and interorganizational communication, possible sources of creative stimulation are limited and good ideas may never reach those who have the power to authorize their implementation. This last point illustrates the way in which communication and motivation are linked. If creative ideas repeatedly achieve nothing because of poor communication, the motivation of organizational members to continue to be creative is likely to be reduced.

A good example of the way that unsupportive organizational characteristics can impede individual creativity is given by Kilbourne and Woodman (1999). They describe how an employee of Chrysler produced an idea for a fold-down car seat which took six years before it was successfully implemented. To achieve this, the employee had to persist in the face of scepticism from a culture that saw only managers as a potential source of creative ideas and a hierarchical structure which meant that creative ideas had to negotiate layer after layer of decision makers. The authors stress that these characteristics of Chrysler are not at all unusual or atypical. Organizations require some degree of stability and certainty to function efficiently; however, this need can easily come to dominate the equally important need to enable creative change. In part, Kilbourne and Woodman argue, this is because forces of organizational conservatism reinforce individual conservatism in cognitive functioning – our tendency to seek to manage the potentially overwhelming amount of information in our environment by simplifying and routinizing it. The interaction between person and organization is thus central to understanding creativity at work.

Enhancing creativity: implications for practice

Organizations have a wide range of strategies and techniques available to them if they are concerned to enhance the creativity of their members. No one approach can be said to be decisively better than the others; what managers must do is decide which best fits their needs and resources. The introduction of idea generation techniques – especially those which do not require extensive training – is probably the cheapest option and may show benefits quite quickly. It is most appropriate where the requirement is for a means to improve the effectiveness of existing problem-solving groups, such as project development teams. On its own, however, it is not likely to have a pervasive effect on creative performance in the wider organization. For this, the longer-term strategies of creativity training and selecting and assessing for creativity are needed, with their correspondingly larger investment of resources. Looking to organizational characteristics which might be inhibiting creativity is important to the effective implementation of any training or selection initiative. Of course, the four strategy types we have discussed – idea elicitation techniques, creativity training, selection and assessment, and changing organizational characteristics – are not mutually exclusive; far from it. A multistrand creativity enhancement programme which includes elements of all the approaches is most likely to be successful, although organizations may find it too costly, and be concerned about keeping control of changes which could touch upon every aspect of organizational life.

One of the barriers to the adoption of creativity enhancement techniques is that their benefits are not easily predictable. This is partly because of the severe lack of evaluation studies carried out in real-world settings looking at the outcomes that matter to organizations. It is also because creativity is essentially unpredictable; it can be influenced by so many things not within the direct control of management. Cautious managers may decide that the strategies we have examined are not worth the risks of disruption, wasted resources and possible demoralizing failure. Against this, for many managers the greater risk is in *not* responding creatively to the threats and opportunities of a rapidly changing environment. Creativity enhancement is no miracle cure for organizational ills, but used intelligently it can be a way of loading the dice in an organization's favour.

Suggested reading

Evans, J. R. (1991) *Creative Thinking in the Decision and Management Sciences*, Cincinatti, OH: South-Western.

Kabanoff, B. and Rossiter, J. R. (1994) 'Recent developments in applied creativity', in C. L. Cooper and I. T. Robertson (eds) *International Review of Industrial and Organizational Psychology, Volume 9*, Chichester: Wiley.

Purser, R. E. and Montuori, A. (1999) *Social Creativity: Volume II*, Cresshill, NJ: Hampton Press.

West, M. A. (1997) *Developing Creativity in Organizations*, Leicester: BPS Books.

3 Psychological approaches to creativity

After reading this chapter you should be able to

- describe different approaches in research into individual creativity
- identify different perspectives to creativity
- evaluate Wallas's (1926) model of the creative process
- discuss social psychological approaches to the study of creativity.

Why is it important in a book on the psychology of organizational innovation and change to consider theoretical approaches to creativity? We believe that there are two reasons. One we addressed at the start of the previous chapter: that an important aspect of understanding innovation is understanding how and why new ideas emerge in organizations. The other is that throughout its development the innovation research field has utilized concepts, models and theories from creativity research. The fact that it has often done so implicitly and sometimes inappropriately makes it all the more necessary for the student of organizational innovation to gain some awareness of creativity research traditions. To that end, we open this chapter with a short historical account of the field.

Creativity research: a brief history

Psychological research is as prone to fluctuations in fashion as any other area of human enterprise; topics move in and out of favour as a result of changes in political climate, economic conditions and media preoccupations, as well as through theoretical developments within the discipline itself. The topic of creativity illustrates this better than most. The scientific study of creativity goes back to the very dawn of psychology, with Galton's attempt to explain the exceptional creative abilities of eminent artists and scientists, published as 'Hereditary Genius' in 1869. In the early part of this century, creativity attracted the interest of psychologists and psychiatrists from a variety of backgrounds, including psychoanalysts such as Sigmund Freud and Carl Jung. Graham Wallas in 1926 provided a description of the creative process as consisting of stages of preparation, incubation, illumination and verification, which remains influential to this day. However, the dominance of behaviourism, with its insistence that psychologists should study only observable behaviour, led to a neglect of creativity in the 1930s and 1940s.

A dramatic revival in creativity research came in the 1950s when it leapt to the top of the agenda, especially in American psychology, following J. P. Guilford's presidential address on the subject to the American Psychological Society in 1950. Subsequently, a series of major conferences was held on creativity in science, industry, education and the arts. The renewed interest was strongly motivated by the perceptions of American academics and policy makers that enhanced creativity in all spheres of life – but particularly the economic – was vital for the development of the United States into a modern superpower. Competition with the Soviet Union also played a key role in turning the spotlight on scientific and technological creativity. As Vernon (1970) says: 'it was the advent of Sputnik in 1957 that shocked America into asking whether its educational system was failing to produce sufficient original scientists to maintain its technological lead in the modern world' (page 11).

The profile of creativity research declined somewhat in the 1970s, though a steady level of output continued; Barron and Harrington (1981) estimate an average of 250 new articles, books and dissertations published on the subject per year. The 1980s saw some significant new directions in creativity research emerging, such as the social psychology of creativity and the use of computers to construct cognitive simulations of the creative process. Building on these developments, the 1990s saw a resurgence of interest in creativity amongst psychologists from varied backgrounds, including cognitive, social and life-span developmental. Several key collections of articles have been published which attempt to draw together the burgeoning body of research and redefine the field for the twenty-first century (e.g. Isaksen *et al.*, 1993; Montuori and Purser, 1999; Runco and Pritzker, 1999).

Post-war research into creativity has had a very strong applied emphasis, as is evidenced by the attention given to idea generation techniques such as brainstorming and synectics, and training programmes such as Parnes' Creative Problem-Solving. One consequence is that psychologists studying organizational innovation have been able to draw readily on the creativity tradition – for example, when tackling issues such as how leadership styles, organizational climate and organizational structure influence innovativeness.

The scope of this chapter

With so vast a field we must of necessity be highly selective in what we cover in the present chapter. Given the aims of this book, our choice has been to concentrate on those parts of the literature which throw most light on creativity in organizational settings. This does not mean that only applied research will be discussed, but it does mean that some large areas such as creativity in children will be neglected. Our overview of the research literature on adult creativity is divided into six broad areas representing the main approaches to the subject: creativity and personality traits, the study of creative lives, creativity as a mental ability, psychodynamic perspectives, humanistic perspectives, and the social psychology of creativity. Inevitably, some studies do not fit neatly into one approach, but this categorization of the literature does reflect the main differences amongst researchers in their orientations to the subject. Throughout we will highlight the relevance of each approach to understanding creativity in organizational settings, helping to put the applied research discussed in the previous chapter in a broader theoretical context.

Creativity and personality traits

The trait approach has been central to creativity research since the renewal of interest in the area in the 1950s. Literally hundreds of papers have been published describing attempts to identify personality characteristics associated with creativity across a wide range of areas of human endeavour, including science, mathematics, engineering, literature, music and art. Typically, measures of a variety of personality traits are correlated either with real-world creative achievement criteria, or with creative ability test scores, in order to identify consistent personality differences between the more and less creative subjects. From the mass of data such studies have produced there is a reasonable consensus that certain traits tend to be associated with relatively high levels of creativity. They include (amongst many others):

tolerance of uncertainty and ambiguity
self-confidence
unconventionality
originality
intrinsic motivation
above average intelligence
determination to succeed.

This is not to say that all people showing high levels of creative achievement or ability will possess all these traits, but that at least some of them are discernible in most highly creative individuals (Barron and Harrington, 1981).

We cannot assume that, because we can identify characteristics which are associated with creativity in general, the 'creative personality' is the same for all types of persons and all areas of creative endeavour. Indeed, research has shown that the general consensus described above conceals important differences in the personality correlates of creativity by age, sex, and occupation or profession. To take one example, Getzels and Csikszentmihalyi (1976), in their influential longitudinal study of creative artists, showed clear differences between those choosing to follow careers in fine and applied arts.

Although the trait approach has been able to identify characteristics associated with high levels of creativity in different domains, it has been much less successful in shedding light on the origins of individual differences in creative performance. Cross-sectional studies, in which the measures correlated with each other are taken at one point in time, can be no more than suggestive of the causal links between variables (see Chapter 1). MacKinnon (1962), for example, found that eminent creative architects (as rated by their peers) were high on the trait of 'independence', which might indicate that independence contributes to creative achievement. But as his was a cross-sectional study, this finding could equally well indicate that creativity contributes to the development of an independent personality. Most studies of creativity and personality are cross-sectional. Longitudinal studies – which do offer the possibility of establishing causality – are rare, largely for practical reasons as they require research projects lasting many years, perhaps decades. Returning to the example of architects, if we wanted to establish the direction of the relationship between creativity and independence, we might measure these two variables early in the careers of our subjects, and at regular intervals afterwards for perhaps ten, fifteen or even twenty years.

The trait approach is chiefly concerned with identifying creative potential and predicting creative behaviour, a worthwhile endeavour, especially for the application of psychology to real-world issues such as the facilitation of organizational innovation. However, there is a tendency to see the identification of creativity-relevant traits as a goal in itself rather than as a means to the end of increasing our understanding of the nature of creativity. Although trait studies have drawn on major theoretical areas which do seek to produce such understanding (such as cognitive, psychoanalytic and humanistic) they have played only a limited role in the development of these theoretical traditions.

The study of creative lives

While the personality trait approach is interested in characteristics associated with creative performance, measurable in the population at large, the psychological study of creative lives focuses on the way in which creative talent emerges and develops over the lifespan of particular individuals. Very often, research focuses on the lives of people of widely acknowledged eminence in their domain of activity – great scientists, musicians, writers, and so on. Other studies have examined the lives of people working in occupations where creative ability is of central importance, such as fine and applied arts. Two broad research strategies can be identified here: *retrospective* studies, using biographical data, and *prospective* studies, often employing multiple methods to track the development of creative ability and achievement.

Retrospective studies

Attempts to explain the creative achievement of eminent people using largely biographical data go back to the roots of scientific psychology (Galton, 1869), and several major studies – some involving hundreds of cases – were carried out in the first half of this century (e.g. Cox, 1926; Raskin, 1936). Some of the best-known work of this type is that of Harvey Lehman (1953, 1965), who concluded on the basis of an enormous volume of biographical material that the peak years for quality of creative output are in the 30s. He did, though, recognize considerable variation from this for specific professions, with musicians peaking earlier and philosophers much later than the overall average. The lifespan approach continues to provide significant insights into the nature of creativity, as will be seen below when we examine the work of Dean Keith Simonton and Howard Gruber. For occupational psychologists, it is potentially applicable to areas such as selection and assessment and career development.

When we consider the lives of eminent creators, one of the most striking features is the variation in what might be termed their creative careers: when they produced their first acknowledged major work, when their creative peak was reached and how long it lasted, whether their work was immediately recognized or only after considerable delay, what their total output was, and so on. Taking the example of classical composers, some, like Beethoven and Tchaikovsky, continued producing major works until the ends of their lives, others declined in creative output or – as in the cases of Sibelius and Rossini – effectively 'retired' from composition decades before their deaths (Swafford, 1992). It may seem a vain effort to attempt to make any predictions about the creative careers of classical composers in the face of such variation, but in fact Simonton (1991) has done so with considerable success. Using a theoretical model developed in his previous work on eminent scientists, he was able to predict from biographical information the timing of creative 'landmarks' (e.g. first, last and best major works) and overall levels of creative accomplishment. For the composers a key predictor was not chronological age, but the age at which a musical career was embarked upon – that is, the first music lessons and the first serious attempt at composition.

Simonton shows there are consistencies behind the variation in creative careers, but his method does not allow much insight into why the variations in initial creative potential and in the timing of careers occurs in the first place; for instance, why one composer had his first musical lesson at age five and another at ten. Though not encompassed in the model, Simonton acknowledges the likely influence of social factors such as the presence or absence of a mentor for a young composer. The importance of a mentor figure to the development of exceptional creativity has been noted by other writers, including Csikszentmihalyi (1996) and Walberg, Rasher and Parkerson (1980).

Case studies of individual lives

To complement the sort of large-scale analyses carried out by Simonton, there is a need to look also at individual creative lives in depth.

Some of the most important contemporary work of this type has been carried out by Howard Gruber and his colleagues (Gruber and Davis, 1988). They have used a case-study approach, examining the creative works and biographical and autobiographical material relating to their subjects who have included Charles Darwin, William James and Dorothy Richardson. Unlike earlier psychoanalytic case studies of creative lives, they are concerned with how eminent creative people work and with the developmental process across the whole career, rather than with unconscious motives for creativity and the role of early development and experience. They have described an 'evolving systems approach' to the understanding of creative lives. Creative achievement is not seen as the result of sudden inspiration, arising out of the unconscious or some metaphysical source. Rather, it is based on the evolution of ideas over extended periods of time:

> Perhaps the single most reliable finding in our studies is that creative work takes a long time. With all due apologies to thunderbolts, creative work is not a matter of milliseconds, minutes, or even hours – but of months, years, and decades.
>
> *(Gruber and Davis, 1988, page 265)*

In Gruber and Davis' approach, the creative person is seen as a system consisting of three interacting subsystems: knowledge, purpose and effect. Thus creative achievement arises through knowledge and skills in a particular domain (or domains), a sense of direction or vision in the creative career, and feelings towards particular projects. A fourth element which is also integral to creativity is the 'milieu', or social and physical world in which the person lives. The work of the Russian composer Shostakovitch was deeply influenced by the difficulties he faced in developing his career in the Soviet Union under Stalin. Similarly, the artistic and scientific achievements of Leonardo da Vinci were shaped by the culture of Renaissance Italy. In recognizing that creativity is not just the product of individual characteristics and abilities, Gruber and Davis have much in common with the social psychological approaches of Amabile (1983) and Csikszentmihalyi (1988).

The use of psychobiographical methods to study creativity has several advantages over other strategies. By studying an individual's creative production across the entire lifespan we can examine the fullest possible range of influences, in particular those which are of a long-term nature which would not be apparent in a 'snapshot' at one moment in time. At a pragmatic level, by selecting individuals of undisputed eminence, problems of defining and measuring creative talent are largely side-stepped. Finally, the use of psychobiographical data enables creative lives to be seen in their social and historical contexts, something which is all too easily neglected in other types of creativity research. The most obvious problem for the psychobiographical approach is that it relies on the quality and accuracy of data available. Researchers have tackled this chiefly through rigorous selection criteria, such that only those for whom adequate data are available are included. This can have unfortunate consequences, particularly in the under-representation of women, as was the case in Simonton's (1991) study. It also limits research only to those who are eminent enough to have generated a substantial body of biographical material. We cannot assume that conclusions drawn from studies of famous creators are applicable to the general population – even to those whose creative achievements are well above average. A recent study by Worth (2001) examining 'everyday creativity' in a varied group of adults provides a rare example of the biographical approach applied to a non-eminent sample.

Prospective studies

The limitations of retrospective studies lead us to the second strategy for research on creative lives: longitudinal studies in which researchers follow the creative careers of a cohort of subjects over an extended period of time. L. M. Terman's huge study – published in five volumes -- which followed a thousand gifted children through into adulthood is a classic example of this approach. One of the most widely-cited longitudinal studies of creativity was initially carried out by Getzels and Csikszentmihalyi (1976) in which the authors followed the careers of a group of 31 fine arts students from entry to art college to five or six years after graduation. This showed problem-finding ability to be a strong predictor of creative success, along with a number of biographical characteristics: birth order (first and only children were more successful), parental education and wealth (students with well-educated and better-off parents were more successful). Only one of the many measured personality traits predicted later success – low concern for social approval – and divergent thinking skills were also not important. Further publications have documented the later development of this cohort (e.g. Csikszentmihalyi, Getzels and Kahn, 1984). Of particular interest is Freeman's (1993) study of 54 of the original sample. Based on lengthy semi-structured interviews, he traced the way in which the social conditions facing aspiring artists shaped the development of their careers and their ability to perform creatively in their field. That there are relatively few such studies in the literature is not a reflection on their value, but rather that they are costly and difficult to carry out, as they require the involvement of subjects and the research team to be maintained over many years.

The most direct application of the creative lives approach to work organizations has been the development of biographical inventories for use in selection and assessment, discussed in Chapter 2, although these are much less common than personality or ability-based measures. The important insights this approach has provided into creativity as a characteristic which develops, or evolves, over the lifespan have been largely neglected by researchers and practitioners concerned with organizational creativity. In concentrating on selecting 'creative people' or providing training to boost creative performance, organizations may be overlooking the need to support the development and realization of creative abilities in the longer term.

Creativity as a mental ability

As we have seen, creativity is commonly defined either explicitly or implicitly as a mental process (or combination of processes). Describing the nature of the process has therefore been a major concern of researchers in this field and has generated a very large literature. We have already seen in the previous chapter how applied research in this area has had an impact on organizations through selection and assessment for creativity, idea generation techniques, and creativity training. Here we will concentrate on four strands of work within the 'mental ability' approach: the relationship between creativity and intelligence, creativity and thinking styles, creativity and altered states of consciousness and creativity, problem solving and imagery. This last topic leads us into key debate, over whether or not creativity involves a special type of thinking, distinct from 'ordinary' problem solving.

Creativity and intelligence

Early researchers assumed a strong relationship between creativity and intelligence, largely on the basis of studies such as those by Cox (1926) using biographical data on 'geniuses' and Terman (1947) who followed the achievements of a thousand gifted children from primary school through to mid-life. Studies of gifted and talented individuals clearly indicate that their IQ test scores are in the upper range, and it seems likely that high intelligence is a prerequisite for exceptional creativity. However, where researchers have examined the relationship between general intelligence and creativity amongst those with relatively high IQ scores, they have consistently found correlations to be weak – there is no guarantee that because someone is highly intelligent they will be highly creative (Barron and Harrington, 1981).

Other evidence suggests that particular components of intelligence are associated with creative achievement in particular areas. Anne Roe (1952) found that experimental psychologists scored higher on spatial and mathematical intelligence tests than on verbal, whilst the reverse was true for other psychologists and for anthropologists. Chauncey and Hilton (1983) found that the achievements of research scientists were unrelated to their general intelligence, but were related to some extent to scores on a measure of quantitative ability. There are strong grounds for domain-specific measures to be used in testing for exceptional ability, and consequently for the use of domain-specific creativity tests in occupational settings: 'Giftedness was found to be much more domain-specific than was first understood: psychologically different for math than for art, for writing than for leadership' (Wallach, 1985, page 117).

Creativity and thinking styles

Much attention has been paid by researchers to the association between creativity and styles of thinking, in particular to how it relates to divergent and convergent thinking. As we saw earlier, many 'creativity' tests are largely or wholly tests of the ability to think divergently rather than convergently. This is an indication of the extent to which divergence and creativity came to be seen as virtually synonymous, especially in the arguments made in the 1960s in support of 'progressive education' in North America and Europe. The assumption is also present in the work of popular psychology writers – most famously Edward de Bono – who have decried the overemphasis on logical thinking abilities in Western education and devised techniques for enhancing more creative thinking styles.

There is good evidence that people do have clear preferences for divergent or convergent thinking styles, and that the nature of the education children receive plays an important role in this. Probably the best-known work in this area is that of Liam Hudson (1966), who studied the divergent and convergent thinking styles and arts or sciences preferences of English schoolboys. However, it is a mistake to consider divergent thinking to be synonymous with creativity; given that almost every definition of creativity stresses the criterion of appropriateness (see Chapter 1), Barron and Harrington (1981) argue that the production of any new idea requires the use of both styles of thinking. A wide range of evidence shows that general divergent thinking tests are only slightly better predictors than IQ tests of real-world creative achievement (Wallach, 1985). This is not to say that divergent thinking *is not* a useful skill, nor that the nature of our education system *does not* overemphasize convergent abilities: both may well be true. There has been something of a rehabilitation of the divergent thinking concept in creativity research over the last decade, with leading researchers stressing its importance while at the same time arguing for a more sophisticated theoretical understanding than was apparent in much of the earlier work (e.g. Basadur, 1997; Runco, 1993). What is evident from decades of research is that we cannot hope to enhance creative performance solely by providing training in divergent thinking.

A different approach to thinking styles and creativity is that of Michael Kirton (1976, 1989) and his colleagues. He has devised a measure which locates people on a dimension labelled adaption–innovation, where the poles represent different styles but not different levels of creativity. Thus the adaptor expresses creativity through making modifications within the existing paradigm (i.e. the existing rules, practices and expectations), whilst the innovator expresses creativity by breaking out of the existing paradigm. There have been some doubts raised over Kirton's claim that style and level of creativity are independent of each other, both on psychometric and conceptual grounds (Payne, 1987; Taylor, 1989). Nevertheless, the KAI has been widely used by researchers and practitioners in organizations (see Table 2.1, Chapter 2).

Creativity and altered states of consciousness

There is a common and long-standing notion that states of consciousness differing from the 'normal' may be associated with creativity. In particular, artistic creativity has been at various times linked to divinely inspired rapture, madness and the influence of psychoactive drugs. In attempting to understand such apparent associations, psychologists have addressed two broad questions; first, whether and to what extent various kinds of altered state are able to enhance creativity, and second, what cognitive and social psychological processes might underlie the influence of particular states. For the sake of clarity, we will examine the research evidence in relation to three general categories of altered state: drug-induced states, meditation, and the impact of specific psychological disorders (especially bipolar disorder).

Drugs and creativity

Empirical research into the effects of drugs on creativity is circumscribed by ethical and, for many substances, legal concerns. Despite this, evidence of an association can be found in the literature, though the relationship is by no means a simple or unambiguously positive one. Ten Berge (1999) reviews two major sets of studies carried out with European artists in the 1960s prior to the criminalization of hallucinogenic drugs. Results were apparently somewhat contradictory, with participants in the French study (led by Robert Volmat) generally feeling more positive about the creativity-enhancing effect of the experience than the German (led by Richard Hartmann). Ten Berge suggests three factors which may in combination explain the different outcomes of the studies. First, the studies differed in the choice of drug and dosage used. The French study used psilocybin (derived from 'magic mushrooms') in quite a moderate dose, whilst Hartmann used higher doses of the more powerful synthetic hallucinogen, LSD. Thus the more negative evaluations of the German participants may be associated with the different quality of the experience between the two drugs (a generally recognized phenomenon) and/or the duration and intensity of the drug effects. Second, the physical settings differed, with Hartmann putting his participants in a bare white room within a psychiatric institute, whilst Volmat's investigations were carried out in the artists' own studios. Finally, there were likely to have been differences in expectations between the groups. Although limited information is available about the professional status of participants in both studies, there are grounds to suggest strongly that the artists in Volmat's research were mostly at an earlier stage in their careers than those in Hartmann's. Ten Berge argues that the disruption to normal modes of thought, perception and action produced by hallucinogens would be more likely to have been seen as a threat by established artists and an opportunity to those whose personal style is less fixed.

> Generally speaking, one might say that established artists will feel more anxious about a *breakdown* than ambitious youngsters aiming for a *breakthrough* in their artistic development and/or career, especially since at the time stylistic continuity in one's work still counted as a sign of authenticity. (page 271)

Ten Berge's point about the importance of expectations is confirmed in an experimental study by Lapp, Collins and Izzo (1994), looking at alcohol and creativity. They used what is known as a 'balanced placebo design', whereby participants either received a small dose of vodka in tonic water or pure tonic water, *and* were either told that they had or had not taken any alcohol. After the drink all participants undertook a creativity test based on the combination of images. The highest scores were obtained by those who *thought* they had consumed alcohol, whether or not they had actually done so. The authors suggest that cultural expectations that alcohol use 'permits' divergence from normal modes of thinking and behaving enabled those who believed they had taken alcohol to risk more radical solutions to the creativity task. As with the studies reviewed by Ten Berge, it appears that it is the meaning of the drug experience to the person which impacts on creativity, not the purely pharmacological effects of the drug itself.

Meditation

Meditation has been employed as a form of spiritual practice for thousands of years in India and the Far East. It came to public prominence in Europe and North America in the 1960s, especially through the proselytising activities of the Transcendental Meditation (TM) movement. It is now commonly used in the West to achieve deep relaxation and enhance personal well-being, without necessarily being linked to a project of spiritual growth. Claims for its positive relationship with creativity centre on the state of calm attentiveness to oneself and ones environment achieved through developing skills in meditation. According to West (1997), this 'mindfulness' enables the meditator to become more aware of taken-for-granted processes and assumptions within organizations, thus opening up the possibility for creative change: 'This present-centred awareness of work is a valuable well-spring for creativity' (page 46). Gowan (1978) argues on the basis of the scientific literature and his personal experience as a meditator that meditation enhances creativity through increased access to the preconscious elements of the mind – that which is potentially accessible to consciousness but normally beyond everyday awareness. We will see in the section on the psychodynamic approach to creativity that some post-Freudian theorists see the preconscious rather than the unconscious as the source of creative impulses. An empirical study by Travis (1979) supports this view, finding that involvement in a TM training course was associated with a significant post-test gain in figural flexibility and originality on the Torrance Tests of Creative Thinking.

Creativity and mental illness

The idea that high levels of creativity are associated with mental illness has a very long history. Plato famously saw the creation of poetry as a manifestation of madness, and the image of the artistic 'mad genius' was heavily reinforced by the Romantic movement of the late eighteenth and nineteenth centuries. Within psychology, Freud saw a close relationship between artistic creativity and neurosis, as Woodman (1981) points out: 'the Freudian position is that mental illness and creativity have identical origins in that they both arise from conflict within the unconscious' (page 45).

Attempts to investigate this proposed relationship empirically have mostly focused on one types of condition; bipolar disorder. This is characterized by sudden changes in mood varying in severity according to the particular form of bipolar disorder present. In the best-known form – manic-depressive illness – the mood swing is often very extreme, from deep depression to an elated, euphoric, manic state.

The evidence for a significantly higher than normal rate of bipolar disorder in creative people – especially in the arts – is strong (e.g. Andeasen, 1987; Jamison, 1989). The case for a direct link between the nature of thought processes in bipolar disorder and heightened creativity was first made by Kraepelin in the 1920s, and more recently has been promoted particularly by Kay Jamison (1989). She argues that manic-depressive illness – especially in the manic phase – facilitates creativity through access to more unusual and original associations (Jamison, 1993), a point supported by another major writer in this area, Ruth Richards (1994). Weisberg (1993), in contrast, is not convinced that the high prevalence of bipolar disorder amongst artists should be explained in terms of creativity-enhancing thought processes. Taking the example of the manic-depressive composer Robert Schumann, he argues that if mania led to qualitatively superior creative thinking, one would expect Schumann to have written a higher proportion of his greatest works during periods of mania than at other times. However, Weisberg's analysis shows that whilst Schumann was at his most prolific during periods dominated by manic episodes, the proportion of acknowledged masterpieces to lesser works did not differ from other, non-manic periods. This, he contends, suggests that mania may lead to a greater volume of creative output, but not to a better quality.

Weisberg suggests that we can look to other explanations than the quality of thought processes to understand the link between bipolar disorder and artistic creativity. It is possible in some cases that far from causing creativity, bipolar disorder may have been triggered by the psychological pressures of high-level creative production. It is also likely that the arts may be particularly attractive to people with bipolar disorders, and therefore 'recruit' them disproportionately. Many of the arts allow for a more unconventional, unstructured and perhaps solitary lifestyle than is possible in other careers, where the socially disruptive nature of manic-depressive illness would make progress difficult. (The much lower rate of bipolar disorder amongst scientists could be seen to support this view.) In fact, the social stereotype of the artist as 'mad genius' may actually work in favour of those individuals who appear to conform to it.

The explanations in terms of social structures and stereotypes do not necessarily conflict with Jamison and Richard's position that manic-depressive thought enhances creativity; it could be that an underlying cognitive advantage is further reinforced by the social factors. Whether one sees these as competing or complimentary theories depends on one's wider understanding of the nature of creativity. Weisberg's problem-solving approach (see below) is at odds with the notion that creativity is linked to 'special' forms of thinking, whilst Richards' evolutionary perspective readily supports such a view. Despite their differences, both authors would agree that it is important not to romanticize manic-depressive illness because of the link to artistic eminence; Richards (1999a) makes the stark point that one in five sufferers who do not receive treatment commit suicide.

Creativity, problem solving and mental imagery

Since the 1970s, the central concern of cognitive psychology has been with understanding the way the mind processes information. Despite growing awareness of the need to examine how cognition functions in the real world (e.g. Neisser, 1982; Cohen, 1996) research remains predominantly experimental and laboratory based. Two main areas of contemporary cognitive psychology have been turned to by creativity researchers, problem solving and mental imagery. The latter has been a fairly recent development in the creativity literature whilst the former has been a key topic from early in the history of this field. Perspectives vary considerably, from those who view creativity as a special form of problem solving to those who see creative production as arising from 'ordinary' problem-solving processes. Many of those who tend towards the former position have been influenced by the work of Graham Wallas, as presented in his 1926 volume *The Art of Thought*. Drawing on autobiographical accounts of eminent creators, such as Mozart and Poincaré, Wallas proposed that there are four stages in the process of creative thinking, which he labels *preparation, incubation, illumination* and *verification* (see Table 3.1).

A famous illustration of this process is the discovery of the structure of benzene by the chemist Kekulé. After thinking about the problem for some time, Kekulé sat dozing by his fire. In his dreams he saw the image of a snake biting its own tail; he awoke suddenly with the realization that benzene had a ring structure. It was then left for him to work this out logically and demonstrate the validity of his solution to his peers.

There is no doubt that as a model of what happens in all instances of creative thinking, Wallas's is too rigid, but the notion that creativity involves a sudden leap of insight continues to be influential and controversial. Insight was central to the explanation of problem solving provided by cognitive psychologists from the Gestalt school, in the first half of this century. According to the Gestalt view, creative problem

Table 3.1	**Wallas's (1926) model of the creative process**		
Preparation	Incubation	Illumination	Verification
The individual turns his or her attention to a task or problem, examining relevant information from his or her own experience and the task environment	Conscious work on the problem ceases; the individual may turn his or her attention to another problem, or simply relax. During this period, Wallas (1926) claims that some degree of unconscious and involuntary (or foreconscious and forevoluntary) work on the problem occurs	The classic 'Eureka!' moment when the core (or even the whole) of the problem solution suddenly springs into awareness	The individual uses logical and rational thought processes to turn the sudden insight into a correct or appropriate solution, apparent as such to others

solving (or 'productive thinking') occurs when the individual suddenly sees how the elements of a problem can be fitted together in a new way to provide a solution. This is not reliant on past experience of tackling similar problems; indeed, Gestalt psychologists such as Kohler and Wertheimer believed that creativity could be blocked by overreliance on well-learnt strategies for approaching problems. Although the Gestalt theories of perception have been shown to be flawed, some contemporary cognitive psychologists have developed new approaches to insight and its relationship to creativity. Sternberg and Davidson (1983) argue that creative achievement is in part due to high levels of an ability they call 'insightful thinking', which has three components: selective encoding, selective combination, and selective comparison. (These are summarized in Table 3.2.)

Weisberg (1986, 1993) is critical of the view that creativity is a 'special' form of problem solving, and especially that it involves unconscious incubation and sudden illumination. He raises serious doubts as to the reliability of many of the classic accounts of illumination, and provides experimental evidence that apparent leaps of insight in problem solving can be seen to involve ordinary processes of trial and error and learning from experience when examined carefully. He does concede that insightful thinking, as described by Sternberg and Davidson, may exist as a distinctive ability, but is sceptical as to whether it plays any major role in creative discovery. Weisberg's work can be seen as supporting – from a very different perspective – that of Gruber and Davis (1988) in their assertion that creative achievement is less to do with the sudden lightning-bolt of insight than the gradual evolution of ideas over long periods of time.

Table 3.2	**Components of 'insightful thinking'**	
Selective encoding	Selective combination	Selective comparison
The ability when faced with a complex problem to identify which bits of information are most likely to be useful in an eventual solution	The ability to recognize the most effective or appropriate way in which the selected bits of information should be combined to solve the problem	The ability to recognize how a new piece of information can be related to existing knowledge in a way which furthers solution of the problem at hand

Source: Based on Sternberg and Davidson (1983).

Since the mid 1980s, mental imagery has grown to become a major research topic in cognitive psychology and allied disciplines. As Finke (1996) notes, it is now generally accepted that imagery is a distinctive cognitive process and that images differ qualitatively from other forms of mental representation. Over the last decade, developments in this area have begun to have an impact on creativity research. A number of studies have suggested a positive association between mental imagery ability and creativity test performance; for example, Gonzalez, Campos and Pérez (1997) found imaging ability was significantly related to fluency, originality, elaboration and resistance to premature closure (as measured by the TTCT). Findings are not consistently supportive of such a link, however. In one recent study, Khasky and Smith (1999) found that training in the use of mental imagery did not lead to higher scores on the TTCT, though the authors themselves conclude that the single session of training given may have been insufficient to have an effect on creative performance.

Finke, Ward and Smith (1992) propose a model of creative cognition called 'geneplore' in which mental imagery plays an important part. The name 'geneplore' derives from their core argument that creative thinking involves a blend of generative and exploratory processes, both of which have conscious and unconscious aspects. Looking particularly at imagery, Finke (1996) describes how creative ideas draw on images that emerge without conscious control *and* on images which are consciously and deliberately manipulated. The combination of these two types of mental imagery facilitates creative solutions which are imaginative and original but at the same time realistic and appropriate.

Is creativity a 'special' ability?

The debate on the role of insight in the creative process is part of a wider controversy over claims that creativity is a 'special' form of thinking. On one side are those who believe that creativity involves the utilization of skills or techniques distinct from those employed in everyday problem solving; this includes advocates of creative thinking techniques such as synectics and lateral thinking (see Chapter 2). Opposing them are writers such as Robert Weisberg and, most vociferously, Herbert Simon, who believe that creativity relies on exactly the same problem-solving skills utilized by everyone in daily life.

Citing as evidence the development of computer programs able to simulate the process of scientific discovery, Simon (1985) argues that all that is required for creative production is normal logical thinking applied to sufficient knowledge of the domain of the problem. Mihaly Csikszentmihalyi (1988) disagrees with this extreme 'rationalist' position, on the grounds that problem solving is not all that is involved in creativity; indeed, he maintains that far more important is 'problem finding' – the ability to identify the key problem in a given domain, and to recognize how existing knowledge can be applied to the problem. This is more a matter of motivation than rationality. (Recent work on the importance of emotion to creativity (Lubart and Getz, 1997) also creates difficulties for Simon's A.I. claims.)

For those interested in creativity in real-world settings, such as work organizations, Csikszentmihalyi's is a crucial point. Much work on creative thinking suffers from a significant weakness as far as the explanation of real-world creative achievement is concerned. By concentrating on the way in which solutions are reached, especially in experimental laboratory conditions or through computer simulations, it frequently overlooks the role of problem finding in creativity. For example, the creative accomplishment of Crick and Watson in discovering the structure of DNA lay not only in the final model they produced but in their recognition that this was the right problem for them to direct their skills and efforts towards. The significance of problem finding has been shown empirically, in Getzels and Csikszent-mihalyi's (1976) longitudinal study and in experimental studies which have shown the importance of questioning and information elicitation in creative performance (e.g. Glover, 1979).

Psychodynamic perspectives on creativity

Psychodynamic theories emphasize the role of the unconscious in shaping personality development and behaviour. They originate in the work of Sigmund Freud and include the modifications and reformulations of his successors in the psychoanalytic movement. In some cases, former followers of Freud split off to found their own distinctive psychodynamic schools – most importantly Carl Jung, whom we discuss below. Since Freud, psychodynamic theorists have shown a strong interest in creativity, especially artistic creativity, and their work has been influential in many of the areas discussed above, such as personality theory, the biographical study of creative lives, and the link between creativity and mental health or ill-health.

We noted earlier that Freud saw a close association between artistic creativity and neuroticism. This arises because of his view that artistic inspiration is derived from sublimation – the redirection of instinctual sexual impulses into activities which are socially acceptable. Sublimation is a 'defence mechanism', a term used by psychoanalysts to refer to strategies for reducing anxiety by distorting or denying the nature of the threat facing the individual. Neuroticism arises through excessive reliance on defence mechanisms, which take up an immense amount of the person's psychological energy and leave him or her prey to overwhelming anxiety when they fail (Fadiman and Frager, 1994). Freud's position on creativity may thus seem a rather negative one. In a frequently cited passage he states that the artist is oppressed by unusually strong instinctive needs and, unable to satisfy these, 'he turns away from reality and transfers all his interest, and his libido too, to the wishful constructions of his life of phantasy, whence the path might lead to neurosis' (Freud, 1963, page 376).

Freud's view of creativity is more ambivalent than would appear from this bald statement, as Storr (1972) points out. Sublimation may result from redirected sexual energy, but it is characterized in psychoanalysis as the most mature of the defence mechanisms, and (one which unlike other defences) is capable of resolving the psychological tensions of anxiety in the long term. This suggests a strength of personality in the highly creative individual superior to the 'ordinary' neurotic, a point supported by the Freudian claim that artists are able to accept and utilize unconscious impulses that others would suppress as socially unacceptable and anxiety provoking (Woodman, 1981). Also, Freud on occasion praises the insights of creative artists (especially writers) into the human condition, a reflection of his own deep interest in literature.

Storr (1972) accepts that creativity can serve as a defence, but argues that it does not always arise for this reason. Freud's explanation is backwards looking, towards the early experiences which he sees as underlying adult anxieties and which creative people deal with through sublimation. In contrast, Storr argues that creativity can have a forward-looking role, in the development of the personality throughout life. In doing so he draws on the work of Carl Jung, Freud's best-known follower who split with him to found an alternative psychodynamic tradition known as 'analytical psychology'. Jung's position on creativity differs from Freud's in important ways, reflecting wider differences in their theories. One of the major causes of his split with Freud was his refusal to accept that the sexual drive underlay all of our psychological functioning and development. Jung therefore also rejected the notion that sublimation is the ultimate source of all creativity. He distinguished between creativity drawing on the unconscious ('visionary creativity') from the 'psychological' type which utilizes the materials of conscious experience (Woodman, 1981). It is in relation to the former type of creativity that Jung's view differs most markedly from Freud's. While Jung accepts that some art is the product of the kind of unconscious conflicts and defence mechanisms that Freud describes (Jung calls this 'symptomatic art'), he maintains that art can also be shaped by the collective unconscious – a level of consciousness below the personal unconscious (Jung, 1966). The concept of collective unconscious refers to the inherited basic structure of the mind, derived from the evolution of the first human beings and common to all people across time and culture. It sets broad limits to the ways we can perceive and experience the world. Although it cannot be accessed directly, even through analysis, it can become manifest in our conscious lives through archetypal images and symbols. Art which is informed by such material has the power to communicate beyond particular societal boundaries; for example, one may deeply affected by an ancient Egyptian statue or an aboriginal rock painting without having any understanding of the cultures which produced these artefacts.

One of Jung's main contributions to our understanding of creativity is his recognition of its potential for facilitating psychological well-being and growth. As suggested above, Jung's psychology is more present and future oriented than Freud's. For Freud, the analyst's task is to help the patient resolve the repressed conflicts of the past in order to overcome current neurosis. For Jung, analysis is also concerned (at least for some patients) with assisting him or her towards a greater degree of psychological integration – a process known as individuation. Jung saw creative activity as potentially playing an important role in achieving individuation and, in the technique known as 'active imagination', encouraged patients to use writing, painting and sculpting to further self-understanding. This approach has had a lasting influence on the use of various forms of creative activity for therapeutic purposes and has helped to construct the argument that involvement in creativity is associated in most people not with mental illness but with personal growth and psychological health (Richards, 1999b).

Many other psychodynamic theorists have addressed the topic of creativity, and the psychoanalytic interpretation of great art and artists remains a popular field – see for example Mary Gedo's analysis of Picasso (1980) and Roman and Stastny's (1987) examination of the German painter Jochen Seidel. For some psychologists, particularly those with a cognitive background, the lack of experimental or other 'objective' empirical evidence for these theories makes them untrustworthy (Weisberg, 1993). Psychodynamic theorists would argue in reply that the kind of phenomena they are concerned with cannot be studied in such ways, as they are concerned with the interpretation of meaning rather than demonstrating a general association between one variable and another. However, some writers within the psychodynamic tradition have urged caution in how it is applied to understanding creativity. Monroe (1991) points out that seemingly autobiographical features of works of art are often intentionally exaggerated by the artist, and that psychobiographical studies should rely on as many different sources of information as possible. The fact that such studies are almost always based on very eminent creators of course necessitates caution in drawing conclusions from them about creativity in the wider population.

Humanistic psychology and creativity

Humanistic psychology is concerned with the individual human being's need to realize his or her full potential in life. It emerged as a distinctive perspective out of the work of writers such as Carl Rogers and Abraham Maslow, in part as a reaction against the hard-line behaviourism which dominated psychology in the middle decades of this century. Humanists insisted that 'the person' should be conceptualized and studied as a whole, and not as a collection of conditioned responses. This requires the consideration of human motivations, needs, attitudes and defences – the types of intangible internal phenomena that behaviourists insisted were unworthy or incapable of scientific investigation.

Creativity figures prominently in the work of humanistic psychologists (Woodman, 1981). It is seen as playing a key role in the process of self-fulfilment (commonly referred to as *self-actualization*), and as a distinctive characteristic of the self-actualized person. Rogers (1954) describes the motivation for creativity as stemming from 'man's tendency to actualize himself, to become his potentialities' (Vernon, 1970, page 140). However, he recognizes that creative products may have negative as well as positive impacts on the individual creator and their wider society. The invention of new methods of pain relief and new methods of torture are both creative acts. He therefore distinguishes between *constructive* and *destructive* creativity, the former arising when individuals are open to all aspects of experience (within and outside of themselves), the latter when they deny or repress large areas of experience. Three 'inner conditions' are associated with constructive creativity. The first, *openness to experience*, refers to a lack of rigidity in beliefs, *concepts* and perceptions, and a tolerance for ambiguity. The individual does not just perceive the world through pre-existing categories but is sensitive to the uniqueness of the particular moment. There are clear parallels here with personality-based studies which have found associations between creativity and traits of tolerance of ambiguity, independence and unconventionality. The second condition, an *internal locus of evaluation*, is seen in the person who evaluates their creative products on the basis of their own personal satisfaction, rather than the praise or criticism of others. Rogers sees this as the most important of the three conditions for constructive creativity. The final condition is the *ability to toy with elements and concepts* – essentially, a playful attitude towards ideas.

While Maslow's humanistic view of creativity is very close to Rogers', his development of 'transpersonal' psychology brings new perspectives to bear on the psychology of creativity (Maslow, 1971). Transpersonal psychology is concerned with experiences that seem to go beyond the personal, which have tended to be neglected by mainstream psychology and are commonly understood in religion as 'spiritual' or perhaps 'mystical'. Transpersonal psychologists seek to study such phenomena systematically, not only because of their intrinsic fascination but also because of their possible implications for recognizing and fulfilling the full extent of human potential (Frager, 1989). Creativity has long had strong associations with the spiritual; in the notion of 'divine inspiration', for example, and in the parallels between moments of creative insight and so-called 'peak' experiences. Also, the products of creativity can themselves provoke in the viewer or listener a sense of being taken beyond one's self. Fontana (1997) argues that by studying holistically such creative experiences we may gain important insights into 'transpersonal levels of mind' (page 35). In terms of our understanding of creativity itself, the transpersonal approach is perhaps of greatest value in drawing attention to the transformational potential of creative action, for both creator and spectator alike.

The humanistic view of creativity has probably had its most direct impact in the areas of counselling and psychotherapy. It has also had a strong, though less direct, impact on researchers and practitioners concerned with creativity and innovation at work. The association between creativity and personal fulfilment at work is widely accepted; it can be seen to underlie conceptual discussions of the nature of innovation and creativity (e.g. West, 1990; King and West, 1987) and recommendations for managing creative people (Lovelace, 1986).

Two main criticisms may be levelled at the humanistic approach to creativity. First, it probably overstates the association between creativity and psychological health. While Maslow, Rogers and their followers may well be right to reject the Freudian view of an essential connection between creativity and neuroticism, it remains the fact that for some, involvement in creativity does not seem to confer psychological health or personal growth. Indeed, some eminent creators find the creative process a painful and unpleasant compulsion rather than a life-enhancing experience. Such negative examples may be in a small minority, but they help to emphasize that the equation of creativity with health is not a universal one.

Second, humanistic psychology tends to portray the influence of the social world on the creative person in almost wholly negative terms. Society is seen as creating inhibitions, anxieties and rigidities which serve as psychologial barriers to the individual manifesting his or her 'true' inherent creativeness. This neglects the fact that much (perhaps most) creativity is a collective endeavour between people – the lone creator, producing their great works in isolation from society, is very much a construction of the nineteenth century Romantic tradition, one whose influence on psychological thinking in the area has been strongly criticized (Montuori and Purser, 1995) and which may have a malign effect on creative people themselves (Freeman, 1993). The hostility to the social in the work of Rogers and Maslow is very much a product of their time, reflecting an understandable distaste for the very conformist and intolerant nature of cold-war America in the 1950s and early 1960s.

Personal construct theory and creativity

The Personal Construct Psychology (PCP) of George Kelly is often included within the humanistic tradition by reviewers (e.g. Woodman, 1981) but offers a very different conceptualization of the person and of creativity from Maslow and Rogers. Butt (2001) has recently argued for the alignment of PCP with social psychology as a theory fundamentally concerned with social action and interaction, whilst others have elaborated it as a cognitive theory (e.g. Mancuso, 1996). Whatever way his theory is defined, a central point is that Kelly does not believe in any essential drive towards self-actualization in human beings. Rather, he famously described people as acting like scientists, constantly trying to understand the physical and social world which they inhabit. He maintains that our understandings are structured in the form of 'personal constructs' which interpret aspects of experience and enable us to anticipate future situations. The configuration of constructs employed by a person constitute his or her unique construct system. This is not a fixed and rigid personality structure as in trait theories but is open to change and growth in the light of new experience.

Kelly's interest in creativity is not in terms of explaining how and why eminent creators produce great works of art, scientific breakthroughs and so on. Like the humanistic psychologists, he is more concerned with the creativity required for growth and change and the factors which facilitate or inhibit this. Kelly (1955) talks about the 'creativity cycle' which consists of successive loosening and tightening of the construct system. Loosening brings a greater openness and flexibility to construing, allowing new and different interpretations and anticipations to be utilized. A creative act, according to Kelly, inevitably starts with loose construing, and a person who uses only tight constructs (i.e. unambiguous and definite) is not capable of creativity. However, loose construing on its own will also not give rise to creativity – tightening of the system is required to enable the new idea to be stated in a clear, verifiable form: 'In creativity, as in other kinds of human activity, optimal functioning is a matter of balance. The creative person must have the important capacity to move from loosening to tightening' (Puhakka, 1994).

Social psychological approaches to creativity

The five approaches to creativity discussed above represent long-established traditions in the literature. In contrast, a distinctive social psychological approach has emerged much more recently; it can be dated to the publication of Theresa Amabile's book *The Social Psychology of Creativity* in 1983. Central to her argument is the 'intrinsic motivation hypothesis', which states that people will perform more creatively if they are motivated by interest in the activity itself (intrinsic motivation) rather than by the promise of rewards or threat of punishments (extrinsic motivation). In a series of experiments and later field studies she highlighted the characteristics of the immediate social environment which tend to facilitate or inhibit the intrinsically motivated state and thus creative performance. She showed that factors such as competition, pressure and rewards contingent on performance generally led to reduced creativity, whilst freedom from time and other task constraints resulted in increased creativity.

Amabile does not argue that motivational state alone determines the level of creative performance. Two other components are included in her model of creativity. 'Skills in the task domain' include knowledge about the area of the task, relevant technical skills and any special talent for the area. 'Skills in creative thinking' embrace appropriate cognitive and work styles, and implicit or explicit understanding of how novel ideas are generated. Creative performance depends on the combination of all three components of the model. Thus an eminent creator in one field – say, theoretical physics – might lack the task-domain skills in a different area – such as life drawing – and fail to perform creatively, regardless of high levels of intrinsic motivation and skills in creative thinking. Amabile also proposes that the three components have their main impacts at differing points in the process of creativity, as shown in Figure 3.1.

Motivational state is of most importance at two stages: at the start of the process – the 'task presentation' stage – where the creative task is identified either by the individual or by someone else; at the third 'idea generation' stage, where the individual produces possible responses in the search for solutions or ideas appropriate to the task at hand. At this stage skills in creative thinking are also highly influential in the quality of potential solutions produced. Idea generation is preceded by a

Figure 3.1   **Amabile's componential model of creativity**

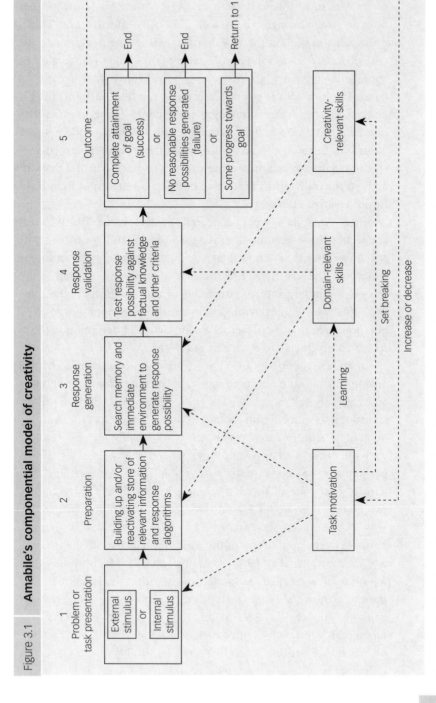

Source: Reproduced by kind permission of the author from Amabile, T. M. (1983) *The Social Psychology of Creativity*, New York: Springer-Verlag.

'preparation' stage, where the individual musters information relevant to the task or problem, both from his or her existing knowledge of the domain and through the search for new information. This relies principally on skills in the task domain, as does the penultimate stage of the process, 'idea validation', where the individual evaluates the appropriateness of ideas generated at the third stage to the task at hand. If a new idea is either accepted or rejected outright, the process ends at the fifth stage, 'outcome assessment'. Sometimes an idea will not be judged as wholly appropriate but will have made a significant contribution towards a task solution; in these cases the process returns to the beginning again, and the experience gained in the first attempt adds to the individual's repertoire of domain-relevant skills available for future creative efforts.

Since Amabile's work appeared in the early 1980s, creativity researchers have become increasingly aware of and concerned with the social conditions which facilitate or inhibit creativity. In an integrative review of the creativity literature, Mumford and Gustafson (1988) discuss the importance of 'attributes of the situation conditioning the individual's willingness to engage in creative behaviour' (page 28). They also point out that social factors are important in determining the extent to which products are evaluated as creative.

Amabile's theory locates the creative process within the person, arising through the effects of motivational state, domain-relevant skills, and creativity-relevant skills. The role of the social world on this process is through its influence on the three components (especially motivation). Such a position places Amabile's work solidly in the tradition of individualistic social psychology, where the person is viewed as participating in, but essentially separable from, society. This contrasts with a more 'social' social psychology, which attempts to understand psychological processes – even those conventionally viewed as 'mental' – as occurring in the interaction between people. The best-known example of the application of this kind of social psychology to creativity is Csikszentmihalyi's (1988) 'systems model', which argues that it is wrong to view creativity as located solely within the individual. He takes the example of the renaissance painter Botticelli, who for centuries was held in little critical esteem until his work was re-evaluated in the nineteenth century by critics such as Ruskin. This raises the question of whether Botticelli's creativity resides in his paintings or in the judgements of the critics; Csikszentmihalyi argues that it resides in both. Creative production requires the existence of a body of knowledge within a culture (for instance, how to use paint to make representational images on canvas), an individual creator to apply and transform that knowledge (Botticelli), and a group of people with the authority to validate a product as creative (Ruskin and his fellow critics). While the individual creator is usually accorded the primary role in the creative process, this is purely convention. All three of the components (which Csikszentmihalyi terms 'domain', 'person', and 'field' respectively) are essential elements of the creative process.

Csikszentmihalyi's systems model has been very influential in drawing attention to the social context of creativity and is widely cited in the literature. However, it has often been interpreted and applied in a way which is closer to individualistic social psychology than a thoroughly social approach. Despite Csikszentmihalyi's insistence that focusing first and foremost on the person (rather than field or domain) is 'purely arbitrary' (1988: page 329), many writers utilizing the model do just that. For example, Ford's (1995) 'Multi-domain model' elaborates in considerable detail the intrapersonal aspects of creative action in organizations – knowledge, beliefs, motivation, goals, sense making – but deals with domain and field in a rather cursory manner (see Figure 3.2). Even in some of Csikszentmihalyi's own more recent work, the person seems to have returned to centre stage, whilst the dynamics of domain and field are undertheorized (e.g. Csikszentmihalyi, 1996). In contrast, Freeman's systems model-based analysis of American artists' careers, mentioned earlier, gives full attention to all three components and genuinely interrogates the nature of the links between them (Freeman, 1993). We would argue that the real value of Csikszentmihalyi's original formulation of the systems model for a social psychology of creativity will become apparent only when (like Freeman) more researchers take seriously the need to avoid a drift back towards individualistic accounts.

As the newest of the six approaches to creativity research discussed here, the social psychological approach has had the least opportunity for its implications to filter through into practice in organizations. The role of high levels of discretion in facilitating creativity has been recognized for some time, through the work of management gurus like Rosabeth Moss Kanter (1983). Amabile's model provides a theoretical framework for explaining why this should be the case (i.e. the 'intrinsic motivation conducive to creativity. More generally, the social psychological approach

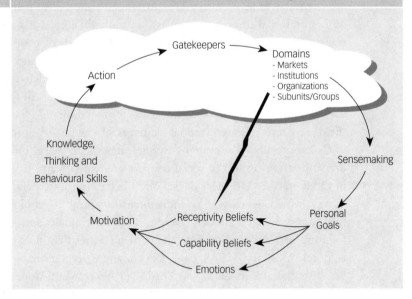

Figure 3.2 **A multi-domain model of creative action taking**

Source: Ford, Cameron and Gioia, Dennis (1995) *Creative Action in Organizations*, Sage.

highlights the limitations of a wholly individualistic view of creativity. Simply selecting highly creative individuals or providing creativity training is not enough to ensure that creativity actually manifests itself in the day-to-day activity of the organization. Finally, the social psychological approach – especially Csikszentmihalyi's work – makes clear that what constitutes creativity inevitably depends on subjective judgements within a relevant field of activity or social setting. Organizations concerned about their own creative performance should therefore consider exactly what creativity means to them, before they take any action to attempt to influence it.

A synthesis of approaches

Although the different approaches to creativity have fluctuated in their prominence and influence within the research community, it would be wrong to see them as inevitably in competition with each other. It is quite possible to view each as addressing a different facet of the phenomenon of creativity; indeed it may well be that the strongest advances in understanding the psychology of creativity will come from attempts at a synthesis of approaches. This is the stance taken by Mumford and Gustafson (1988) who describe creativity as a 'syndrome' comprised of cognitive, personality, developmental and situational elements. We have shown here and in the previous chapter that there are actual or potential applications within organizations of research into each of these elements. Recognizing the multifaceted nature of creativity will enable managers to draw on a wider range of possible strategies for enhancing creative performance than would be available if they conceive of it as solely a matter of thinking styles, or individual disposition, or organizational climate.

Suggested reading

Barron, F. and Harrington, D.M. (1981) 'Creativity, intelligence and personality', *Annual Review of Psychology* 32: 439–76.

Freeman, M. (1993) *Finding the Muse: A Sociopsychological Enquiry into the Conditions of Artistic Creativity.* Cambridge: Cambridge University Press.

Runco, M. A. and Pritzker, S. R. (eds) (1999) *Encyclopedia of Creativity* (2 vols), San Diego CA: Academic Press.

Sternberg, R. (ed.) (1988) *The Nature of Creativity,* Cambridge: Cambridge University Press.

4

Innovation and the social psychology of groups

After reading this chapter you should be able to

- discuss social psychological approaches to research into work group innovation
- discuss work and organizational psychological approaches to work group innovation
- describe likely relations between the following group character-istics and innovation
  (a) leadership
      group composition
      group structure
      group climate
      group longevity
- critically appraise team-building interventions as a means toward enhancing work group 'innovation'

In the previous two chapters we have concentrated on the individual's role in organizational creativity and innovation. We have seen how psychologists from many different perspectives have attempted to account for human creativity and have examined critically some of the ways in which their work has been applied within organizations. In so doing, we have made it clear that selecting creative individuals and enhancing the creativity of existing organizational members is by no means a sufficient condition for successful innovation. At the end of Chapter 2 we stressed that innovation is a social process, involving interaction and communication within and between people in a whole range of social structures, from the immediate work group through the department or division, to the organization as a whole and the wider society. Similarly, in Chapter 3 we have shown that creativity is as much a social as an individual phenomenon.

In the present chapter we will examine the ways in which the psychological processes operating within and between groups can contribute positively and negatively to innovation in organizations. We will draw on two main sources to inform our examination. First, we will look at some of the implications of the social psychological literature on groups, especially in relation to processes of social influence and decision making, and social identity theory. We will also consider the relevance to this area of social constructionist approaches which are critical of mainstream social psychology. Second, we will examine empirical evidence from occupational psychology and allied disciplines regarding factors that inhibit or facilitate innovation in real-world work groups. The final section of the chapter looks in more detail at the issues related to team building and innovation in organizations.

Defining the term 'group'

Before we can proceed, we need to think about what is meant by the term 'group'. A key distinction made by social psychologists is between 'membership groups' and 'reference groups'. The former are groups to which a person belongs by some verifiable criterion. We, the authors of this book, objectively belong to the groups of 'university lecturers', 'chartered psychologists' and 'white British males'. How important these groups are to us, and whether we feel positive or negative towards them, is irrelevant; if we fulfil the factual criteria for membership, then members we are. In contrast, reference groups are those groups with whom a person identifies; we compare ourselves with them in order to make judgements about ourselves, and we take our values and norms from them. It may well be that many of our membership groups are also reference groups (and vice versa), but it is not necessarily the case. A person may belong physically to a group without feeling any sense of identity with it. Equally, they may identify with a group of which they are not a member. People in organizations are likely to identify with a range of reference groups, some more strongly than others. How they react to innovations introduced by the organization, and how well they perform as innovators themselves, will be heavily influenced by these identifications, and by the type of interaction between groups within the organization.

Social influence in groups

The origins of modern social psychological research into group processes lie in work undertaken in the United States in the 1950s, which was predominantly concerned with how groups influence individuals to conform to their norms and values, and comply with their judgements and expectations. The series of studies carried out by Solomon Asch introduced the dominant experimental paradigm and remains amongst the most famous in the history of social psychology (Asch, 1956). The original experiment involved a naïve subject who had volunteered to take part in a supposed perception experiment. The subject sat in a semicircle with six others, who were secret confederates of the experimenter, and each was asked to judge which one of three lines was the same length as a designated target line.

The task was actually very easy – in the control condition where judgements were made in private, unseen by other groups members, subjects had an error rate lower than 1 per cent. But in the experimental condition, on 12 of 18 trials the naïve subject heard five confederates announce the same wrong judgement before he or she was requested publicly to make his or her judgement. The error rate on these critical trials shot up to 37 per cent. There was considerable variation between individual subjects, but of 123 subjects only about a quarter made no errors. In interviews afterwards it was evident that subjects found the unanimous errors made by their companions puzzling and worrying, and that as the trials progressed they felt increasingly uncomfortable with their own deviance and isolation from the rest of the group.

Asch's findings have been shown to be highly consistent across different cultures and times (although there has been a minority of studies which failed to obtain the effect). Variations on this basic experiment have been carried out by Asch and later researchers. Two findings are of particular interest. First, Asch himself showed that the size of the majority made little difference to the conformity effect. A majority of two leads to a reduced effect (conformity on about 13 per cent of trials) but the full effect was apparent with a majority of three, and it did not become significantly greater when the majority was increased to 16. Later research has found some incremental increase in conformity with larger majorities, but with diminishing effects for each additional majority member. Second, research by Allen (1975) and colleagues has shown that the addition of a single supporter for the naïve subject drastically reduces the conformity effect to 5.5 per cent of trials.

There is good empirical evidence that conformity with the majority is positively related to group cohesiveness. In other words, the more strongly members are attracted to a group and wish to remain part of it, the more likely they are to conform to the majority view within the group, and the greater effort they will make to resolve discrepancies between each other's positions. High cohesiveness leads to an active concern with maintaining a uniform group position; persistent deviants will be subject to strong persuasive pressure, and eventually if they do not conform, to exclusion from the group. Such pressures are commonplace in organizations and, as we will see later, the impact of cohesiveness on group innovation has been a key topic in applied research.

The Asch studies, and many others like them, demonstrated that groups can exert powerful pressures for conformity with the majority position. There have been numerous attempts to provide a theoretical explanation of how and why this occurs. While they differ in emphasis and detail, at the heart of most of them is the notion of social dependence; that, as human beings, our view of ourselves and our world (especially our social world) is dependent on others. This has led to the development of what is known as the 'dual process model' in which conformity is seen to result from two distinct processes. One is informational; we look to others for an explanation of the world around us, especially where there is ambiguity. The other is normative; we look to others for an indication of what is expected of us, in order to obtain acceptance and approval from the group. It is commonly held that informational influence produces lasting, internalized changes in our attitudes and beliefs, whilst normative influence leads to a public display of conformity without necessarily any private changes in attitudes and beliefs. While it is now clear that it is wrong to consider informational and normative processes as entirely separate (Turner, 1991), the basic propositions of the dual process model remain widely accepted.

Conformity and innovation

It would be easy to draw the implication from this research that because groups exert strong pressures to conform, they are therefore inhibitive of innovation at work. This would be a gross oversimplification. The crucial issue is exactly what kinds of behaviours and attitudes any particular group tends to conform to. In some organizations, or parts of organizations, innovation and creativity may be the predominant values, and innovativeness may therefore be facilitated by group conformity pressures. We might expect to see pressures to conform by innovating in companies which have been explicitly built around a philosophy of innovation. Nystrom (1990) describes one division of the Swedish chemical company EKA Nobell where norms for innovation appeared to override all else. It is hard to say how exceptional such examples are, but we can safely assume that for many organizations fear of failure and the desire to preserve the status quo *do* result in pressure to conform to norms of conservatism and caution. In such circumstances, the social psychological literature on conformity discussed above can suggest strategies to prevent new ideas from being stifled by forces of conformity. For example a potential innovator would be advised, on the basis of the studies by Allen and colleagues, to try to find at least one ally before confronting the group, as this would be expected to reinforce greatly his or her ability to withstand normative influence. However, the traditional approach to conformity does not offer an explanation of how the minority might actually convert the majority to its position. We turn our attention now to the issue of minority influence.

Minority influence

Until the mid 1970s, research into social influence in groups was almost exclusively concerned with how and why majorities influence minorities to conform with them. It was the European social psychologist Serge Moscovici who was chiefly responsible for drawing attention to the fact that influence can work the other way; that sometimes minorities succeed in changing the position of the majority – a phenomenon he termed 'minority influence' (Moscovici, 1976). In a series of experiments he and his colleagues demonstrated that a minority which stuck consistently to their position could elicit change in the majority position. Furthermore, the change was likely to be long lasting and internalized rather than simply an outward manifestation unaccompanied by a genuine shift in perceptions, beliefs or values. Moscovici and his followers see minority influence as an important engine for social change, pointing to the way that protest movements such as those for Women's Suffrage or Black Civil Rights can alter majority public opinion in their favour if they present a consistent and confident position. The term 'innovation' is actually used by Moscovici to describe the type of social influence associated with minorities.

Social psychological research into minority influence does provide a possible explanation of how a minority within an organization (or some subdivision of an organization) can go beyond the position of 'deviant' resistors of conformity pressures to that of active promoters of innovation. There are lessons for would-be innovators regarding how they should present their minority view in order to maximize their influence; the effectiveness of a consistent and coherent argument has been shown in numerous studies. However, consistency alone is not enough, as is shown by several studies which have found consistent minorities unsuccessful in influence attempts (Mackie, 1987). In order to be influential, a minority must present their view in a way which does not lead to them being categorized by the majority as an 'out-group'. If the minority are seen as outsiders, then their opinions can be safely disregarded. If, however, they are seen as insiders, sharing the values and interests of the majority, then their alternative position must be taken seriously. Thus, if the government is attacked on its health policy by the opposition, it probably will not reconsider its programme in the light of their arguments. If the attack comes from a usually loyal group of its own back-benchers their opinions are more likely to be taken seriously.

One set of minority-influence studies of especial relevance to organizational innovation are those carried out by C. Nemeth and her colleagues. They have been explicitly concerned with creativity as an outcome of minority influence. In one experiment (Nemeth and Wachtler, 1983) involving a problem-solving task, the real subjects were exposed to a minority of confederates who consistently proposed alternative solutions to those of the majority. While the majority did not adopt the specific strategies of the minority, in subsequent tests they were significantly more creative than a control group not exposed to a minority. These findings suggest the value of an organizational climate in which members feel able to voice ideas which depart from dominant group norms, as exposure to minority views may make the majority think more critically and creatively about their established ways of doing things.

A final comment is required regarding the implications for organizational innovation of minority-influence research. Just as we observed earlier that the pressures for conformity within groups need not always operate against innovation, so we would stress here that a consistent minority can influence a group against new ideas as well as towards them.

Group decision making

Organizational innovation is not wholly a decision process, but it is a process in which decision making plays a prominent part. Furthermore, decisions about innovations at many points in the process are commonly made by groups. The decision to introduce a new product might be made by the senior management team of an organization; a specially constituted project team might be responsible for decisions about the design and manufacture of the product; these or other groups might be responsible for decisions about the testing and evaluation of prototypes and the marketing, distributing and advertising of the final product. Given that the above is not an exceptional scenario, the potential relevance of social psychological research into group decision making to our understanding of innovation in organizations is apparent.

Group polarization

One area of interest is the phenomenon of *group polarization*. This was first observed by Stoner (1961) who found that decisions made by groups after face-to-face discussion tended to be riskier than those made by group members individually. This was labelled the 'risky shift' phenomenon. It came as a considerable surprise to social psychologists because at the time the prevailing view of groups was as forces for conformity, and by implication conservatism in decisions. Subsequent research indicated that group decisions were not riskier than individuals' in all cases; for some decisions groups were consistently less risky. 'Group polarization' is a more accurate description because what appears to occur is that group decisions become polarized in the direction of the shared values of group members. For example, groups of middle-class American college students tend to polarize towards riskier decisions if the question is about business opportunities but towards less risky decisions if the question is whether two people should marry despite doubts about their relationship.

Given that innovation often entails risk, we would expect differences in innovation decisions according to whether they are made by groups or individuals. However, it would be wrong to make any general predictions about all innovation decisions, as the direction in which polarization occurs may be influenced not only by values in the wider society but also by those prevalent in a particular organization. For instance, in an organization where there is a strong fear of failure, groups may be more cautious than individuals in decisions about innovation. In an organization which encourages risk and is relatively forgiving of failure in pursuit of it, we might see riskier group than individual decisions.

Group composition

Some writers have argued for the superiority of group decisions over individual decisions on the grounds that groups can by definition draw upon a greater range of experience and intellectual ability than a lone individual. Another advantage is that if people take part in reaching a decision as a group they are more likely to feel personally committed to it than if the decision is made by a leader and presented to them as a *fait accompli*. (Note the similar point made in relation to brainstorming groups in Chapter 2.) However, the social psychological literature draws attention to circumstances in which groups are prone to making poor decisions. I. Janis (1972) describes the phenomenon of 'groupthink' where members become more concerned about protecting the identity and convivial atmosphere of the group than with coming to optimal decisions. He points to historical examples of this such as the Bay of Pigs fiasco in 1961 where the policy-making team, headed by President Kennedy, overlooked glaring flaws in the plan to instigate the overthrow of Castro's regime in Cuba because they were unwilling to listen to the views of 'outsiders' or to accept any arguments which might disturb the cohesion of the group.

This has important implications for group-level innovation in organizations. Many team-building initiatives are designed to maximize the cohesion and sense of identity within the group, but Janis's work suggests that such groups are most likely to suffer from 'groupthink'. Unless measures are taken to guard against it, there is a danger that highly cohesive teams may be insufficiently critical of innovations they propose or support, and fail to give adequate consideration to alternatives. This could lead to a deterioration in the quality, though not necessarily the quantity, of innovations produced by the group. Groupthink may be combated in a number of ways. Recruiting members with diverse backgrounds and viewpoints will increase the likelihood that a variety of approaches to problems will be considered, although too much diversity may encourage conflict and make it difficult for a consensus ever to be reached. One or more member(s) of the group may be assigned the role of 'devil's advocate', charged with the task of actively seeking weaknesses in innovation proposals.

Social identity and innovation

Our discussion so far has focused on processes within groups: conformity, minority influence and decision making. There is also a substantial social psychological literature on relationships between groups which can inform our understanding of organizational innovation. We will concentrate here on a theory of intergroup processes which has been highly influential in European social psychology over the last two decades: Henri Tajfel's social identity theory (Tajfel, 1978, 1982; Hogg and Abrams, 1988). Unlike the areas we have discussed so far, this theory is concerned with reference groups rather than membership groups. The basic proposition of social identity theory is that people seek to achieve and maintain a positive image of themselves, and that one of the principal ways they do this is by comparing groups they identify with ('in-groups') favourably with those they do not identify with ('out-groups'). The theory makes predictions about the circumstances in which group identifications are likely to be strengthened or alternately in which individuals will try to leave a group. It has been used to explain conflict and discrimination between groups in a wide variety of settings; for instance, between nurses of different grades (Skevington, 1981) and between the police and local community in the Bristol St Paul's riot of 1980 (Reicher, 1984). Social identity theory can be used to make sense of positive and negative reactions to innovation from groups within an organization. Research examining how specific innovations develop over time has shown that different groups within organizations often have different perceptions of, and attitudes towards, the innovation in question. Aydin and Rice (1991) showed that differences in the 'social worlds' of the various occupational groups in a hospital were a major determinant of individual attitudes to a new medical information system. Social identity theory suggests that such differences may constitute an attempt to increase differentiation between in-group and out-group(s), rather than simply being due to groups having different knowledge about the innovation. Whether an innovation is resisted or accepted may therefore depend on whether those with whom it is associated are viewed as a negative or positive reference group by other groups. Where identification of an innovation with an out-group causes resistance, management might attempt to reduce it by weakening that identification, perhaps by vigorously promoting the innovation as 'belonging' to the organization as a whole.

As with conformity, minority influence and group polarization, social identification processes will not affect all innovations in all organizations to the same degree and in the same direction. Contextual specifics must always be taken into account. We discussed above how it could sometimes be advantageous for managers wishing to facilitate an innovation to downplay its association with one particular group. This strategy is especially likely to be appropriate where the major concern is that a particular innovation is fully implemented with as little disruption as possible. In other situations, stimulating groups to initiate innovations might be of greater importance to management than smoothing the implementation path of innovations already adopted. Strengthening group identities to encourage competition might be the best strategy here (although keeping competition from spilling over into open conflict can be hard to achieve).

Social identity theory is a potentially valuable tool for analysing the role of groups in organizational innovation. There remains, though, a dearth of real-world studies to examine the utility of the theory in this context, and even in the area of intergroup relations – the core focus of the theory – organizational research remains scarce. Hartley (1996) has questioned whether the dramatic effects shown in experimental studies from even the most trivial sources of group identification will occur in organizational settings. Many of the features of real-life groups that are very likely to influence behaviour – leadership, shared history, expectations for the future – are not present in most experimental groups which have no history, no common goals beyond the experiment, and are often composed of schoolchildren or students. On a theoretical level, she suggests that it may be useful to distinguish identification with the group from the wider concept of social identity as something relatively stable and enduring:

> Perhaps what we are witnessing is less a permanent social identity but rather the process of group identification. This may be characterized as more unstable, less enduring, and importantly, arising in part out of the interactions, perceptions and practices of group and intergroup relations.
>
> *(Hartley, 1996, page 416)*

Social constructionism

A radically different understanding of intergroup relations is offered by social constructionists, which rejects the notion of a universal cognitive process of social categorization that is the basis of social identity theory. Social constructionism is a broad movement in social psychology which focuses not on abstract internal mental processes but on the everyday actions and interactions which make up the social world. Although there are many different theoretical strands within social constructionism (see Burr, 1995), all make the central point that language does not simply describe social reality but also constructs it. Thus if a psychologist were to interview a work group member about the nature of her team, her responses would be viewed as an attempt to build a particular representation of the team (and of herself) in the specific context of the interview, not simply as a description of her feelings about the team. To take the hypothetical example further, our interviewee might compare her team favourably to others in the organization in terms of its creativity. A social identity theorist might see this as evidence of an internal psychological process of categorisation resulting in in-group bias. A social constructionist researcher, in contrast, would seek to understand what the interviewee was trying to achieve by this representation at this point in the interview. Perhaps she was trying to claim an association with the desirable quality of creativity, without appearing boastful are conceited by stressing her own personal creativity?

In social constructionist theory, accounts are never purely personal products, emerging from within the individual's private world. Instead, the individual is seen as drawing on a range of ways of representing experience (often referred to as 'discourses') which they have internalized through their interaction with the social world. The focus of social constructionist research methods – of which discourse analysis is the most prominent (Burman and Parker, 1993) – is therefore on the nature of discourses used in particular social settings and what these tell us about wider social relationships.

A number of important criticisms have been levelled at social constructionism – or at least at certain forms of the approach. Some argue that it removes notions of personal agency, seeing people's actions as determined by the discourses that make up the social world. At its most extreme, it may be seen as losing any sense of 'the person' at all (Crossley, 2000). Critics have also pointed out that the emphasis on the variety and flexibility of discursively constructed identities neglects the fact that people generally experience their identity as relatively stable, and have a sense of what is or is not their 'true' self (Butt, Burr and Epting, 1997). Psychologists need to take seriously this experience of a continuing 'core' self, without falling into the trap of simply accepting lay accounts as literal fact. The arguments about personal agency and stability of identity are commonly made by writers who are broadly sympathetic to social constructionism, and can be seen as attempts to influence the ways in which its ideas develop. Other critics, of course, are not persuaded by the central arguments against a cognitive-based understanding of social identification, and continue to view social identity theory as the most convincing explanation of the processes involved (Abrams and Hogg, 1990).

As yet there have been few attempts to apply a social constructionist approach to issues relating to groups and innovation. Bouwen and Fry (1996) has presented a social constructionist interpretation of group development which has implications for innovation. He has also used a similar approach to examine organizational learning and innovation (Bouwen, De Visch and Steyaert, 1992). More recently, Symon (2000) has used discourse analysis to examine 'resistance' to innovation, showing how those opposed to a particular change produce accounts which turn proponents' arguments back against them. She emphasizes the importance of identities (both the participants' own and those of rival groups), not as the relatively stable self-definitions of social identity theory but as ways of presenting self and others in the specific context of the interview, constructed to serve a specific rhetorical purpose – undermining the need for the change in question.

We would expect social constructionist work to expand in this area in the near future, and see it as valuable alternative to more traditional approaches – especially because of its ability to explore group identification in the context of innovation without reducing the former to individual cognitive processes. An approach which rigorously interrogates the way language is used is particularly welcome at a time when the terms 'team' and 'innovation' have become managerial buzzwords, often extolled uncritically in popular literature.

Social psychological theory and organizational innovation

We have argued for the relevance of four important areas of social psychological research into group processes in understanding innovation in organizations. This is not a new observation; McGrath (1985) and the present authors (King and Anderson, 1990) have contended that social psychology can help to provide a theoretical foundation for research and practice which is largely absent in much of the literature on innovation at the group level. It can also help to make sense of findings from existing group-level studies of innovation, which frequently focus on a small number of variables and fail to address adequately wider intra- and intergroup processes. Social psychology itself may benefit by observing how well its theories are able to predict and explain the behaviour of real work groups involved in innovation processes. Unfortunately there remains as yet little in the way of synthesis between occupational and social psychology in this area.

While social psychology has much to offer in increasing our understanding of innovation at the group level, we must emphasize that it has limitations too. Mainstream social psychology has relied heavily on laboratory experimentation (often exclusively using university students as subjects), and many theories have not received a great deal of testing in real-world settings to examine their applicability. There has been a long-running and vigorous debate within social psychology over the experimental approach, with some critics arguing that its findings represent little more than artefacts of the laboratory situation (Gergen, 1978) whilst supporters emphasize the value of the control the laboratory allows the researcher which cannot be achieved in field research (Turner, 1981). 'The social constructionist approach, which arose in part from dissatisfaction with experimental social psychology, offers the potential for fresh, radically different perspectives on work group innovation, though the question of whether and how it can be applied to real-world problems remains contested' (King, 2000).

What cannot be denied is that the world outside the laboratory is vastly more complex than that within it, and it is this which constitutes the principal problem in applying social psychological theories to organizational innovation. People at work commonly belong to a wide range of groups, identifying with each to different degrees and in different ways. A further limitation to the applicability of social psychological research is that much of it has focused on groups where all members are of equal status and power. This is particularly true in the area of social influence, and reflects the dominant experimental paradigm (e.g. the Asch conformity studies) where groups of real subjects and stooges are asked to perform some kind of task or activity. In real organizations, status and power differentials within and between groups are the norm, and will affect innovation processes significantly. If a minority of one is opposing a proposed innovation at a board meeting, it makes a considerable difference whether that minority is a relatively junior newcomer to the board or the managing director. In highlighting these limitations we are not saying that it is impossible to apply social psychological theories of group processes to the real world of organizations, only that they should be used with caution given the current lack of work-based research.

Studies of work group innovation

Having reviewed the key findings of social psychological research and their generalizability to organizational innovation processes, we now move on to research which has focused specifically upon organizational settings and the role of work groups in the innovation process. While work group innovation has been relatively neglected by occupational psychologists, compared with individual and organizational levels of analysis, there has been sufficient research to enable some conclusions to be drawn about factors which tend to inhibit or encourage innovation. We will concentrate here on five principal research areas:

1 leadership
2 group composition
3 group structure
4 group climate
5 group longevity.

The final part of the chapter will consider the fashionable but problematic area of team building and its potential for enhancing organizational innovativeness.

Leadership

A democratic and participative leadership style is commonly recommended as encouraging group innovation, reflecting similar prescriptions made for organizational leadership. The rationale is straightforward: it is widely agreed that creativity is facilitated by high levels of discretion (Nicholson and West, 1988) and that people feel more committed to changes if they have participated in decisions about them. The role of the group leader is therefore to provide direction whilst allowing members as much say in decisions and as much freedom to approach tasks in their own way as is practicable. A positive association between group innovativeness and participative leadership style has been found in several studies, such as those by Farris (1973) with research laboratory teams and West and Wallace (1991) with primary care teams.

It should not be assumed that a participative leadership style will always be the most effective for facilitating group innovation, or that greater participativeness will always lead to greater innovativeness. Manz *et al.* (1989), considering data on seven major innovations from the Minnesota Innovation Research Program, argue for a contingency approach, as different leadership styles were effective for different innovations and at different stages in the innovation process. The present authors have also suggested that leaders need to modify their styles over the course of introducing an innovation as different tasks become salient (Anderson and King, 1991), as shown below in Figure 4.1. There is a great deal left to find out about how leaders facilitate or inhibit innovation in groups (although it seems safe to predict that a rigidly authoritarian style would rarely be optimal).

Greater participation in itself does not necessarily lead to enhanced group innovation. In Farris's (1973) study, for instance, the most innovative teams were not those which were most democratic but those in which the leader exerted a moderate degree of control. This makes sense when it is recognized that innovation is not just a matter of generating as many creative ideas as possible but of successfully turning

| Figure 4.1 | **A contingency model of leadership in groups to support innovation** |

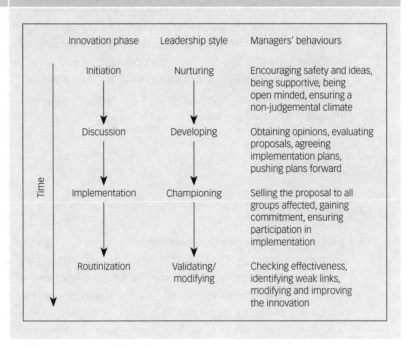

	Innovation phase	Leadership style	Managers' behaviours
Time	Initiation	Nurturing	Encouraging safety and ideas, being supportive, being open minded, ensuring a non-judgemental climate
	Discussion	Developing	Obtaining opinions, evaluating proposals, agreeing implementation plans, pushing plans forward
	Implementation	Championing	Selling the proposal to all groups affected, gaining commitment, ensuring participation in implementation
	Routinization	Validating/ modifying	Checking effectiveness, identifying weak links, modifying and improving the innovation

Source: Reproduction by kind permission of MCB University Press Ltd, from Anderson, N. R. and King, N. (1991) 'Managing innovation in organizations', *Leadership and Organization Development Journal* 12(4): 17–21.

ideas into reality. If the leader does not impose some degree of control and direction upon the group, then it is easy for the very freedom which encouraged the initiation of an innovation to make it difficult to form a clear implementation strategy and carry it through to completion.

Much of the research on leadership and innovation in work groups focuses on formally appointed leaders. However, in many groups an individual assumes a leadership role informally, as a result of personal qualities and intragroup dynamics. This is particularly the case in an autonomous work group, a form of organization which has risen in prominence in recent years (see the later section on 'group structure'). Guastello (1995) argued that in groups faced with creativity-related tasks, emergent leaders would not only be facilitative of others' creativity, but would also demonstrate creativity themselves. In a study of groups of university security officers involved in a training programme he found support for both these hypotheses.

When considering the relationship between leadership and group-level innovation, the question of the direction of causality must also be borne in mind. In most studies it is hard to be sure whether a particular leadership style has contributed to a group's innovativeness, or whether the style adopted by the leader is a result of the group's innovativeness in the past. One can imagine the latter case occurring where a group is allowed greater freedom and participation in decisions because of its success in an earlier innovation project. Longitudinal studies are required, following work groups from their inception, or from the moment when a new leader joins them.

Group composition

Matching people to roles

Various aspects of group composition have been considered in relation to innovativeness. Some writers have argued that highly innovatory teams need to match individuals to the requirements of particular roles. To take one example, the Team Management System (TMS), developed by Margerison and McCann (1990), identifies nine types of work which a team may be involved in and describes nine distinctive work preferences. They hypothesize that team effectiveness will be greatest where there is maximal correspondence between the work preferences of individual members and their roles within the team. Where there is a major mismatch, options include redesigning jobs, personal development in less preferred types of work, delegation or reallocation of tasks, or the mismatched person(s) leaving the team. The TMS and similar packages (e.g. Belbin, 1981, 1993) are attractive to organizations and to management consultants because they offer a relatively simple 'fix' to problems of team effectiveness which corresponds well with common-sense observations of teams at work. Few managers would disagree that people differ in the types of work they perform best, and that an effective team needs to include members who between them are adept at the various tasks and functions required of them. A well-designed assessment package may help organizations to achieve this. (For a review of the validity of such tests, see Bartram *et al.*, 1995.) However, models of this type present a rather static picture of group functioning. They do not pay much attention to the way that groups change over time as a result of interactions amongst members and with other groups or individuals in the organization. Building an effective team is depicted as a rational process of fitting person to role; in reality, interpersonal relationships, concerns about status and power, and many other factors can considerably complicate matters.

Homogeneity/heterogeneity

When making prescriptions about the matching of people to roles in a group it is important to consider how group innovation is influenced by the homogeneity of members. A highly homogeneous group is one in which members have a great deal in common with each other, as opposed to a highly heterogeneous group in which members differ markedly from each other. Similarities and differences may be on many dimensions: age, sex, tenure, professional allegiances, attitudes, and so on. The social psychological literature on group decision making, discussed above, suggests that high homogeneity may inhibit innovation in some circumstances. A highly homogeneous group is likely to draw on a narrower range of experiences and expertise than a more heterogeneous group, and where homogeneity is accompanied by strong attraction to the group, the 'groupthink' phenomenon may lead to poor-quality innovation decisions. It is worth recalling that research on brainstorming groups (discussed in Chapter 2) consistently shows that heterogeneous groups outperform homogenous groups in idea generation.

Conversely, there are possible disadvantages to high heterogeneity. There are more opportunities for clashes of values and opinions in a group with considerable differentiation amongst members than in a more homogeneous one. Even where this does not lead to overt conflict, it is likely to be a difficult and protracted task to bring the whole group to consensus on innovation decisions. It may also be more difficult to promote a sense of common purpose, or 'shared vision' – something which is frequently cited in the occupational psychology literature as a key facilitator of innovation (West, 1990). Finally, innovation is unlikely to be the only significant function of a group; managers need to consider whether any advantages in terms of innovativeness accruing from heterogeneity will be offset by detrimental effects on other aspects of group functioning. The task of the manager in constituting a group for whom innovation is an important goal is to decide upon the appropriate degree of homogeneity, in the light of the specific requirements and organizational context facing the group.

Diversity

During the 1990s, diversity became a key topic in work/organizational psychology and allied disciplines, and it shows every sign of continuing to occupy a central role in the twenty-first century. There is considerable disagreement over its definition, with debate concentrating on the issue of whether a narrow or broad definition is most appropriate. Narrow approaches generally define diversity in terms of gender, race/ethnicity, disability and other culturally related categories, and they tend to be used where issues of discrimination and exclusion are the main focus of research (e.g. Morrison, 1992). Broad definitions include any characteristic which organizational members may use to differentiate themselves from others. They would include, along with the categories already mentioned, such things as job function, tenure, professional affiliation, values and even personality characteristics. Broad definitions are commonly used where there is the intention to develop an overarching theoretical explanation for the effects of difference *per se*, such as through applications of social identity theory (e.g. Brewer, 1996). Nkomo (1996) sees problems with both types of definition in that neither gives proper weight to the complexity of diversity; rather than attempting to produce explanations of a unitary phenomenon (be it narrowly or broadly defined), she argues that psychologists should seek to clarify and better understand the many different facets of diversity in organizations.

Despite differences in approaches to defining diversity, there is general agreement that studying diversity means studying identity – people's sense of who they are and how they differ from or are similar to others. Thus O'Reilly III, Williams and Barsade (1998) state that 'a group is diverse if it is composed of individuals who differ on a characteristic on which they base their own social identity' (page 186). The emphasis on identity helps to distinguish the concept of diversity from the heterogeneity/homogeneity dimension discussed above. The latter is generally used in a way which takes little or no account of how people see themselves and simply reflects categories the researcher chooses to employ. Diversity, in contrast, requires attention to the subjectivities of research participants, though of course studies vary in the sophistication of their understanding of identity.

Research into work group diversity is a major subset of the wider diversity literature, and some of this material has dealt directly with innovation and change. This is one of the few areas of group innovation research which has drawn strongly on social psychological theory, in particular on social identity theory. O'Reilly et al. (1998) looked at the impact of diversity on team innovativeness in a major US clothing manufacturer with a reputation for the successful management of diversity. (Innovation was divided into a creativity measure, covering the generation of new ideas and an implementation measure.) They found evidence for different effects from different types of diversity. Ethnic diversity was associated with increased innovation (though not for all mixes of ethnicity). Tenure diversity was negatively related to innovation implementation, though this seemed to be related to the high levels of conflict associated with high tenure diversity. Gender diversity was unrelated to innovation. The general pattern of findings was in keeping with predictions from social identity theory, but some of the detail could not be explained purely in terms of social categorization processes. In particular, the fact that only certain configurations of ethnic diversity were associated with team innovativeness is hard to account for if we make the reasonable assumption that all the categories used (Asian, African-American, Hispanic and White) were meaningful and salient to an American population.

Social identity theory has evident strengths for understanding diversity in terms of the way people categorize themselves and others. However, some authors have questioned its underlying assumption that the social categorization processes it describes are universal. Triandis (1996) comments that 'research on diversity must take the issue of context more seriously' (page 230), whilst Nkomo in the same volume cautions against the possible limitations of social identity theory in this area: 'A research approach that emphasizes experimental control and universal psychological processes may not be appropriate if the objective is to illuminate the more contextually structured and socially constructed aspects of diversity' (page 252). She calls for a greater emphasis on social and cultural context in diversity research; we would echo this in relation to the specific focus on how work group diversity relates to innovation.

Group structure

The formal structure of a group may influence its innovativeness. Meadows (1980) applied the concepts of 'organic' and 'mechanistic' organizational structures (developed by Burns and Stalker, 1961) to work groups. An organic group tends to approach tasks in an integrative way, rather than breaking them down into separate subtasks assigned to individual members. Its boundaries of responsibility, authority and influence are not rigidly set, but are to a large extent dependent on the demands of particular situations facing the group. There is a high volume of interpersonal communication, which is characteristically lateral rather than vertical in direction (i.e. between colleagues of similar status, rather than between superiors and subordinates), and supportive rather than directive. There is also a high degree of involvement in decision making amongst group members. Finally, members of organic groups show strong commitment to the skills and values of their profession, above commitment to the particular organization. Mechanistic groups have the opposite characteristics, being highly formal, hierarchical and heavily reliant upon rules and procedures.

Meadows showed that the organic/mechanistic concepts could be applied to groups in industrial organizations, and that those groups whose tasks involved the highest levels of innovativeness – such as telecommunications research teams – tended to be the most organic, whilst those with a low requirement for innovativeness – such as clerical and stenographic groups – were the most mechanistic. What this research does not allow us to tell is whether differences in innovativeness amongst groups with the same function are associated with differences in organicity of structure. Are the most innovative R&D teams the most organic in structure? Even if they are, we are still left with the familiar question of direction of causality: do groups become more innovative because of their highly organic structure, or do they become more organic because they are highly innovative?

Many of the characteristics of organic-structured groups can be seen in autonomous work groups. These are groups with a high degree of authority and responsibility for the way they conduct their activities, commonly consisting of members of similar status (Guzzo and Dickson, 1996). Such groups generally make decisions collectively, and leadership is participative, often emergent rather than imposed. Carletta, Garrod and Fraser-Krauss (1998) carried out a study comparing autonomous and traditional groups in medium-sized UK manufacturing companies in terms of communication patterns within meetings. They found that although the meetings of both types of groups were dominated by conversations between pairs of members, in autonomous groups participation was more equal with more individual members involved in pairwise interactions. However, if autonomous groups became too large they became more centralized in formal discussions and lost the advantage over traditional groups in terms of participation. The authors argue that innovation will be facilitated in small autonomous groups. They also make the point that organizations can support the kind of communication patterns that enhance innovation by encouraging diverse interactions outside of formally constituted groups. Carletta *et al.* give the example of the highly innovative 3M company, which has strongly emphasized the importance of interaction outside of immediate work roles, through measures such as multidisciplinary technical forums and a policy of allowing members time to pursue their own ideas.

Group climate

Climate has been defined as 'the feelings, attitudes and behavioural tendencies which characterize organizational life' (Nystrom, 1990). It can also be seen as the prevailing atmosphere or mood within a group or organization. One aspect of climate which has been widely considered in relation to group innovation is cohesiveness – the extent to which members are attracted to the group and wish to remain part of it. There is a strong argument for high cohesiveness having a positive effect on group innovation, as it results in the individual gaining great satisfaction from group achievements, whilst feeling that the responsibility for any failures will be shared by the group as a whole. Once again, though, we would warn against overgeneralizing this relationship between cohesiveness and innovativeness. Cohesion is often strongly related to homogeneity, because similar people are more likely to be attracted to each other than dissimilar people, and/or because over time members of a cohesive group come to share attitudes, perceptions and values. As such, high cohesiveness is a common characteristic of groups in which 'groupthink' occurs, and thus may operate against innovative performance. Studies in organizations tend to show complex relationships between cohesiveness and group innovation, in which other variables, such as group size, have an important influence.

Recent research has moved on to look at facets of climate other than cohesiveness. West (1990) proposes 'climate for excellence' and 'participative safety' as two of the four factors in his theory of group innovation. The former refers to a climate in which the quality of decision making and task performance is highly valued, whilst the latter describes a climate characterized by supportive interpersonal interactions resulting in group members feeling safe to propose and develop radical and risky new ideas. The four-factor theory, and the Team Climate Inventory (TCI) derived from it, are discussed in more detail in the section on team building, below.

Group longevity and development

A weakness of both social psychological and occupational psychological research into groups is that it often neglects the fact that groups change over time. There has been some work examining the effects of group longevity on innovation; that is, whether the length of time that a group has been together influences its innovative performance. Katz (1982) found that R&D teams tended to perform less well the longer they had been together, although it should be noted that he was concerned with overall performance rather than specifically with innovativeness. Several writers have argued for the advantages of relatively short lifespans for groups, on the basis that long-standing groups can become very habit bound and resistant to change in their approach to problems (e.g. Lovelace, 1986). For some types of group, restricting the lifespan is not difficult; project teams, for instance, can be set up with the clear understanding that they will be disbanded once the project is completed. For other groups, where there is not a natural end-point to their existence, breaking them up simply on the grounds that they have been together 'too long' may be highly disruptive to the organization and damaging to the motivation of individual members. This may outweigh any potential benefits in terms of innovativeness, and it is worth stressing that the empirical evidence for a negative relationship between group longevity and innovativeness is – as yet – not substantial. If there is a genuine problem caused by the hardening of habits of thought and behaviour, managers might be best advised to consider other ways of stimulating innovativeness, perhaps introducing a number of new members to the group, or focusing strongly on creativity and innovation in personal and team development activities.

An understanding of the temporal context of group innovation requires researchers to look beyond the rather limited concept of longevity, and examine the processes that unfold in groups over time. There have been few studies of this type focusing specifically on innovation, but some of the wider literature on temporal processes in work groups is of clear relevance. This includes work which concentrates on processes within groups, and that which is concerned with the influence of the wider environment on the group. In the former category, Connie Gersick's work on task performance and group development has been highly influential. She has shown that groups do not evolve new ideas gradually, but rather undergo what might be termed 'quantum leaps' in their development. In experimental studies she found that groups of fixed longevity when given a simulated project task commonly underwent a significant change in their approach at roughly the midpoint in their life-span (Gersick, 1989). More recently, Gersick (1994) has examined pacing effects in real-world organizational settings. Kelly, Futoran and McGrath (1990) showed that performance effects associated with group deadlines varied according to the kinds of temporal-related problems experienced earlier. Where groups had encountered 'capacity' problems (i.e. getting work finished on time), they tended to speed up their activities subsequently. Where groups had encountered 'capability' problems (i.e. succeeding in overcoming task difficulties) they subsequently slowed down their performance – perhaps to ensure they thought more deeply about their task, as McGrath (1996) suggests.

These findings relating to how groups pace their activities are potentially of great interest to innovation researchers, though the relative scarcity of field studies means that we can only be speculative about the implications for real-world groups. Kelly *et al.*'s (1990) findings, for instance, may suggest that groups which have repeatedly been given inadequate time to complete tasks will tend to become focused on speed rather than quality, with a possible deleterious effect on innovation. Simply raising awareness about these phenomena would seem valuable. Group leaders and managers need to recognize that levels of activity in an innovation project will tend to change over time, and that this is not necessarily a reflection of the degree of effort and commitment in group members. 'Attempts to force the pace', especially early in the process, may be ill-advised; similarly we would concur with McGrath (1991; 1996) in warning against normative fixed-stage models of group development.

When considering temporal issues in terms of the relationship between the group and its environment (within and outside of the organization), the concept of 'entrainment' is particularly important. Ancona and Chong (1999) define entrainment as 'the adjustment of the pace or cycle of an activity to match or synchronize with that of another activity' (page 36). They argue that group processes in organizations are entrained by a whole range of temporally patterned activities in the wider organization and outside it. These may include such things as planning and financial cycles, seasonal variations in demand, and changes in personnel through recruitment and retirement (to name but a few). Such entraining forces can have a major impact on group innovation processes. They can provide what Ancona and Chong call 'windows of opportunity' which enhance the likelihood of successful change in specific limited time periods. Alternately they may impede change, perhaps by diverting organizational energy and resources from an innovation attempt which is ill-coordinated with cycles of activity outside the group. Ancona (1990) documents just such an occurrence in a US education department change programme, where innovative teams were constituted in September, but because of the department's cycle of activities were largely unable to begin initiatives until January. The result was a loss of momentum in the programme and consequently of team commitment.

A final point relating to the temporality of group innovation is raised by West (2001). He questions whether the innovation process in groups is more accurately seen as a 'normal' ongoing activity, paradoxically happening in many groups as part of routine group development over time; rather than a discrete set of events representing an aberration to 'normal' group processes (see also King, 1992). It may sound a contradiction in terms to talk of innovation being a routine group process, but there may well be elements of this as work teams develop and change their social and task processes as part of the natural evolution of the group over time. West (2001) goes further and argues that bureaucratic forms of work organization prevalent in the 1950s, 1960s and 1970s stifled the natural innovation potential present in many work groups, resulting in a fallacious view of innovation as being an abnormal, infrequent interruption to the usual social functioning of the group (see also Chapter 5).

Team building and innovation

Team building as an organizational training intervention is very much in vogue presently; it has its roots in organization development (OD) as described in Chapter 7. Modern-day team-building techniques vary enormously from short *in situ* meetings to discuss particular aspects of the team's performance, to extended off-the-job training courses addressing every facet of the team's climate, structure, task objectives and mission. Some common examples are:

- on-site team meetings to 'take stock' of progress on a particular project
- on- or off-site workshops to discuss the team's decision-making and problem-solving style
- on- or off-site workshops to examine the team's interaction with other parts of the wider organization
- off-site outdoor-type courses, where the team is given a series of physical tasks to accomplish.

Team-building interventions are normally focused upon the tasks of the team, as opposed to interpersonal relations and processes which are more the focus of traditional T-group training. Interventions aim to improve, amongst other things, group decision-making processes, interpersonal communication, group cohesion and unanimity, problem-solving capacities, creativity and innovation, participation, and group mechanisms for coping with external work pressures and demands. However, several reviews of the research into the efficacy of team-building techniques have noted a lack of rigorous evidence to support their transferable benefits back into the work setting (e.g. Porras and Silvers, 1991; Porras and Robertson, 1993). Most team-building interventions appear to be 'validated' at best by self-report attitude questionnaires completed by team members at the close of the training course and there remains a paucity of studies demonstrating real improvements in team functioning due to team building. More concerning, perhaps, is the mystique which has built up around the technique which shrouds the fundamentally simple aim of any team-building intervention – to improve decision-making and problem-solving processes in teams. Mayer (1990) describes a three-day team-building workshop offered commercially to organizations in California:

> The workshop is consonant with the integrated learnings on human potential of the past few thousand years and resonant with the modern findings of humanistic and transpersonal psychologies ... reported results cover an extraordinary range: increased job effectiveness, upgraded leadership, improved public speaking, greater assertiveness, improved work and family relationships, greater managerial effectiveness, a wide variety of personal growth experiences, spiritual development, healings, etc.
>
> *(Mayer, 1990, page 117)*

Unfortunately, no evidence whatsoever is given to vindicate these rather bizarre claims. Although this lack of validation is undoubtedly worrying, there are compelling reasons to expect that team building will increase in importance over the foreseeable future as a strategy to enhance innovation. *Ad hoc* project teams are being used more frequently by organizations seeking increased flexibility and speed of response to environmental changes, new manufacturing methods require group-level co-operation to function effectively, and team working is becoming increasingly common in areas of the public sector undergoing rapid structural change (Hosking and Anderson, 1992). So, it is imperative that the conditions for effective team building are articulated and the efficacy of different team-building interventions demonstrated. Porras and Robertson (1993) lay down five major conditions for effective team building:

1 a legitimate need for the team's existence (formal or informal task interdependence between team members);

2 a genuine desire to improve team functioning (as opposed to acquiescence to political pressures to go through the motions of attending team-building courses);

3 a willingness by the team to be introspective and to improve its own functioning and performance;

4 an allowance of sufficient time by the organization to engage in team-building activities;

5 an openness amongst team members to accept candid feedback and a willingness to respond constructively.

It would be sensible to check these conditions before initiating any team-building intervention as part of an organization's innovation strategy. Otherwise, regardless of how well designed the training is, it is likely that team building would have only a restricted impact, at best.

We conclude this section by presenting a case study (Box 4.1) illustrating West's (1990) four-factor theory of team climate and innovation, and the application of the Team Climate Inventory derived from it, in one particular organization.

Implications for practice

Although there has been less research on group innovation than at the individual and organizational levels, there is enough work to offer some suggestions to managers and group leaders for enhancing innovation. All such recommendations, however, must be preceded by a warning that they always need to be considered carefully in the context of particular groups, involved in particular types of innovative activities, and in particular organizational contexts. Social psychological understandings of group processes need to be applied critically, not treated as recipes to be followed without question. It is in this spirit that we draw the following implications for practice from the literature.

Social influence and decision processes in groups

Groups at work are likely to be subject to a variety of forms of social influence, often including conformity pressures. This is not necessarily a bad thing for innovation; some organizations may benefit from group members conforming to norms and values for being creative and taking risks. Where the climate and culture is substantially anti-innovation, however, conformity will tend to be associated with the inhibition of innovation. In the longer term this is not a problem that can be solved at the group level alone; it requires organizational-level change. Group-level change can contribute, though, by harnessing the innovative potential of minority influence. Leaders can try to ensure that dissenting voices are heard rather than punished; they may even encourage certain members to fulfil a 'devil's advocate' role.

Social constructionist approaches show how interactions within a group construct the way it sees itself and its world, including its stance towards innovation. Groups may construct an identity which is anti-innovative, for instance through reiteration of 'cautionary tales' about past failed innovations, and through talk which centres on the positive aspects of the status quo. In such cases, change to a more innovative outlook requires the group to draw on different ways of constructing its identity and its position towards innovation; members are more likely to embrace change if the status quo is seen in terms of stagnation or inertia rather than stability. This kind of change cannot be achieved by diktat, and attempts to manipulate people covertly through discourse have a strong likelihood of backfiring. It is far better if the group as a whole can be persuaded to reflect upon how it constructs its identity through its daily interactions. One useful strategy can be to enable members to see how other, more innovative groups, operate in order to expose them to unfamiliar discourses of group performance and innovativeness.

Group leadership, structure and composition

As a broad generalization, innovative groups tend to have participative leaders, organic structure and are not excessively homogenous in membership. Managers need to be very aware, though, that this combination of characteristics is in no way a guarantee of innovative-ness. Some configurations of group, organizational and innovation characteristics can necessitate a more directive leadership style or a more formal and centralized structure. Some groups with very diverse membership may fail to innovate because of conflict, or simply because they cannot understand each other's perspectives. The common recommendation for the kind of group described at the start of this paragraph should therefore always be considered in the light of the specific characteristics of an individual group (including its organizational context and the type of innovation it is mostly concerned with).

Temporal aspects

We have stressed that innovation is a process that unfolds over time in a group; it is not a single decision or a one-off event. As such, managers, group leaders and members need to be aware of the common temporal patterns in group development, such as the 'mid-point effect' in the nature of group processes in time-limited projects (which includes most innovation projects). They also need to recognize the importance of co-ordinating group activities with the temporal patterns and cycles of activity in the wider organization and environment so as to ensure that potentially valuable innovations do not fail through simple mis-timing.

It is clear then that our understanding of work group innovation is at an early phase of development. We are far from the point of being able to 'socially engineer' groups to be highly innovative, despite the claims of some team-building programmes, and the desirability of so doing is open to debate. The downside of intervening to maximize group innovativeness remains virtually unexplored – could it lead to feelings of burn-out or exploitation amongst group members, for instance? We would like to conclude by restating our earlier point that few, if any, groups exist with the sole objective of being innovative, even in areas such as R&D. Innovation is not an activity which occurs in isolation from other work group functions in organizations, and managers need to be wary of the possible knock-on effects of strategies which promise a 'quick fix' to enhance group innovativeness.

Box 4.1	**Climate and team building in NHS management teams**

One aspect of intrateam functioning often addressed by team-building interventions is the climate of relationships between individuals. Reichers and Schneider (1990) define climate as 'the shared perception of the way things are around here. More precisely climate is shared perceptions of organizational policies, practices and procedures, both formal and informal. ... Multiple climates are thought to exist in organizations' pages 22–3. ▶

As part of a three-year research programme into change and innovation in the British National Health Service (NHS), Anderson and West (1999) developed a five-scale facet-specific measure of team climate – the Team Climate Inventory (TCI) based on West's (1990) four-factor theory of innovation and team climate. The objective was to measure climate in a number of NHS management teams and to relate it to the teams' interactions in formal team meetings and also to their performance and innovativeness over time. Four main research questions were generated.

1 What factors act as helps and hindrances to innovation?
2 What distinguishes between highly innovative and less innovative teams?
3 How does the innovation process develop over time?
4 What practical measures can be recommended to facilitate innovation and match the demands of the work to team innovativeness?

Focusing on the final question, the researchers conducted more in-depth interventions with a small sample of the participant management teams using the TCI as their base-line measure of climate.

The Team Climate Inventory (TCI)

The TCI comprises 44 items which load onto five climate scales.

1 *Participative safety* – how participative the team is in its decision-making procedures and how psychologically safe team members feel it is to propose new and improved ways of doing things.
2 *Support for innovation* – the degree of practical support for innovation attempts contrasted against the rhetoric of professed support by senior management (many organizations have an abundance of the latter but a scarcity of the former!)
3 *Vision* – how clearly defined, shared, attainable and valued are the team's objectives and vision.
4 *Task orientation* – the commitment of the team to achieve the highest possible standards of task performance, including the use of constructive progress monitoring procedures. ▶

5 *Social desirability* – a check scale which indicates excessive faking and impression management by respondents.

The TCI underwent over four years of psychometric development and validation prior to publication, but its administration is essentially simple. All team members complete the measure and return it to the researchers who them score up, profile the team against established norms, and then feed back the results to the team.

To illustrate the use of the TCI in team building we describe below the characteristics and TCI profiles for two of the management teams involved in this study – 'Team A' and 'Team B'. For obvious reasons, some details have not been divulged to protect the anonymity of the teams, but the results themselves are based upon the actual team climate profiles obtained.

Team A

Team A was the senior management team of an acute hospital in the north-east of England. The unit boasted speciality departments in microsurgery, ear, nose and throat (ENT), and obstetrics and gynaecology. It possessed a total of 170 patient beds supported by some 970 medical and administration staff. The management team comprised five individuals: the unit general manager, accountant, director of nursing, personnel director, and the director of works. A closely knit team, this group had been together for over four years in all, a fact which the UGM was evidently proud of. Indeed, the UGM's style of management may have contributed to this – she was a highly charismatic leader, much respected and admired by the team and by staff in the hospital. Her major weakness seemed to be trying to do too much by herself and taking on every aspect of the hospital's strategic planning process personally, steadfastly refusing to involve any of her senior colleagues by delegating planning tasks to them.

Team B

An entirely different team in many respects, Team B was responsible for the day-to-day management of one of the ▶

largest general hospitals in the UK. Based in a major Midlands city centre, this unit employed over 3,100 staff in total. Including all wards, there were some 300 patient beds and, importantly, the unit was one of the first in the country (so called 'First Wave') to become an NHS trust hospital. This meant that the management team had greater autonomy from the local regional health authority, but that income was dependent upon local community doctors referring their patients to the hospital for treatment. It had also resulted in greater decentralization in decision making so that the management team alone could decide upon all issues of resource allocation within the hospital. Of course, this had also led to much political intrigue and lobbying by all departments. Quite content to preside over a degree of interdepartmental rivalry, the chief executive had radically restructured the management some months previously. It now comprised eight members – the chief executive himself, three directors of patient services representing each of the major clusters of medical specialities in the hospital, the unit business manager, finance director, director of human resources, and the director of community services. To describe the chief executive as a politically adept manger would be to understate the case – he was remarkably skilled at getting the best out of senior staff and had been known to pit managers against one another. Competition for resources was intense and the final decision over all types of resource allocation (finance, staff, services, etc.) was always the sole responsibility of the chief executive.

TCI profiles and team-building interventions
Both teams completed the TCI and Figure 4.2 shows their resultant profiles.

Team A
Team A profiled as high on Participative Safety, Support for Innovation, and Task Orientation, but lower on some facets of Vision, and also scored very highly on the Social Desirability check scale. This suggests a team climate where individuals actively participate in decision making, where information is shared as necessary and where individuals feel safe with one another at ▶

work. Conversely, it also suggests that whilst there is some enacted support for innovation, this falls far short of articulated or professed levels of support – a common finding when using the TCI. More concerning perhaps are Team A's scores in relation to the Vision scale. There appears little clarity over team objectives and some doubt over the value of these objectives in the view of team members, but perceived attainability and sharedness of objectives are higher. A further potential area for development is the middling score on appraisal on the Task Orientation scale – the extent to which team members constructively appraise each other and check progress. But these results are all influenced by Team A's profile on the Social Desirability scale which clearly indicates likely faking in the team's portrayal of itself in a too positive light. Thus, we may treat the more flattering points of the profile with some scepticism since those factors would be likely to be less impressive.

Given these profiles, what teambuilding interventions could be recommended to Team A? Certainly, an opening gambit would be to give survey feedback (see Chapter 7) on this profile in order to get behind the social desirability response. Here, the team builder would question, constructively but with tenacity, the team's responses to the TCI, probing for agreement that the team really does concur with this profile. Second, a series of team-building meetings designed to clarify, discuss and agree the team's vision/objectives would be advisable. Although levels of perceived sharedness and attainability are higher, attention needs to be given to the clarity of team objectives and to their perceived value to team members. A third issue warranting attention is the team's mid-scale scores on appraisal. Whilst not an immediate cause for concern, it is apparent that the team would benefit from closer self-monitoring and critical appraisal of progress. Again, workshop sessions could be developed as part of a team-building intervention to improve this aspect of team climate.

Team B

Again referring to Figure 4.2, Team B showed an entirely different profile to Team A. This team profiled as low on all aspects of Safety apart from interaction frequency, very low on enacted support ▶

119

Figure 4.2 **Team Climate Inventory – profiles for Team A and Team B**

SCALE/SUB-SCALE: LOW SCALE SCORE	STEN 1	2	3	4	5

PARTICIPATIVE SAFETY: The team meets only infrequently and/or some members participate only partially in decision making. There is a lack of trust between team members. Individuals do not feel safe to make proposals to the team. Individuals may not be contributing fully towards team objectives.

Information Sharing: The team shares information only to a limited extent or infrequently. Individuals tend to keep information to themselves.

Safety: Individuals do not feel safe within the team. Team members do not trust one another particularly. Individuals guard themselves at work.

Influence: Team members do not influence each other. Individuals' views are often overlooked or disregarded. There is little give and take.

Interaction Frequency: The team meets only infrequently. Team members do not keep in regular contact. Team members interact only irregularly.

SUPPORT FOR INNOVATION: Little articulated or enacted support for innovation is given. Stability is favoured above change. The team commits few resources to innovation.

Articulated Support: The team professes support for stability above innovation. Top management in the organization does not favour creativity. Assistance in developing new ideas is not always readily available.

Enacted Support: Little practical support is given to the team to develop creative ideas. There is too little time to be innovative. Few resources are available to introduce new ideas.

VISION: The team lacks a clear, shared, attainable vision/set of objectives which is valued by all team members.

Clarity: Team members are unclear about the objectives of the team.

Perceived Value: Not all team members are convinced of the value of these objectives. Individuals perceive team objectives as only partially worthwhile.

Sharedness: Team objectives are not shared by all team members. Some team members do not agree with all team objectives.

Attainability: Team members feel objectives may be problematic to achieve in reality. Team members perceive the objectives as unrealistic.

TASK ORIENTATION: The team is not fully committed to achieving the highest performance possible. Team members may not critically appraise their work. Help in developing new ideas may not be readily available.

Excellence: Team members are not necessarily all committed to achieving the highest levels of performance. The team lacks agreed criteria to measure excellent task performance.

Appraisal: Team members rarely critically appraise potential weaknesses. Team members rarely monitor colleagues' work performance.

Ideation: Team members seldom provide useful ideas and help, nor build upon the ideas of other team members.

SOCIAL DESIRABILITY: Low social desirability response – likely accuracy over social and/or task climate.

Social Desirability: Social Aspect: Team members sometimes feel tense with each other. There is sometimes disharmony between team members.

Social Desirability: Task Aspect: Team members sometimes feel the team functions below par and/or fails to meet some of its performance targets.

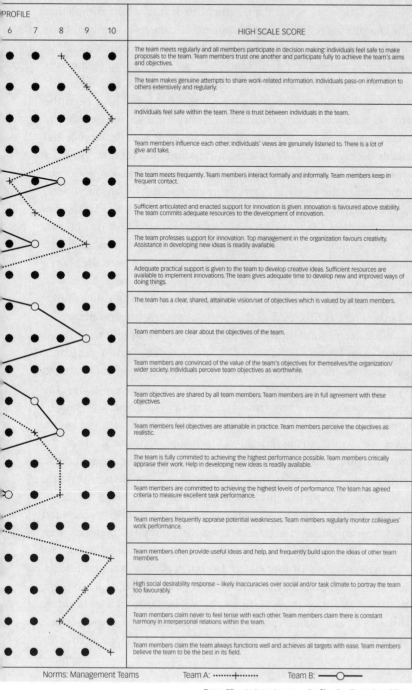

PROFILE

| 6 | 7 | 8 | 9 | 10 | HIGH SCALE SCORE |

The team meets regularly and all members participate in decision making: individuals feel safe to make proposals to the team. Team members trust one another and participate fully to achieve the team's aims and objectives.

The team makes genuine attempts to share work-related information. Individuals pass-on information to others extensively and regularly.

Individuals feel safe within the team. There is trust between individuals in the team.

Team members influence each other. Individuals' views are genuinely listened to. There is a lot of give and take.

The team meets frequently. Team members interact formally and informally. Team members keep in frequent contact.

Sufficient articulated and enacted support for innovation is given. Innovation is favoured above stability. The team commits adequate resources to the development of innovation.

The team professes support for innovation. Top management in the organization favours creativity. Assistance in developing new ideas is readily available.

Adequate practical support is given to the team to develop creative ideas. Sufficient resources are available to implement innovations. The team gives adequate time to develop new and improved ways of doing things.

The team has a clear, shared, attainable vision/set of objectives which is valued by all team members.

Team members are clear about the objectives of the team.

Team members are convinced of the value of the team's objectives for themselves/the organization/ wider society. Individuals perceive team objectives as worthwhile.

Team objectives are shared by all team members. Team members are in full agreement with these objectives.

Team members feel objectives are attainable in practice. Team members perceive the objectives as realistic.

The team is fully commited to achieving the highest performance possible. Team members critically appraise their work. Help in developing new ideas is readily available.

Team members are committed to achieving the highest levels of performance. The team has agreed criteria to measure excellent task performance.

Team members frequently appraise potential weaknesses. Team members regularly monitor colleagues' work performance.

Team members often provide useful ideas and help, and frequently build upon the ideas of other team members.

High social desirability response – likely inaccuracies over social and/or task climate to portray the team too favourably.

Team members claim never to feel tense with each other. Team members claim there is constant harmony in interpersonal relations within the team.

Team members claim the team always functions well and achieves all targets with ease. Team members believe the team to be the best in its field.

Norms: Management Teams   Team A: ⋯⋯＋⋯⋯   Team B: ——O——

for innovation, but higher on the Vision scale. Task Orientation was lower but we would also note that the low Social Desirability scores suggest little impression management or faking whilst completing the questionnaire. This profile suggests a climate of minimal trust and participation between team members, despite regular meetings and contact between individuals. It seems that the team was meeting but under a negative climate of distrust and perceived unsafety. Perhaps one contributor to this could well have been the interdepartmental competition and rivalry for resources within the management team – a point strongly suggestive of developmental needs during any subsequent team-building intervention. Another point of note is the discrepancy between articulated support for innovation (the levels of support as professed by team members) and actual support (as perceived by team members). It appears team members felt that the rhetoric far outweighed reality in terms of the support of resources (time, finance and personnel) to implement innovative solutions. Finally, we would note the team's lowest possible subscale score on appraisal – very little self-evaluation appears to be going on in comparison with other similar management teams used as the norm group for this profile.

What team building interventions would be appropriate based upon Team B's profile on the TCI? First, a series of non-threatening exercises to encourage interpersonal trust and co-operation could be recommended. Almost certainly, this would involve taking the management team away from the hospital site for a few days to preclude ongoing work pressures from interfering with the event. Exercises would strongly reinforce the superordinate goals of the organization and would emphasize the need for collaborative efforts and co-operative task performance to achieve overriding objectives. Supportive interpersonal behaviours could be high-lighted and any destructive rivalry or intrateam competitiveness fed back to individuals via classic 'sensitivity training' methods (see Chapter 7). A second intervention could be recommend to address the twin concerns of low enacted support for innovation and low levels of self-appraisal by the team. Here, the aim would be to make the team aware of these results (i.e. survey feedback) to facilitate discussion and action planning over measures to redress these aspects of team climate and to engage in team-building exercises ▶

to encourage appraisal via process management of interpersonal interactions. In this team's case, both interventions would be interdependent and the team builder would undoubtedly need to be diplomatic and tactful in relation to the chief executive's management style. Of course, finally, it should be noted that such team-building interventions, although highly useful, would have limitations upon just how much the functioning of the team could be improved. This 'ceiling' of improvement will be unknown before team building begins but will become apparent over times as the intervention process moves forward.

Suggested reading

Agrell, A. and Gustafson, R. (1996) 'Innovation and creativity in work groups', in M. A. West (ed.) *Handbook of Work Group Psychology*, Chichester: Wiley.

O'Reilly, III, C. A., Williams, K. Y. and Barsade, S. (1998) 'Group demography and innovation: Does diversity help?', in D. H. Gruenfeld (ed.) *Managing Groups and Teams: Vol. 1, Composition*, Stamford, CN: JAI Press.

Wetherell, M. (1996) *Identities, Groups and Social Issues*, London: Sage.

5

The antecedents of organizational innovation

After reading this chapter you should be able to

- overview the likely relations between organizational innovation and its people, structure, climate and culture, and environment;
- identify how different types of organization structure, facilitate or hinder innovation;
- identify and utilise the major typologies of innovation.

Organizational innovation research has been driven by the desire to answer the seemingly straightforward question: what is it that makes some organizations more innovative than others? Researchers have searched for factors which help or hinder organizations in their attempts to innovate, hoping to be able to describe reliably characteristics of high and low innovative organizations. This approach has its roots in sociological and social anthropological work on the diffusion of innovations, which seeks to explain how new ideas, products or processes spread through a population. Examples of diffusion as varied as the spread of snowmobiles in the Arctic, commercial dairying in Mexico and medical innovations in the British NHS can be found. The most influential theoretical work in this area has been that of Everret M. Rogers, who has identified the characteristics of early and late adopters of innovations, at the individual and organizational levels. (See Rogers (1983) and Brown (1981) for good accounts of this literature.)

A vast number of different factors have been examined as possible facilitators or inhibitors of innovation. It is not possible to discuss all of them in the space available here, and indeed some are of only marginal interest from a psychological perspective. We will therefore concentrate on four important groups of influencing factors:

1 people
2 structure
3 climate and culture
4 environment.

We will conclude by considering the strengths and weaknesses of this 'antecedent factor' (King, 1990) approach to the study of organizational innovation.

People

When trying to explain why some organizations are more innovative than others, one of the first factors at which researchers looked was – not surprisingly – the characteristics of people within the organization. Leaders and other top decision makers were the principal focus of early studies, and have continued to receive a good deal of attention, though more recent research has broadened its scope to consider other influential individuals, such as internal change agents and informal 'ideas champions'. The personal characteristics of non-managerial, non-professional members of organizations are rarely considered, except in the context of resistance to change (see Chapter 8).

Leaders

Early research into the influence of leaders on organizational innovation frequently focused on individual characteristics: personality traits, values and beliefs, experience and knowledge, and so on. In one study, for instance, it was found that 'elite' values amongst organizational leaders were predictive of high levels of innovation (Hage and Dewar, 1973). The problem for studies of this kind is that they have not been able to identify characteristics which predict innovation in all types of leader. Furthermore, in many studies where leader characteristics are found to be associated with organizational innovation, other variables show a stronger relationship or have a major modifying effect. In Kimberly and Evanisko's (1981) study of American hospitals, aspects of organizational structure proved better predictors of innovativeness than leader characteristics, whilst in Lawrence Mohr's (1969) research into the characteristics of local health officers, leader values were much more strongly related to innovation in organizations with high resources than in those where resources were low.

In the face of these difficulties, studies of innovation and leadership changed emphasis, from asking what innovative leaders are like to asking what they do; in other words, to examining their leadership style. By the early 1980s a considerable degree of consensus had emerged about the style required for innovative leadership. Drawing heavily on the work of organizational gurus like Tom Peters and Robert Waterman (1982) and Rosabeth Moss Kanter (1983), writers in Europe and North America stressed the need for a participative, democratic style of leadership which encourages subordinates to be involved in innovation decisions and to feel able to suggest novel ideas without fear of censure. A second vital aspect of innovative leadership is, they assert, the ability of the leader to provide a vision of where the organization is going to which organizational members can commit themselves.

More recently, academic and managerial writers have argued that transformational leadership is facilitative of innovation. This concept was developed by Bass (1985) to refer to leaders who inspire followers to act together towards shared goals. It comprises components of charisma, inspiration, intellectual stimulation and individual consideration, and has much in common with the kind of participative and visionary styles recommended in the early 1980s.

Participative, visionary and/or transformational leadership continues to be identified as an antecedent to organizational innovation in both academic and popular management writing. There is certainly some evidence from empirical research to support such claims. Howell and Higgins (1990) found transformational leader behaviours to be associated with the championing of technological innovation. Shin (1997) found that a 'vision setter' innovation style was more strongly linked to innovation in human service organizations than other less transformational styles. Ruigrok, Achtenhagen, Rüegg-Stürm and Wagner (2000) presented a case study of a leading construction industry firm which showed the importance of the spread of a 'shared leadership' style to the enhanced innovativeness of the company. However, there is also debate as to how generally effective for innovation these styles are. Many critics argue for a contingency approach, whereby the type of leadership required depends on factors such as the nature of external demands on the organization and the attitudes of organizational members towards change (Dunphy and Stace, 1988). Where an organization faces a threatening, turbulent environment, with members who are suspicious of change, leaders may need to be directive rather than participative in order to implement innovations. Against this view, the positive relationship between vision-setting style and innovation in Shin's study was unaffected by environmental and organizational characteristics, but it should be noted that this research only involved one type of organization (non-profit human services) in one particular geographic location in the USA.

Evidence against a universal prescriptions for innovation-facilitating leadership style comes from Manz, Bastien, Hostager and Shapiro (1989), who examined the influence of leadership on the development of seven major innovations (as part of the Minnesota Innovation Research Program; Van de Ven, Angle and Poole, 1989). They concluded that different leadership styles were required for different innovations, and at different stages in the process. In a later publication based on the same longitudinal research data, Van de Ven, Polley, Garud and Venkataraman (1999) argue that organizations need to be able to call on a range of different leadership styles to meet different circumstances in what they call the 'innovation journey' from initial idea to implementation.

Change agents

Research into the influence of individuals other than leaders on organizational innovativeness has concentrated on formal change agents and informal ideas champions. A change agent may be defined as a person who has been given explicit responsibility for overseeing the introduction of a specific change (or set of changes) within an organization. He or she may be a member of the organization (an 'internal change agent') or an outside consultant ('external change agent'). Everret Rogers (1983) proposes eight actions and characteristics which are likely to be positively related to successful innovation adoption by the client organization. They are based on research which has concentrated mainly on external agents, though many are applicable to internal ones as well.

1 The amount of effort the change agent makes to contact clients.
2 An orientation towards clients rather than towards the change agency.
3 The degree to which the innovation programme is compatible with clients' needs.
4 The empathy of the change agent with clients.
5 The degree to which the change agent and his or her clients share the same outlook and background.
6 The change agent's credibility to clients.
7 The extent to which the change agent is able and willing to work through opinion leaders in the organization.
8 The extent to which he or she is able to increase the clients' own ability to evaluate innovations.

We discuss the skills, knowledge and abilities required by change agents further in Chapter 7 on organizational development.

Idea champions

The individuals who take prime responsibility for the introduction of innovations often are not formally appointed change agents, but rather 'ideas champions' who feel a strong personal commitment to a particular new idea and are able to 'sell' it to others in the organization. Such champions may not be senior members of management – for instance, a technical specialist might identify a particular piece of technology which he or she believes would significantly improve organizational performance if adopted. Research shows that two crucial factors determining whether ideas champions are successful are personal power in the organization (see Frost and Egri, 1990a, 1990b), and ability to access and utilize wide communication networks. The two are, of course, likely to be interrelated but are not synonymous, as effective networking depends on personal characteristics, not just position. Howell and Higgins's (1990) study mentioned earlier showed that informal ideas champions showed the inspirational qualities of transformational leaders. In a study of large, mature organizations, Dougherty and Hardy (1996) found that ability to 'work' powerful networks was a key factor in the outcome of idea championing. Senior, long-serving members of staff were often able to succeed in championing through their credibility and extensive personal networks where newer staff found their efforts frustrated. This research also showed that whilst idea champions could succeed in facilitating specific innovations in the face of anti-innovation structures, processes and values, sustained innovation required appropriate organizational characteristics – champions alone were not enough, however personally effective.

Organizational structure

The importance of an organization's structure for its ability to innovate has long been a major theme in the literature. But what exactly is meant by the term 'organizational structure'? John Child defines it as follows: 'The formal allocation of work roles and the administrative mechanisms to control and integrate work activities including those which cross organizational boundaries' (Child, 1977).

Mechanistic and organic structures

The work of Burns and Stalker (1961) set the agenda for subsequent research and for the recommendations of popular management writers in the 1980s which have had a powerful influence on practice. Burns and Stalker studied British firms from a variety of industries in the 1950s. On the basis of their findings, they located organizational structures on a continuum of 'mechanistic' to 'organic'. The characteristics of organizations at either end of the dimension are shown in Table 5.1.

Burns and Stalker state that organizational structure should be related to the environment in which the organization operates. Where the environment is very stable and predictable, a mechanistic structure is suitable; people know what is expected of them and can concentrate on performing their tasks efficiently. At the time of Burns and Stalker's work, much of Britain's established manufacturing industry, such as textiles, operated in this way. However, where the organizational environment is one of change and unpredictability, mechanistic organizations lack the flexibility to cope and an organic structure is required. This enables the organization to change direction rapidly in response to market demands, and to take advantage of new technologies. Burns and Stalker identified these structures in industries

Table 5.1	**Characteristics of mechanistic and organic organizations**	
	Mechanistic organizations	Organic organizations
	Hierarchical structure, with stable divisions/departments based around functions	Flat structure, with temporary work groups/teams based around specific projects
	Vertical communications dominate	Lateral communications dominate
	Rigid job definitions, set by senior management	Flexible job definitions, defined by individuals through interaction with colleagues
	Power and authority based on seniority in hierarchy	Power and authority changing with changing circumstances; based on individual skills and abilities

Source: Based on Burns and Stalker (1961).

such as electronics, where in the 1950s new products were being developed and new markets opening up at an enormous rate.

The American researchers Lawrence and Lorsch (1967) took Burns and Stalker's approach a stage further. As well as saying that different types of overall structure were required according to environmental conditions, they claimed that in turbulent environments a greater degree of structural differentiation between departments (or other subunits) is required than in predictable environments. Thus in a firm facing an unstable market, the production department (where tasks are quite clearly defined) would have a more mechanistic structure than the sales department, which needs to respond quickly to changing demands, and to seek new outlets. In a firm whose market is highly predictable, both these departments would have the same kind of mechanistic structure.

During the 1970s, criticism of structural contingency theories such as that of Burns and Stalker mounted. They were seen as focusing too strongly on rather abstract concepts relating to organizational structure and neglecting processes within organizations that shaped the way they functioned – especially decision making. There were also strong criticisms made of the methodologies used in empirical studies. (See Pettigrew and Fenton, 2000, for an overview of these critiques.) By the late 1970s, configuration theories had largely replaced the structural contingency theories in attempting to understand how forms of organizing relate to performance (including innovation). These theories also tried to relate types of organization to the circumstances in which they operated, but did so in a more multidimensional way than the mechanistic/organic distinction. They also put a strong emphasis on linking structure to strategy (e.g. Miles and Snow, 1978; Miller and Friesen, 1978; Miller, 1986).

New forms of organizing

Just as the early 1980s saw a profusion of texts by management 'gurus' on the structural and cultural requirements for achieving success through innovation, the 1990s saw an explosion of interest in new forms of organizing. We will consider the nature of these new forms shortly; first, it is important to recognize the context within which this literature has developed. It is very much a product of a set of social, economic, political and technological changes that have had a worldwide impact over the last decade or so. These include globalization, expanding markets and changing consumer behaviour, growing concerns about the environment and, of course, the Internet. In terms of what the new organization should (or actually does) look like, structural recommendations follow a similar pattern to those of the 1980s: delayering, project-based organization, cross-functional links and increased use of autonomous units. However, the importance of structure *per se* is much diminished; a common theme is that organizing should be around processes and strategies, not structures. Indeed, the most radical suggestions relating to virtual organizations (e.g. Handy, 1996) paint a picture of a future where the physical organization exists in only the most minimal form. Even in less extreme formulations, there is a shift in emphasis towards the importance of relationships, often conceptualized in terms of intra- and interorganizational networks.

Despite the volume of literature in this area, there is a rather limited amount of evidence that organizations are really changing in the direction described, or that new forms necessarily encourage innovative performance. In this context, the INNFORM research programme recently reported by Pettigrew and Fenton (2000) is of special importance. This international programme consisted of a survey of large and medium-sized organizations in Europe (and subsequently the USA and Japan), supplemented by case studies of individual innovative organizations. The European survey shows between 30 per cent and 51 per cent of organizations exhibiting specific structural changes of the kind noted above over the period 1992–1996, and also a substantial proportion showing changes in processes and the nature and management of organizational boundaries. However, only a very small number of organizations showed substantial changes in all three areas (structure, processes and boundaries) – as few as 4.5 per cent of the sample. It is notable that this minority do show on average a much higher performance than the other organizations included in the study.

An optimum structure for innovation?

There is currently no shortage of prescriptions for the kind of structure organizations should adopt in order to facilitate innovation and change. Most retain the early 1980s emphasis on flat structures, temporary project-based teams and cross-boundary communication. To these are generally added the 1990s concerns with networks, autonomous units and virtual aspects of organization through the use of the Internet and associated technologies.

To a large extent, the psychological rationale for the effectiveness of such structures is in terms of job discretion and idea ownership through participation. High discretion is consistently found to predict innovation and creativity at work (West, 1987; Hill and Amabile, 1993), both through the motivating effects of a sense of control over one's own work and by removing hierarchical barriers to trying new ideas. Idea ownership stems from participation in idea generation and decision making; in the context of teamworking, ownership associated with autonomy and participative leadership may encourage the development of an innovative group identity. The emphasis on lateral communications and network building can also be supported from psychological theory, in terms of both access to diverse sources in initiating innovations (see Chapter 4) and opportunities for influence and persuasion in adopting and implementing them (Weenig, 1999; Dougherty and Hardy, 1996).

It is useful to draw managers' attention to the psychological arguments in favour of certain kinds of structure when seeking to facilitate innovation, but it is dangerous to present them as a universal recipe for innovative success. All of the positive aspects mentioned above have a potential down side; high discretion can be anxiety provoking for some people, participative decision making can result in a tortuous path through adoption to implementation, strong group identities and diversity can both be causes of harmful conflict. Structural recommendations must be considered in the light of the history and current circumstances of a particular organization. For instance, managers may intend the introduction of autonomous work groups as a means of stimulating innovation through enhanced discretion and participation, but it may be experienced as a lack of support and direction if the staff involved have historically felt abandoned and unsupported by management.

Organizational climate and culture

The 1980s and 1990s saw a shift in emphasis in the search for antecedents of successful innovation, away from characteristics of people and structures towards less tangible features of organizations – in particular their climate and cultures. Gareth Morgan (1986) states that 'effective organizational change implies cultural change' (page 138), and this message has been very much taken to heart by management writers and consultants. Whereas in the 1970s a change agent might recommend that an organization adopts a more organic structure in order to become more innovative, since the 1980s he or she is as likely to suggest a change of logo and the distribution of a glossy internal newsletter to all members of staff. That organizations see the value in such measures is evidenced by the sum of around £50 million spent by British Telecom on introducing its new logo in the late 1980s.

It is not only in relation to innovation that climate and culture have become major preoccupations within occupational psychology – a substantial literature has built up looking at how they relate to such things as organizational commitment and leadership. In spite of this, there remains a lack of clarity and constituency in how the terms are used, and a considerable degree of overlap between them. No one pair of definitions would meet with universal approval, but those of Nystrom (1990) are reasonably representative of the majority. He defines organizational culture as 'the values, norms, beliefs and assumptions embraced by participants' (page 147) and climate as 'the feelings, attitudes and behavioural tendencies, which characterize organizational life and may be operationally measured through the perceptions of its members' (page 148).

Climate

Ekvall (1996) draws a useful two-way distinction in conceptualizations of climate. First, some writers treat it as effectively synonymous with culture by including values, beliefs and norms within the concept, whilst others strive to maintain separation between the concepts through a narrower definition of climate. Second, for some theorists, climate exists in the perceptions of the organizational members, arising from the nature of their interactions (e.g. Schneider, 1975). Others, including Ekvall himself, view it as an objective feature of the organization: 'climate is regarded as an attribute of the organization, a conglomerate of attitudes, feelings and behaviours which characterizes life in the organization, and exists independently of the perceptions and understandings of the members of the organization' (Ekvall, 1996, page 105).

This distinction reflects different underlying assumptions about the nature of people and organizations, with the former position typifying symbolic interactionist, phenomenological and social constructionist views, whilst the latter is characteristic of the positivist views of most of mainstream psychology (including occupational psychology). Most research has taken the latter stance, and used survey methods to examine the relationship between climate variables and innovative performance. Common recommendations for climates supporting innovation emerging from such work include openness to change, risk taking, tolerance of debate and disagreement, and playfulness (e.g. West, 1990; Nyström, 1990; Ekvall, 1996). Not all researchers support the notion that overall climate predicts innovation. Klein and Sorra (1996) provide evidence from organizational case studies to suggest that research should focus on 'climate for implementation' in relation to specific innovations rather than general climate factors of the kind mentioned previously. Scott and Bruce (1994) found a rather weak mediating influence of climate on individual innovation, and suggest that its importance might be overstated in the literature.

Despite the dominance of the objective view of climate, it is open to serious philosophical and methodological criticism. If the climate concept is concerned with such things as feelings and attitudes, it is hard to see in what sense these can be independent of organizational members' perceptions and understandings, as Ekvall claims. A non-objectivist approach has the advantage of focusing on climate as arising through the way people engage with each other in the daily activity of the organization. This emphasis on relationships and interaction is in keeping with developments in the literature on organizational structure and form, noted earlier. Qualitative methods which are sensitive to the subtleties of workplace interactions and place climate in organizational context are well suited to address such issues. Carrero, Peiró and Salanova's (2000) recent study of radical innovation using a grounded theory approach, which identified 'implementation climate' as an emerging theoretical category, is a good example of this.

Structural approaches to culture

Approaches to culture may be categorized as either structural or interpretative (Wilson, 1992). The former focus on the link between culture and organizational structure. One well-known structural typology is that proposed by Charles Handy (1985), who identifies four types of culture; they are described below, with implications for organizational innovation highlighted.

Role cultures are typical of the classic bureaucratic model of organization, where the structure is one of multiple layers of hierarchy, each reporting to the one above. Key values are adherence to and expertise within clearly defined roles – ambiguity of any kind is highly threatening, and as a result formal rules, regulations and procedures abound. Given these characteristics it is not surprising that role cultures are generally not held to be effective innovators. They function best in stable, predictable environments, where they may actually be quite successful at managing non-radical changes which do not threaten the fundamental organizational structure. However, they are too inflexible to cope well with radical change.

Power cultures are often found in organizations which have grown up around one strong, authoritative individual. Handy likens the structure to that of a web, with its maker – the spider – in the centre. Status, obedience and control are highly valued, as in role cultures, but unlike classic bureaucracies, in power cultures the central authority tends to function through *ad hoc* decisions made to deal with particular circumstances rather than through the imposition of fixed rules and regulations. This enables such cultures to respond to and initiate change more rapidly than role cultures. When the organization is small enough for the power figure to exert effective hands-on control, and when staff members largely share his or her vision, Handy argues, power cultures can be very effective innovators. However, if they grow to a size where the power figure cannot maintain central control over everything that is happening in the organization, the dangers of innovation attempts meeting unforeseen hindrances are greatly magnified. Power cultures may also inhibit effective innovation because of the limited discretion offered to most members. Lack of autonomy amongst those distanced from the centre may lead to their dissatisfaction and unwillingness to put in the extra effort needed to make innovations imposed from above work. Equally, they are unlikely to initiate innovations themselves.

Task cultures are associated with matrix structures. They stress flexibility, adaptability and egalitarianism within project teams, lateral rather than vertical communications, and place a high value on individual and group achievement. They are commonly considered the most favourable towards innovation, and are routinely prescribed as the ideal type by both popular and academic management writers. As in our earlier discussion of organizational structure, we would warn against the view that any single type of culture is always the most appropriate for innovation. Whilst task cultures do have clear positive features, there are circumstances where they will be less effective than other types. A small organization with a power culture may be faster to respond to an unexpected new market opportunity. A role culture may be more successful at introducing some externally imposed innovations such as new health and safety regulations.

Person cultures emphasize individual autonomy and interpersonal relationships above all else. They are therefore associated with highly decentralized and informal structures, where control is exercised through mutual accountability. Organizations such as workers' co-operatives, communes and professional partnerships (e.g. lawyers, general practitioners) are examples of person cultures. Because of the maximizing of individual discretion, person cultures can help facilitate high levels of individual creativity. However, this may not always translate into organizational level innovation, because of the need to achieve consensus by persuasion. Additionally, the value placed on the quality of interpersonal relationships means that if problems occur in relationships they can have a devastating impact on the whole organization.

Interpretative approaches to culture

Interpretative approaches view culture in terms of the symbols, rituals and myths pervading the organization. Managing change therefore involves the manipulation of these symbolic elements of culture, and the communication of them to staff and customers. This can be seen in the way in which many British banks transformed themselves in the 1980s. High counters and glass screens were replaced by open-plan layouts, with tables and armchairs for customers. Staff uniforms were modernized. Accounts were referred to as 'products' and given names such as 'Orchard' and 'Meridian'. These changes were a response to the novel experience of genuine competition arising from the financial deregulation of the 1980s. They reflect a recognition that it is not enough simply to introduce new services; both customers and staff must be persuaded that banks – once the epitome of tradition and stability – have become dynamic, client-orientated organizations.

Ideas about the need to manage culture as a means of managing change, and about the types of culture that are desirable, have been accepted very readily by organizational change practitioners. Careful examination of their foundations in empirical research, however, shows them to be rather insubstantial. There have been relatively few studies examining the influence of climate and culture on organizational innovativeness compared with the amount of attention given to leadership and structural variables. Nor have there been many evaluation studies of the impact of cultural change programmes on medium- or long-term organizational innovative performance. Nystrom's (1990) study in a large Swedish chemical company, EKA Nobell, is a rare example of an attempt to test empirically the dimensions of climate and culture which are associated with innovativeness. He found that the most innovative division of the company had a climate that was high on playfulness, support for ideas, freedom and challenge, and which strongly encouraged risk taking and debate. Its culture emphasized creativity and change above all else, including profitability and customer orientation, and there were high levels of conflict and disharmony. These findings suggest that allowing pro-innovation values to become too dominant may in some instances have significant detrimental effects on an organization; priorities other than innovation for its own sake must not be neglected.

An important realization when considering the influence of organizational culture on innovation is that in almost all organizations there is not one unitary culture to which all members exclusively belong. Organizations, like the wider societies they exist within, consist of a series of subcultures, some of which may be highly congruent with the overall culture whilst others may be antagonistic to its values. When using cultural change to facilitate innovation, the manager or other change agent needs to be sure he or she is aware of the existing subcultures, which may not all respond in the same way. The successive changes in the British National Health Service since the mid 1980s provide a good example of the importance of subcultural values in organizational change. The then Conservative Government promoted a managerial model closer to that of business, followed by the introduction of an 'internal market' for health care in which district health authorities and some general practitioners (known as 'fund-holders') purchased care from 'providers' – hospitals and community services. A great deal of the resistance to these changes by doctors and nurses can be seen as a clash between the new culture, emphasizing managerial values, and the established subcultures of these groups which maintain that decisions about the provision of health care should be based on professional judgements, not market forces. The new Labour Government's abolition of GP fundholding in 1997 was in part a recognition of the scheme's perceived mismatch with health service culture. Ironically, Labour soon faced its own problems with proposed innovations that were seen as threatening the NHS culture in the form of increased private sector involvement in the running of the health service. On a much smaller scale, Meston and King (1996) showed that an innovation in staff training in a nursing home for older people was much less successful than managers had hoped because it was perceived to undermine the family-like culture of the home.

There is no doubt that understanding organizational climate and culture can take us further in making sense of innovation and change than a focus solely on more tangible aspects such as leadership styles and formal structure. However, there is a need for caution, as there are dangers in overemphasizing the extent to which climate and especially culture can be 'managed'. An organization's climate and culture (or climate*s* and culture*s*) have deep roots in its history and in the personal experiences of its members. These cannot be magicked away by a change of logo and the distribution of a mission statement, as managers sometimes seem to hope will happen – perhaps under the influence of overoptimistic culture change 'experts'. In any case, there is something worrying about efforts to impose a complete set of values and perceptions on organizational members from on high, as writers such as Morgan (1986) and Hollway (1991) point out. Such attempts have an unpleasant whiff of authoritarianism about them.

Environment

In seeking to identify factors which help or hinder innovation, it is not enough just to look at features of the organization itself: its people, structure, climate and culture. It is also necessary to look at the environment within which the organization exists, and the way it interacts with that environment. Of course, in an economic analysis of organizational innovation, a wide range of factors in both the physical and commercial environment would need to be considered, but from a psychological point of view two areas are of principal interest – the ways in which the organization communicates with its environment and the assumptions and expectations about its environment that it holds.

Much research has examined how the quantity and quality of communication with the environment influences the organization's ability to innovate. Studies have shown innovativeness to be associated with the existence of boundary-spanning roles within the organization (Tushman, 1977) and with professionalization of organizational members (Daft, 1978). In both cases, the relationship with innovativeness can be understood in terms of organizational knowledge of innovations. Individuals in roles which cross organizational boundaries, and professionals who have access to formal and informal networks of fellow professionals, have the opportunity to come across new ideas which could be applied within their own organizations. We have already seen that issues of intra- and interorganizational boundary management loom large in the literature on new forms of organizing for innovation (Pettigrew and Fenton, 2000).

The extent to which an organization engages in an active search of the environment for new ideas to adopt (commonly referred to as 'environmental scanning') depends on its perceptions of its own relationship with its environment. Such perceptions have been used as the basis for classifying organizations into 'strategic types'. Miles and Snow (1978) identify four strategic types: defenders, prospectors, analysers and reactors. Taking the first two of these as examples, defenders are organizations which see their environment as essentially stable, and therefore are concerned with the efficiency of existing operations in order to dominate their market niche. Prospectors in contrast see their environment as uncertain and turbulent, and therefore place a high value on innovation. Meyer (1982) looked at the responses of American hospitals of different strategic types to a crisis caused by a doctors' strike. He observed that the prospector-type hospital responded to the crisis by defining it as a 'good experiment' and increased its innovative activity, whilst the defender-type hospital fell back on its financial slack to carry on business as usual.

The concept of entrainment which we discussed in Chapter 4 is as important for the organization/environment relationship as it is for the work group/organization relationship. Just as a group or team needs to co-ordinate its innovation efforts with the temporal sequences of the wider organization, so the organization must entrain its innovative activity to patterns and cycles in its environment. These might include predictable seasonal variations in supply and demand, the activities of competitors, and legislative or other political changes. Again, boundary-spanning roles can be of great assistance in achieving such co-ordination.

It is convenient for the purposes of simplification, but essentially inaccurate, to draw a clear boundary between organization and environment, as people within organizations simultaneously exert influence on and are influenced by the 'outside world'. The ways in which they see themselves and their environment are inextricably intertwined. Morgan (1986) argues that some organizations fail to innovate because they have a rigid view of themselves as entities separate from their environment. He gives the example of typewriter manufacturers who failed to take account of changes in computer technology which led to the development of word processors because they did not see microprocessing technology as being part of their environment. To have done so would have required a change in the way they perceived themselves.

Types of innovation

Researchers have long recognized that facilitating and inhibiting factors might differ for different types of innovation. This is implicit in work which has restricted its focus to a specific type: for example, managerial innovation (Kimberly, 1981), product innovation (Normann, 1971) and medical innovation (Stocking, 1985). Unfortunately, attempts to systematically compare innovation types remain relatively uncommon.

Innovation typologies

There are numerous ways in which innovations can be categorized; four useful methods are by the sociotechnical system within which they occur by classification as product or process innovation, by characteristics of the innovation itself, and by the source of the innovation. Table 5.2 gives examples of each kind of typology.

Sociotechnical systems

Fariborz Damanpour and William Evan (1984) distinguished between technical innovations, which occur within the primary work activity of the organization, and administrative innovations, which occur within the social system and are concerned with the organization of work and the relationships between organizational members. In a study of American public libraries they found that the adoption of administrative innovations often triggered technical innovations, but the reverse did not occur. Damanpour (1990) has since added a third category, ancillary innovations. These are innovations which span organizational–environment boundaries, and go beyond the primary work functions of the organization. In the libraries they included career development and adult education programmes for the community. Damanpour found that organizational performance was best predicted by adoption of administrative innovations, but that technical innovations were perceived as more effective than the other two types. This is in line with Nelkin's (1973) claim that unrealistic expectations are often placed on technological innovations to solve organizational problems.

Table 5.2	**Typologies of innovation**		
Sociotechnical systems	Product and process	Innovation characteristics	Innovation source
Damanpour (1990)	Damanpour and Gopalakrishnan (2001)	Zaltman, Duncan and Holbek (1973)	Anderson (1992)
Technical New products, services or processes directly related to primary work activity	*Product* A new good or service introduced to meet the needs of an external user or the market	*Programmed–Non-programmed* Whether or not innovation is scheduled in advance. (Non-programmed innovations can be further divided into *distress* or *slack* types)	*Emergent* Innovations based on ideas emerging from within the organization itself
Administrative Changes to social relationships and communication, and rules, roles, procedures and structures related to them	*Process* New element(s) introduced to the production or service operations of an organization	*Instrumental–Ultimate* Whether innovation is introduced to facilitate a further innovation or as an end in itself	*Adopted* Innovations copied from other similar organization(s), often with subsequent modifications
Ancillary Innovations crossing boundaries between organization and environment		*Radicalness* The extent to which the change is both novel and risky	*Imposed* Innovations which an organization has been forced to make by some external regulatory or legislative power

Product and process innovations

A distinction has often been made between these two types of innovation (Abernathy and Utterback, 1978; Barras, 1986). In a recent paper, Damanpour and Gopalakrishnan (2001) define product innovations as 'new products or services introduced to meet an external user or market need' and processes innovations as 'new elements introduced into an organization's production or service operations' (pages 47–8). They show that in a large sample of US banks ($n = 101$), product innovations are introduced at a higher rate and speed than process, which they explain in terms of managers' perceptions that the former will confer greater competitive advantage. However, the banks who showed the greatest co-ordination of the two types of innovation also showed the highest performance, a finding in keeping with previous research in other sectors (e.g. Ettlie, 1995, in manufacturing; Pisano and Wheelright, 1995, in pharmaceutical companies).

Characteristics of the innovation

Zaltman *et al.* (1973) offer a typology consisting of three dimensions of innovation characteristics:

1 programmed–non-programmed
2 instrumental–ultimate
3 radicalness.

The first dimension distinguishes between those innovations which are scheduled in advance – perhaps as necessary consequences of another innovation – and those which are not. Non-programmed innovations are further subdivided into *slack* innovations, which occur as a result of the availability of slack resources, and *distress* innovations, which are immediate responses to crisis. The first author has suggested a third subcategory of *proactive* innovation, where an individual or group tries to draw the organization's attention to an area where the need for change has not previously been recognized (King, 1990).

The second dimension is concerned with whether an innovation is introduced as an end in itself (ultimate) or as a means to facilitate the adoption of a further innovation (instrumental). The final dimension of radicalness is conceptualized by Zaltman *et al.* (1973) as the product of an innovation's novelty and riskiness; a highly radical innovation is one which is both very novel and very risky.

Of these three dimensions, only radicalness has been the subject of much discussion in the literature. It is widely assumed that more radical innovations will stimulate greater resistance to change than less radical ones, because they challenge the perceptions and assumptions of the status quo. A study by the first author in a hospital ward found, however, that radicalness was not necessarily associated with resistance, owing to a prevailing pro-change climate. The same study found that on dimension one, pro-active innovations were more likely to meet obstacles to adoption and implementation than other types, and that their success was particularly dependent upon the status of their initiators (King, 1989).

It is disappointing that there have not been more attempts to use Zaltman *et al.*'s typology in empirical research, as it provides a useful framework for examining how innovations vary by type. West and Anderson (1992) have used a typology derived in part from it in a study of top management teams in the British National Health Service, adding to the dimensions of novelty and radicalness those of *magnitude* and *effectiveness*. It is to be hoped that this line of research will be further developed in the future.

Innovation source

Innovations may be classified according to whether they are initiated within the organization (emergent), are adopted from other organizations (imported) or forced upon the organization from outside (imposed). We will see in the next chapter that there is evidence to suggest that the innovation process develops differently for these different types (Sauer and Anderson, 1992). It is also likely that there will be differences in antecedent factors and in reactions to innovations according to their source.

General or specific theories of innovation?

Cooper (1998) criticizes attempts to examine differences in innovation process and outcomes in terms of single dimensions, such as radicalness or technical-administrative. Most innovations, he claims, can meaningfully be classified on two or more dimensions, and the interactions of dimensions are likely to relate to important differences in innovation processes and outcomes. For example, a radical technological innovation may have different antecedents, and provoke different reactions, from a radical administrative innovation. He proposes a three-dimensional typology of incremental–radical, product–process, and administrative–technological to be used as the basis for future research in order to more accurately reflect the complex character of real-world innovations.

This argument raises the question of whether we should seek to produce general theories of innovation at all. If distinct types of innovation differ in antecedents, development and impact, general theories may do more harm than good, oversimplifying the field and leading to misleading universal prescriptions. Against this, if all attempts to generalize across types are abandoned, the field is likely to become even more fragmented than it already is. We have argued in several places in this book for a more contextually aware approach to understanding innovation and creativity at work, and from this position feel sympathy with those who urge caution about general theories. It is preferable to build tentatively towards a more generalized understanding through the accumulation of context-specific evidence rather than to propose grand, universal models that through averaging out differences, may bear little resemblance to any one real case.

Strengths and weaknesses of research into the antecedents of innovation

The continuing influence of diffusion research can be seen in two pervasive features of the antecedent factors approach to organizational innovation. First, there is an emphasis on the innovation adoption decision, the point at which the organization makes a firm commitment to introduce an innovation. Research tends to be little concerned with what happens to the innovation after it has been adopted. This is problematic, as the fact that an innovation has been adopted is no guarantee that it will be successfully implemented and routinized into organizational life. In most organizations it is possible to find examples of innovations which meet such a fate.

Second, cross-sectional research designs dominate; comparisons across organizations at one point in time are made, in order to identify what it is which makes some more innovative than others. Innovativeness is usually defined in terms of the number (and less often, the quality) of innovations adopted. This is equivalent to the comparisons of early and late adopters of innovations carried out by diffusion researchers. The limitation of such designs is that they are of little use in establishing cause and effect. The finding that organizations with organic structures are more innovative (Burns and Stalker, 1961) is generally held to show that organic structure facilitates innovation. But it could equally be the case that engaging in high levels of innovation causes the organization to adopt a more organic structure. To determine which interpretation is most valid, studies which trace innovation processes and organizational performance over time are necessary. We will consider the process approach to innovation research in the next chapter.

A further weakness of the literature on antecedents of innovation is its tendency to be normative; that is, to suggest that particular features will facilitate innovation in almost any organization. Popular management texts are probably the worst offenders here; as we have seen, they have encouraged the emergence of a 'new orthodoxy' which recommends participative leadership, organic structure and a strong task culture as the universal recipe for innovation. This is in spite of the widely acknowledged lack of consistency in relationships between specific antecedent factors and innovative performance. The danger of such normative assumptions is that they can make managers over-confident of their ability to manipulate all aspects of an innovation's progress, through adherence to a simple 'cookbook' of instructions. As we will see in the next chapter, serious doubts have been expressed about how manageable organizational change processes really are.

Despite these limitations, there are some advantages in taking the antecedent factors approach. One is that it provides the opportunity to integrate different levels of analysis – something which occupational psychology rarely achieves. Researchers can assess the relative influence of individual, group and organizational characteristics on innovativeness and examine how they interact with each other, though in reality most studies only look at one or at best two of these levels. Large-scale surveys across varied organizations are useful as a way of identifying the range of variables that can influence innovation, though they cannot adequately explain how and why innovations are initiated, or which factors are influential at different points in the process of adoption and implementation. To continue to make a significant contribution, antecedent factors research needs to move on to more sophisticated questions than the compelling but overly simplistic one of what makes some organizations more innovative than others. The kind of question that managers really need answering is: 'which parts of our organization need to become more innovative, and in what ways?'

Implications for practice

Given our scepticism regarding general theories of antecedents to innovation, and our warnings regarding universal prescriptions, the implications we draw from this literature for managers must be more suggestive than directive. There is no 'cookbook' that can guarantee success. Nevertheless, in some areas theory and evidence are sufficiently well developed to offer worthwhile advice, though it should always be considered carefully in the context of particular organizational circumstances and innovation characteristics.

Regarding leadership, the common recommendation for participative style does have a plausible rationale in psychological theory, and is supported by evidence. In some circumstances, though, it may not be effective; for instance where there is a combination of high uncertainty, environmental turbulence and strong resistance to change, or where different groups take opposing views on an innovation, reflecting deep-seated cultural differences between them.

There is no single ideal organizational structure to facilitate innovation, but a combination of social, economic and technological changes in the late twentieth century have tended to confer advantages to those using some of the structural features associated with so-called 'new forms of organizing'. These include an emphasis on intra- and interorganizational networks and relationships, the use of autonomous units where creativity is especially important and an avoidance of overly-rigid hierarchies. Perhaps most important is the notion that organizational processes and strategy should determine structure, and not vice versa.

An understanding of organizational climate and culture is very important if managers are to maximize their chances of successful innovation. They need to recognize that stances towards innovation will reflect feelings, norms and values of particular groups and of the organization as a whole, and that divergence from their own perspective does not necessarily imply wilful intransigence or unthinking resistance to change (see Chapter 8 for a fuller discussion of these issues). One of the advantages of participative leadership and cross-functional or multidisciplinary teamwork is that they can provide an opportunity for people to increase their understanding of each other's point of view.

Suggested reading

Anderson, N. and King, N. (1993) 'Innovation in organizations', in C. L. Cooper and I. T. Robertson (eds), *International Review of Industrial and Organizational Psychology Volume 8*, pages 1–34, Chichester: Wiley.

Cooper, J. R. (1998) 'A multidimensional approach to the adoption of innovation', *Management Decision*, 36(8): 493–502.

Dougherty, D. and Hardy, C. (1996) 'Sustained product innovation in large, mature organizations: Overcoming innovation-to-organization problems', *Academy of Management Journal*, 39(5): 1120–53.

Pettigrew, A. M. and Fenton, E. M. (2000) *The Innovating Organization*, London: Sage.

6   The innovation process

After reading this chapter you should be able to

- describe major models of the innovation process including key stages and validation evidence
- describe the main stage, proposed in Zaltman *et al.*'s (1973) model, and critically appraise this model
- discuss critically the degree to which the innovation process is manageable.

Anyone who has been responsible for managing the introduction of innovations in an organization will know that there is much more involved than taking a single decision to adopt and implement change. Commonly, it requires a range of activities prior to and following the adoption decision, including fact finding, political manœuvring, formal and informal discussions and negotiations, and so on. Yet much of the research into antecedents of innovation reviewed in the previous chapter uses methods which provide only a 'snapshot' of the innovation process at a single point in time (or at best, at two points), examining correlations between various attitudinal and behavioural variables. Everett Rogers (1983) says of this type of research: 'Essentially, this approach amounts to making the innovation process "timeless". It is convenient for the researcher but intellectually deceitful with respect to the process he (*sic*) is investigating' (page 177). He went on to call for more in-depth studies of the progress of particular innovations. Although this might mean studying fewer organizations, he argued that such a strategy would provide much richer insights into the innovation process, allowing the researcher to learn 'more about less, rather than less about more' (page 358). The process approach enables us to examine how innovations occur, how they develop, and why some are more successful than others.

Another strategy is to study innovation processes retrospectively; in other words, to construct innovation histories. A major issue for this type of research is that people tend to reconstruct events from memory in a way which makes them appear more logical and orderly than they were (Bartlett, 1932; Loftus, 1979); also, people may simply forget important details. The implications of this depend on the approach to organizational research that is being taken. If one is concerned with identifying causal factors to enable general predictions about the progress of the process to be made (i.e. working within the dominant positivist paradigm) then ensuring that accounts are as accurate as possible is centrally important. The reliability and validity of innovation histories can be enhanced by triangulation of methods – that is, by using a combination of methods, such as interviews, questionnaires and analysis of documents (such as minutes of meetings). Care must be taken to obtain information from as many groups involved in, or affected by, an innovation as possible. In contrast, approaches such as social constructionism, phenomenology and narrative psychology, which reject the positivist concern with general causal relationships, would treat participant accounts of innovation histories in a different way (e.g. Bouwen, Steyaert and Van Looy, 1996; Symon, 2000). They would find them of interest not for producing accurate pictures of what happened in the innovation process, but for exploring how accounts of innovation are constructed and why different individuals, groups or subcultures within an organization have different perceptions of what happened (King, Anderson and West, 1991). The concern in these circumstances is to have a sufficiently deep understanding of the case and its context to enable a credible interpretation to be produced.

Models of the innovation process

Despite the shortage of empirical studies, writers have been proposing models describing the sequence of events in the innovation process since the field first emerged in the 1960s (e.g. Wilson, 1966; Zaltman et al., 1973; Rogers, 1983). These and most other models have three general features in common. First, they are based largely or solely on theoretical speculation, rather than observations of real innovation processes. Second, they are normative; they seek to describe how innovation 'normally' occurs. Third, they describe the process as a sequence of developmental stages, each of which must be passed through in turn.

Stage-based models

A typical stage-based model is that of Zaltman *et al.* (1973), which describes the process in two main stages, initiation and implementation. These are broken down further into five substages, as shown in Figure 6.1.

In Zaltman *et al.*'s model the division between the two main stages is at the point of adoption of the innovation; that is, the point at which the organization makes a firm decision to implement the innovation. This distinction between pre- and post-adoption stages is seen in most stage-based models. Where they vary is in the extent to which they focus on the process before and after adoption. Some describe the pre-adoption process in much more detail (e.g. Wilson, 1966), whilst others concentrate as much or more on what happens after adoption (e.g. Rogers, 1983). Overall, the majority place greatest emphasis on events leading up to adoption, which is probably due to the influence of the

Figure 6.1   **Zaltman *et al.*'s (1973) model of the innovation process**

INITIATION
Knowledge awareness – the organization becomes aware of the existence of an innovation which it has the opportunity to utilize.
Formation of attitudes – members of the organization form and exhibit their attitudes to the proposed innovation.
Decision – the potential innovation is evaluated and the decision to proceed with it or abandon the idea is made.

IMPLEMENTATION
Initial implementation – first attempts to utilize the innovation are made, often on some sort of trial basis.
Continued–sustained implementation – the innovation becomes routinized as part of organizational life.

innovation diffusion research tradition, which has been principally interested in what leads some individuals, groups, organizations or communities to adopt new ideas sooner than others (Rogers, 1983; Brown, 1981).

The start of the innovation process is conventionally ascribed to the detection of a 'performance gap' – a mismatch between actual and potential performance. Zaltman *et al.* (1973) argue that this may occur in two ways: either the organization realizes that its performance is unsatisfactory, and therefore searches for an innovation that would help close the gap, or it becomes aware of a potential innovation in its environment – perhaps being used by a competitor – and realizes that by introducing the innovation it could improve its performance. Although the performance gap is a useful concept, it would be wrong to suggest that all innovations are triggered in such a way. Adoption of an innovation from the environment is not always a sign that the organization feels it is underperforming. Innovations may also be forced on organizations by legislation; for example, the right to 13 weeks unpaid parental leave introduced by the British Government in December 1999.

It is usual for the end of the innovation process to be portrayed in terms of routinization; the innovation becomes absorbed into the everyday life of the organization until it is accepted as part of a new status quo. Most stage-based models are rather perfunctory in describing how this point in the process is reached, though Rogers (1983) is an exception. He states that following adoption, the innovation will often be redefined as initial problems are identified, leading into the 'clarifying' stage, at which its meaning gradually becomes clear to organizational members. It is only once this has happened successfully – which may require further modifications and redefinitions – that routinization occurs. Kimberly (1981) does not define innovation as a process but as a series of processes which constitute the 'innovation life-cycle'. The last process is 'exnovation', where the organization rids itself of the fully implemented innovation when it becomes obsolete, allowing the life-cycle to begin again with the adoption of a fresh innovation. The process of exnovation is essential to innovation, but has been very much neglected in the literature.

Criticisms of stage-based models

Conventional innovation models have been criticized by Schroeder *et al.* (1989) and the present authors (Anderson and King, 1993), who query whether the limited evidence available supports the existence of stages in the innovation process, and point to the potential dangers of a normative approach. Schroeder *et al.* (1989) put forward an alternative model, based on longitudinal data from the Minnesota Innovation Research Program (see below), which describes a series of common features of innovations but does not attempt to place them in discrete stages.

In a study of the development of innovations on a hospital ward, the first author (King, 1992) found support for the general approach of Schroeder *et al.*'s model, though some of the observations did not appear very applicable to certain innovation examples – generally those which were least radical and/or narrowest in scope. This raises questions as to the generalizability of Schroeder *et al.*'s model, as it was derived from studying large-scale innovations. King also compared Schroeder *et al.*'s model with a conventional stage-based model (Zaltman *et al.*, 1973) and found that the very broadly defined stages of the latter could not be applied reliably by independent raters, and that in many of the innovation examples from the hospital ward there was little evidence that the stages occurred in the order Zaltman *et al.* suggest.

Research at Sheffield University into engineering design innovation *did* find a distinction between idea generation and implementation stages, with participants perceiving individual factors to be more influential at the former stage (personal and job characteristics) and group and organizational factors more important for implementation (Axtell, Holman, Unsworth *et al.*, 2000; Unsworth, Brown and McGuire, 2000). More specifically, the strongest relationships with idea generation were for autonomy and confidence across varied work areas ('role breadth self-efficacy'), and with implementation were team support for innovation and participation in decision making. However, the cross-sectional and retrospective nature of the data means that the findings must be interpreted cautiously; it may be that the division between initiation and implementation appears clearer in hindsight than it does when in the midst of it (King, 1992).

Other studies have also found only limited support for the existence of discrete developmental stages in the innovation process. Pelz (1983), in a study of urban innovations in the United States, found that there were some signs of progression through a set of stages in relatively simple, non-radical innovations, but no such evidence in more complex, radical innovations. Witte (1972) looked at the innovation decision process in the introduction of electronic data processing (EDP) and found that a clear progression through stages occurred in only a minority of cases. More research is needed in differing organizational settings to test the applicability of existing innovation process models, and if necessary to derive new ones grounded in observation of real-world innovations. The evidence so far certainly raises serious doubts as to whether the process usually passes through discrete stages. If stages can only be distinguished in a minority of cases, normative models are of little value in aiding our understanding of the innovation process. In fact, they may be dangerous, in that normative models can become prescriptive. The message that 'this is how innovations normally develop' is very easily translated into one of 'this is how they *should* develop'. We surely need to consider more the mediating and moderating effects of particular circumstances and how these influence the development of different types of innovation.

A further weakness of most current models is that they do not acknowledge that perceptions of the innovation process may differ from different perspectives within the organization. Top management may believe that an innovation has been fully implemented and is in routine use when on the ground it has been effectively abandoned in all but name. An innovation may also develop differently in different parts of the organization, as it is reinvented to suit local conditions, or may meet varying levels of acceptance in different parts of the organization (e.g. Lewis and Seibold, 1993). Aydin and Rice (1991) found that the implementation of a new computer system progressed differently in the different occupational and departmental 'social worlds' that exist within a hospital. The case study in Box 6.1 illustrates how a single innovation can assume different patterns of development within one organization. Examples such as these help to illustrate that innovation is essentially a social process. It is the patterns of interaction between individuals and groups within the organization which determine how innovations progress. Recognition of this has influenced researchers to focus explicitly on social psychological aspects of innovation. Unsworth's

Box 6.1 | **Variation of the innovation process within an organization: the key-worker system at Watersmeet home for elderly people**

The organization

Watersmeet is a local-authority-run home for elderly people in a large British city. Purpose built in the late 1960s, it provides beds for 49 elderly residents sited on three floors. It has a staff of 30, including five 'senior staff' with managerial responsibilities, headed by the principal. The current principal, Mrs Louise Brook, has been in post for four years, and prior to that was deputy principal for just under a year. Her arrival as deputy marked the beginning of a period of considerable change aimed at improving staff morale and attitudes towards residents. The preceding three or four years had been characterized by uncertainty and poor management, which led to a reduced standard of care for residents and seriously damaged the home's reputation with the local community.

The key-worker system

This is a system whereby individual care-workers are assigned special responsibilities for particular residents. It usually involves the allocation of specific tasks such as bathing, shopping and administering medication, as well as generally being aware of the elderly person's wants and needs. It is a common practice in many health and social care settings, aimed chiefly at improving staff/client relationships and facilitating more individualized care.

The first attempt to introduce a key-worker system at Watersmeet was approximately five years ago; the then principal was instructed to do so by higher management in the council's social services department. He had little interest in the idea, and the details were worked out by two of his assistant principals. There were a number of practical problems, such as the fact that a care assistant might be a key-worker for residents across all three floors of the home. Some of these were ironed out, but the system ceased to operate when the principal left due to illness and the home was run by a succession of temporary principals, each of whom had different ideas as to how the home should be run. ▶

> I'd say it fell down when we had the temporary Principals coming in, because we had different kinds of Principals; one would be like a matron type, ... and then there was another one; she just said 'you do exactly what you want' sort of thing, you didn't know where you were.

It was not until the current principal took up her post that the key-worker system was successfully reintroduced. Mrs Brook divided the care assistants into three teams each responsible for one floor of the home. Each team was then expected to operate a key-worker system for their residents. In fact the system developed differently on each floor. On the first floor, the system was fully implemented and is now routinized. Each resident has a pair of key-workers, to minimize the interruption to personalized care which can be caused by staff sickness and holidays. This system is popular with the care assistants, whose only complaint is that they are often too short staffed to run it effectively.

On the ground floor, the key-workers system became unworkable because of another innovation – the conversion of the floor into a short-stay wing. The floor is now used to take in elderly people from the community for periods of a few weeks, often to provide respite for family carers. With an ever-changing set of residents it did not make sense to assign them to key-workers. A modification of the system was tried whereby staff were responsible for particular rooms, but this was unsatisfactory as the workload for individual care assistants could vary tremendously from week to week according to who occupied the room.

On the top floor, the system was tried for a whilst, but then abandoned. Two reasons for this are given by staff. First, they claim that there was a higher proportion of confused and incontinent residents on the top floor than elsewhere in the home, making it hard to assign specific responsibilities to specific members of staff – crises had to be dealt with by whoever was on duty. Second, staff did not like being split into pairs; they saw this as weakening the cohesion of the floor team: 'The way we work now, we get to know all the residents and we're not split as little units in one unit.'

However, the assistant principal who has recently taken over responsibility for managing the top floor, Anna Walsh, is not ▶

convinced that these stated reasons for abandoning the key-worker system are wholly valid. She feels they are to some extent rationalizations, and that the real reasons for the system's failure were suspicion of change in general amongst some of the older staff on the floor, and the rather lukewarm support for the idea from her predecessor as floor manager. She would like to see a key-worker system reintroduced in the near future.

Question

The principal is currently reviewing care practices within the home with her management team. Anna Walsh argues that a uniform key-worker system should be introduced on the two long-stay floors to ensure a consistent standard of care for all permanent residents. Carolyn Smith, the manager responsible for the first floor, disagrees; she thinks that they should accept that what works well for one group of staff might not do so for another. Decision about whether to operate a key-workers system, and what form it should take, should be made for each floor separately.

In the light of your knowledge of organizational innovation and change process, what advice would you give to Mrs Brook on this matter? (You might like to think about this case study again once you have read Chapter 8 on resistance to change.)

(2001) study of engineering design innovation highlighted the key role of interaction processes. King *et al.* (1991) showed that perceptions of the same innovations differed between managerial and non-managerial staff in two homes for the elderly, and offered an explanation in terms of each group's role in the innovation process, stake in the outcome of the innovation, and identity with the organization as a whole. Ramirez and Bartunek (1989) observed increased political behaviour and intergroup conflict between medical, nursing and administrative managers as a result of a management development innovation. Bouwen *et al.* (1992) examined the tension between established ways of thinking ('dominant logics') and new ways required by the innovation ('innovation logics') in four major innovation projects studied longitudinally. They found that conflict was a common feature of innovation, and that the process did not follow a neat sequence of stages.

The most important body of work on the process of innovation comes from the Minnesota Innovation Research Program (MIRP), led by Andrew Van de Ven. He and his colleagues studied 14 major innovations in areas as diverse as a naval torpedo system, a cochlear implant programme, education and hospital management, and the development of a new strand of hybrid wheat. These innovations were studied over several years using a mixture of methods, with the aim of examining their patterns of development over time and identifying factors which shaped the way they progressed and the outcomes they achieved. The researchers sought to highlight common features across the innovations studied without losing sight of the distinctive characteristics of individual innovations.

With regard to the unfolding of the innovation process in the different cases – what Van de Ven *et al.* (1999) call 'the innovation journey' – the MIRP evidence did not support the notion of linear progression through a sequence of distinct stages. Instead, they draw out from their longitudinal data 12 components of the process which were common to most or all of their cases. These are organized into three broad phases: the initiation period, the development period and the implementation/termination period, as shown on Table 6.1. Within these phases, components do not occur sequentially; rather there is a great deal of cycling back and forwards, and overlap between them. Even the main phases are not as clear cut as depicted in conventional stage models such as Rogers (1983) and Zaltman *et al.* (1973). Figure 6.2 illustrates the complex, non-linear nature of their generic process schema, and even this is a simplification of what happens within individual cases.

In attempting to understand the factors which shape the way innovations progress through the process, Van de Ven *et al.* propose a model based on a synthesis of divergent and convergent activities within the organization. Divergent activities involve 'branching behaviour that explores and expands in new directions' (page 184) and include such things as creating ideas and strategies, building relationships and networks, and pluralistic leadership to encourage and balance diverse views. Convergent activities involve integrating, narrowing and focusing on a specific direction of development. They include 'trial-and-error' testing of new ideas, pushing chosen ideas into currency, and unitary leadership to encourage unity and goal consensus. Note the strong parallels between what Van de Ven *et al.* propose at an organizational

Table 6.1	**Process observations from the Minnesota Innovation Research Program**

Initiation period

1. Most innovations have a long gestation period prior to initiation
2. Internal or external 'shocks' trigger initiation
3. Plans are developed, more to 'sell' the idea than as realistic scenarios for development

Developmental period

4. The initial idea proliferates
5. Setbacks and mistakes are frequently encountered
6. Criteria of success and failure often change during the process
7. Organizational members participate in the innovation in highly fluid ways
8. Senior managers and/or investors intervene in the process throughout development
9. Relationships with other organizations develop during the process and shape its course
10. Innovation participants often work with external organizations and agencies to build infrastructures for their innovations

Implementation/Termination period

11. During the innovation, the 'new' and 'old' are linked and integrated
12. The innovation process stops at implementation or is terminated through lack of resources
13. Attributions of success or failure are made, though are often misdirected

level and the literature on individual creativity which also argues for a combination of divergence and converge – for instance, in the work of Basadur and colleagues (e.g. Basadur, Graen and Scandura, 1986) discussed in Chapter 2.

General or type-specific models?

So far, we have talked about the innovation process in the singular, as if a single definition of the process can be given which would be applicable in all cases, regardless of the nature of the innovation and organization involved. In fact, it is very much open to question whether we can and should attempt to devise a universal model of the innovation process.

Figure 6.2 **Key components of the innovation journey**

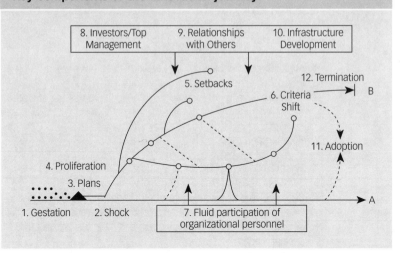

Source: Van de Ven, Andrew H., Polley, Douglas E., Garud, Raghu, and Venkataraman, Sankaran (1999) *The Innovation Journey.* Oxford University Press, New York.

We saw in the previous chapter that there is some evidence of variation between types of innovations in antecedent factors. Equally, a number of studies have suggested that the process of innovation may develop quite differently for different types of innovation. As we have seen, Pelz (1983) found that complex, radical innovations progressed in less of a step-by-step linear fashion than simpler, non-radical innovations. In the first author's study of innovation in a hospital ward (King, 1992), the stage-based model tended to be most applicable in the least radical cases and vice versa. Finally, Sauer and Anderson (1992) found that innovations imposed on an organization from outside had a more complex pattern of development than those emerging from within the organization. So it is likely that different types of innovation will follow distinct developmental paths.

However, just because the innovation process can be shown to differ in some respects across innovation types does not mean that there is *nothing* that is common to all or most cases. After all, Schroeder *et al.* (1989) were able to derive common process observations from seven very different innovations, including a weapons system, a medical innovation and a new hybrid wheat strain. We need to assess what the pros and cons are of putting forward a general model of the innovation process. On the negative side, the main danger is that a general model may come to be regarded as the ideal for all types of innovation. Managers and change agents may try to force innovation processes into the 'correct' mould, regardless of the distinctive requirements and circumstances of particular cases. On the positive side, the provision of a general model does assist comparisons across organizations and innovation types, and through this enables a broader understanding of the psychology of innovation to emerge than would be possible if each type of innovation were studied in isolation. One strategy for future research could be to construct both general and type-specific models. Comparisons between different type-specific models and the generic one would highlight distinctive features of the innovation process in particular circumstances.

How manageable is the innovation process?

There is now considerable evidence that whilst we may distinguish broad phases in innovation development, at a more detailed level innovations rarely progress in a clear and predictable sequence of discrete stages (King, 1992; Pelz, 1983; Unsworth, 2001; Van de Ven *et al.*, 1999). A corollary of this is that innovations frequently show a lack of 'fidelity' (Lewis and Seibold, 1993); that is, a mismatch between the outcome intended by those initiating them and the actual consequences once implemented. Nevertheless, much of the organizational change literature continues to present innovation as essentially controllable. Popular management texts help to convey the impression that managers can ensure that innovation and change have the desired successful outcomes within their organizations if they follow the advice given. More precisely, it is assumed that change can be directed from above and that, as its outcomes are more or less predictable, the final outcome of the process is largely due to the competence and skill of those *directing* the change. Our view is that such assumptions are at best overstated and at worst dangerously complacent, in that most change processes can only be *partially influenced* even by senior executives possessing considerable hierarchical and positional power. We are certainly not saying that managers cannot significantly improve the chances of a change initiative having a successful outcome; indeed, we have written this book with the belief that an informed understanding of the psychology of innovation and change is a valuable asset for a manager. But applying such an understanding cannot guarantee that every innovation attempt will go smoothly to plan, any more than a football manager can guarantee that his team will win every match by buying the best players and providing the best training facilities.

Van de Ven *et al.* (1999) make a similar point when summarizing the main lessons learned from the Minnesota Innovation Research Program. They use the metaphor of navigating an uncharted river to characterize the manager's role in the innovation process; he or she cannot determine where the river goes, but with the right skills can help to steer safely towards a favourable destination. They prescribe that 'innovation managers are to go with the flow – although we can learn to maneuver the innovation journey, we cannot control it' (page 213).

Components of the 'illusion of manageability'

We argue that this general illusion of manageability is composed of three sets of second-order illusory beliefs – the *illusion of linearity*, the *illusion of predictability* and the *illusion of control*. These are illustrated in Figure 6.3, and described in more detail below.

The illusion of linearity

Spurred by a plethora of multistage models of change, almost all of which depict change processes as a neat set of stages, less experienced managers may give too much credence to these oversimplified models in practice. Kurt Lewin's (1951) force field analysis model, which is described in some detail in Chapter 7, is prototypical of stage models of this ilk. The stages *unfreeze–move–refreeze* suggest a simple three-phase process, applicable to all organizational change initiatives on all occasions. We have already seen earlier in this chapter that this assumption is almost certainly unwarranted. Most experienced managers will appreciate these problems inherent in the change processes which may involve

- one step backwards for every two steps forward (or sometimes seemingly the other way around);
- multiple processes of change occurring at several levels of analysis, all at quite different stages of development;
- multiple pressures for moving in different directions – from superiors, peers and subordinate staff.

Figure 6.3   **Illusion of manageability of organizational change**

The illusion of predictability

Stemming from this 'illusion of linearity' is the associated belief that change processes are therefore largely predictable, at least to the extent that the next phase of the process can be accurately anticipated. Research supports the view that organization change procedures contain numerous unanticipated and unexpected events and that major diversions in the planned process may need to be dealt with (e.g. Schroeder *et al.*, 1989).

In combination, the illusion of linearity and the illusion of predictability could lead unsuspecting managers to overestimate their own levels of personal authority and influence over organizational change – this we term the 'illusion of control'.

The illusion of control

It is perhaps reassuring and comforting during periods of rapid change to believe in one's own ability to exert control over unfolding events. The problem is that in many such scenarios, even the most skilled manager equipped with the most well-prepared change strategy will have only limited influence over certain outcomes. 'Entrepreneurs and managers cannot control innovation success, only its odds' (Van der Ven *et al.*, 1999, page 65). The impact of unforeseen events, resistance to the change by those affected by it, adjustments by senior management to the original change agenda, and the emergence of competing vested-interest groups each politicking to subvert the change process in their favoured direction, will all mitigate the degree of control possible.

So, managers charged with the responsibility of 'managing' the change process may well experience a double-bind of feeling that they *should* be in charge of unfolding events but that in reality it is only possible to exert *partial influence* at some stages in the process over some of those involved.

Implications for practice

To summarize, our point is not that managers are impotent to influence change processes, but that, owing to a variety of quite legitimate factors, there is a general tendency to overestimate managerial control in times of change. This 'illusion of manageability' is fuelled both by the popular management literature in this area, but also by the political imperatives managers find themselves under in work organizations. This illusion of manageability has for too long remained unchallenged in the literature and our argument is for a more balanced and cautious account of the extent to which any organizational member, managers included, can exert authority over organizational change processes. It is consequently important for managers to recognize their own limits in change management and that this is not merely an academic point of debate. Realizing these restrictions early on during a major change will facilitate appropriate and balanced action later in the change process when the manager is confronted with the inevitable shocks and surprises that such organizational upheavals generate. Perhaps the two characteristics most required in managing innovation and change processes are *vigilance* in detecting the unforeseen as early as possible, and *flexibility* in reacting to it.

Suggesting reading

Aydin, C. E. and Rice, R. E. (1991) 'Social worlds, individual differences and implementation: Predicting attitudes toward a medical information system', *Information and Management* 20: 119–36.

King, N. (1992) 'Modelling the innovation process: An empirical comparison of approaches', *Journal of Occupational and Organizational Psychology* 65: 89–100.

Van de Ven, A. H., Polley, D. E., Garud, R. and Venkataraman, S. (1999) *The Innovation Journey.* New York: Oxford University Press.

Organization development

After reading this chapter you should be able to

- define the term 'Organization Development' or OD
- describe the OD process in organizations, including key stages and techniques
- discuss the main OD intervention techniques, including
  (a) survey feedback
  (b) quality circles
  (c) process consultation
  (d) team building
  (e) the 'learning organization'
- list criteria against which organizations should select their change agents.

Introduction

Attempting to describe the field of organization development (OD) in a relatively short chapter such as this is tantamount to trying to drape an articulated lorry with a motorcycle cover. In both cases it will fit, but severe choices have to be made early on as to which areas the cover is going to fall upon. OD is nowadays not so much a topic within organization psychology or organization behaviour, as a burgeoning field of professional practice and research in its own right. This blend of theory and practice, which is the essence of modern OD, is one which we shall highlight in this chapter, but the links between the two have proven harder to determine through empirical research into the tangible benefits of different OD projects in organizations. Moreover, as we shall point out, it has been the practitioner wing of the OD discipline which has flourished in recent years whilst applied research efforts have tended to be restricted to case studies of *in situ* OD interventions and cross-sectional questionnaire studies. Fortunately two major reviews of this whole field have been published quite recently (Porras and Robertson, 1992; Sinangil and Avallone, 2001) and the reader is referred to either of these for a more comprehensive and in-depth coverage. Given the width and breadth of OD subject matter, we therefore focus upon issues of current and emerging concern for practising managers and students of organizational psychology. These include the range of intervention techniques in OD, the role of internal and external change agents, process models of OD, and the need for validation studies of OD practice in British and European organizations.

The structure of the chapter is quite straightforward, reflecting our intention to overview the major areas of activity and research in OD but also to highlight issues of emerging import for practitioners and students viewing OD from a distinctively psychological perspective. The chapter is divided into four sections:

- Defining and characterizing OD;
- The OD process;
- OD interventions – organization, team and individual;
- Change agents and their role in the OD process.

Defining and characterizing OD

What is OD? Over the years an increasing number of definitions have been proposed by various authors, but the following are typical and suggest the central characteristics of OD as being a fusion between knowledge and organizational practice:

> a set of behavioural science-based theories, values, strategies, and techniques aimed at the planned change of the organizational work setting for the purpose of enhancing individual development and improving organizational performance, through the alteration of organizational members' on-the-job behaviour.
>
> *(Porras and Robertson, 1992, page 722)*

a system wide application of behavioural science knowledge to the planned development and reinforcement of organizational strategies, structures, and processes for improving an organization's effectiveness.

(Cummings and Worley, 1993 page 2)

an effort planned, organization-wide, managed from the top, to increase organization effectiveness and health through planned intervention using behavioural science knowledge.

(American Society for Training and Development, 1975, quoted in Muchinsky, 1993, page 444)

Organisation Development is a program of planned interventions. Specifically, OD should improve the internal operations of the organization by opening up communication, by decreasing internal destructiveness, such as win–lose conflicts, and by increasing creativity in problem solving. OD includes the following procedures (1) diagnosing the organization's current functioning; (2) planning interventions for improvement; (3) mobilising resources to put the plan into action; and (4) evaluating the effects.

(Berry and Houston, 1993, page 514)

So, OD incorporates a number of key activities and assumptions, including:

- *planned interventions* – including diagnosis of the need for change, prognosis of a specified plan of action, and validation of intervention outcomes;
- *organization-wide programmes* – the unit of analysis is the organization as a whole, although aspects of an OD intervention will focus upon particular departments, subunits, horizontal strata and cohorts or work groups;
- *knowledge-based action* – OD is dependent upon the application of behavioural science knowledge, principles and research. This knowledge base spans areas of organizational psychology, human resource management, organizational sociology, and other relevant topics in organization behaviour;
- *pragmatic improvement of organizational capabilities* – enhancing intra-organizational efficiency and performance, including those capabilities related to individual health and psychological well-being at work;

- *Multiple levels of outcome* – given the range of objectives above, it is common for OD interventions to have potentially measurable outcomes at the organizational, group and individual levels of analysis.

OD is therefore not so much a topic warranting a review of the academic literature, as a vibrant, expanding (and highly lucrative) field of professional consultancy practice derived from a long-standing but ever-developing series of research study findings and theoretical developments. It is consequently fair to describe OD as a practice-led discipline, its Achilles heel being the tendency over recent years for independent consultancies to dominate the entire OD profession, some would even argue to the cost of proper research and validation of consultancy interventions and change management products (Porras and Robertson, 1992; Schein, 1990). Perhaps this is a function of the sheer size of the market for OD in Europe and North America. Accurate estimates are hard to come by, but it is likely that contracts held by consultancies for OD work in the UK alone run to tens of millions of pounds value per annum. In this chapter we therefore also consider a number of issues surrounding ethical professional practice in OD and the skills and qualifications needed to be an effective OD practitioner or so-called 'change agent'. Initially, however, it is necessary to consider the heart of any intervention – the OD process. An example of a real-world planned change intervention in a major company; the 'EQUIP' program in Ford Europe is illustrated on pages 178–83.

The OD process

What does OD involve? This is a more complex question to answer than one might, prima facie, believe. OD is perhaps most accurately viewed as a conglomeration of approaches, techniques and methods derived from an underlying body of management science knowledge, theories and empirical research findings. A classic model of OD was proposed by Kurt Lewin in 1951, commonly referred to as the 'force field' model. It is shown in Figure 7.1.

Lewin described organizations as systems held in steady state, or 'equilibrium', by equal and opposing forces. On the one hand there exists a range of 'driving forces' – pressures for change – including, for instance, competitive pressures, the dispersion of new technology, innovation and

Figure 7.1 **Lewin's 'force field' model of organization change**

Desired balance

Resisting forces

Present balance

System equilibrium

Driving forces

Change strategy:

1. Unfreeze
2. Change: reduce resisting forces; increase driving forces
3. Refreeze

creativity from within the organization, and new legislation governing such things as business practices, environmental concerns, and employee rights at work. Counter-balancing these driving forces, Lewin argued, are a number of 'resisting forces' – including established custom and practice in the enterprise, trade union agreements, the organization's culture and climate, and so forth. Since each set of forces is deemed to cancel the other out, the system is held at an equilibrium position.

As a corollary to his model, Lewin asserted that any organization change process can be conceived of as effecting a move in the equilibrium position towards a desired or newly established position. Lewin proposes a three-stage process change implementation – *unfreeze, change, refreeze*. Here it is assumed that to unfreeze the system one must first investigate the myriad of resisting forces. Any premature unilateral increase in driving forces for change will meet with an equal and opposite increase in resisting forces. Lewin thus emphasized the need for consultation and participation in the change process. Once these resisting forces have been minimized, the change can be implemented and the equilibrium position modified towards the desired balance position. Importantly, for the change to become routinized into day-to-day practice in the organization, Lewin argued for a third stage in the model – that of refreezing the organizational system. Here, a number of strategies for refreezing the system are called for, including, for instance, rewarding the desired behaviours of staff and new rules and regulations to reinforce the change process.

Lewin's force field model has gained great popularity in management training and on OD programmes. Whilst it certainly provides a simple representation of the change process, more recent models have developed and extended this system's approach in more depth. A seven stage model of OD was proposed by Edgar Huse in 1980 based upon Lewin's original model, as shown in Figure 7.2. Let us consider each of the stages:

1 *Scouting* – the organization and OD consultant meet initially to identify and discuss the need for change. The organization explores what skills the consultant has to offer; the consultant elicits data on symptoms and systemic manifestations of problems needing attention.
2 *Entry* – the organization and OD consultant move closer together to agree both a business and a psychological contract. The psychological contract consists of expectations of what each party will give to the other relative to what they expect to receive from the other.
3 *Diagnosis* – the consultant, based upon his or her background knowledge and training, diagnoses the underlying organizational problems and specifies a planned intervention strategy.
4 *Planning* – the organization agrees with the OD practitioner a detailed series of intervention techniques and actions, and a timetable for the change process. Potential sources of resistance and reasons for resistance are noted (see Chapter 8 for more detailed discussion of resistance to change).
5 *Action* – the intervention commences according to the agreed plan. Multiple methods may begin simultaneously, or in complex OD programmes a number of multi-strand projects may run in parallel.
6 *Stabilization and evaluation* – refreezing the system equilibrium in Lewin's (1951) model is termed by Huse (1980) as 'stabilization'. At this point the newly implemented practices, systems and codes of action are routinized into everyday usage in the organization. Following stabilization, the change process is evaluated and its outcomes quantified (see our comments later in this chapter).
7 *Termination* – the change agent intentionally moves on to another client organization – one disarmingly simple rule of thumb used by change consultants is 'getting in, getting on and getting out!' Alternatively, an entirely different OD project is commenced within the same host organization.

Figure 7.2 | **Huse's model of planned organization change**

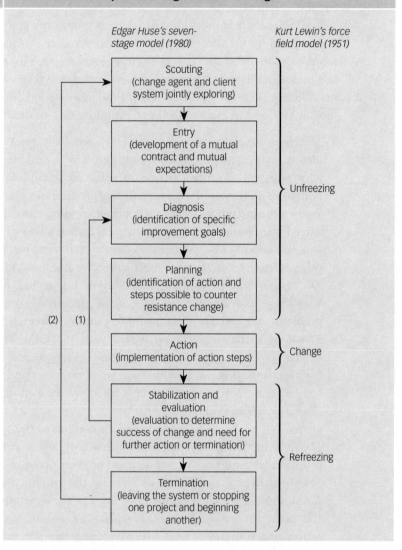

Edgar Huse's seven-stage model (1980)

Kurt Lewin's force field model (1951)

Scouting
(change agent and client system jointly exploring)

Entry
(development of a mutual contract and mutual expectations)

Diagnosis
(identification of specific improvement goals)

Planning
(identification of action and steps possible to counter resistance change)

} Unfreezing

Action
(implementation of action steps)

} Change

Stabilization and evaluation
(evaluation to determine success of change and need for further action or termination)

Termination
(leaving the system or stopping one project and beginning another)

} Refreezing

(2) (1)

Huse's seven-stage model also incorporates two feedback loops as shown in Figure 7.2. The first, loop (1), relates to situations where the planned change has been enacted but, following a mid-point evaluation, its general thrust or specific action points are modified for some reason.

An example would be where an organization has decided to introduce team briefing sessions in order to communicate to staff the vision of senior management. After several such briefings it is found that staff were unhappy that the meetings are exclusively 'one-way' affairs with only management presenting their views and concerns. Upon further evaluation and re-diagnosis, it is decided to modify the team briefing intervention to incorporate an open agenda item whereby staff members can raise any issues or concerns they may have. Thus, the general intention of the OD invention is maintained but its exact style of operation is modified to fit in with factors unknown when the team briefings were originally developed.

The second feedback loop (2) in Figure 7.2 depicts the situation where a major development project has worked its way through to completion and the OD consultant moves on to either an entirely new organization or to a new project within the same host organization. Here, the OD cycle recommences with the consultant scouting for information on the new project and establishing contacts with those concerned with this potential change intervention in another part of the organization.

Edgar Huse's model is a useful heuristic to illustrate the multi-phase process of OD work in organizations. It also hints at the complexity of this type of work, but only in passing. On a more critical note we would highlight three further points of critical importance to modern-day OD interventions which these neat linear models potentially overlook. First, the pace of organization change in today's rapidly developing business environment can result in the refreezing stage never being reached; instead, organizational systems undergo continual change interventions 'one of top of the other' and never revert back to stabilized steady state. Readers who have experienced an organization going through the upheaval of responding to a changing environment will be familiar with this effect. Put simply, change is so rapid and recurrent that the system fails to restabilize itself again before the next change initiative is imposed. Organizations prone to fashion and fads in managerial practice suffer from this effect particularly badly. Some might complain that no sooner had quality circles been imposed than total quality management (TQM) became the whim and then ISO 9000 and BS 5750 were thrust upon staff as the latest saviours of the organization. Importantly, it may well not have been the *content* of these innovations themselves which was at fault but the *process* of attempting to reunfreeze the organization even before the previous change process had been stabilized and the system refreezed.

Second, OD programmes often consist of several projects running concurrently. This multi-channel effect increases the complexity of the change process immensely, with the possibility of numerous individual interventions all at different stages of development and each involving different staff groups. Of course, the more complex the OD project, the more difficult it is to manage effectively (see our discussion in Chapter 6 on the 'illusion of manageability' of organization change). Here, the models proposed by Lewin and Huse again tend to oversimplify the OD effort which, in extremely complex multi-intervention programmes, can take on the guise of an all-out attempt to keep track of numerous, interrelated project themes (Cummings and Worley, 1993).

Third, the whole OD process is critically 'front-end dependent'. By this it is meant that the early-stage skills of the OD consultant to diagnose the problems of the system and to recommend appropriate solutions are all-important. A misdiagnosis could result, for instance, in an organization being poorly advised and even commencing down an incorrect path of intervention for change. The diagnostic process will always be a highly demanding and complex task in any dynamic and amorphous setting of the work organization and so the skills needed by the OD consultant to accurately discharge this responsibility are quite considerable. We return to this issue of consultant skills and abilities later in this chapter, but suffice it to say at this point that the systems models tend to underplay the crucial role of the OD consultant's skills, knowledge and abilities.

Despite these reservations, the models proposed by Lewin (1951) and Huse (1980) are useful guides to the major elements of an OD process. They do not, conversely, hint at the underlying *strategic orientation* of the intervention, the consultant's underlying assumptions of the change process, or at an appropriate toolkit of intervention techniques intended to effect organization change. Here we need to refer to Robert Chin and Kenneth Benne (1976) who identified three major strategies in OD intervention: *rational-empirical, normative-reeducative,* and *power-coercive*. In the first, the *rational-empirical* strategy, organization change and development are seen as processes of rational persuasion as to the benefits of the change for those influenced by it. Once these paybacks have been communicated, it is assumed that any resistance will automatically be minimized (see also Chapter 8). OD is therefore a process of communicating the benefits of change to rational individuals motivated primarily by self-interest. The second strategy, the normative-reeducative, also assumes a model of rational individuals as employees but acknowledges the existence of socio-cultural norms in organizations. Here, OD becomes about challenging established values, beliefs, attitudes and norms, and about re-educating employees into the new methods of working or techniques of production. The final, and perhaps most controversial strategy, the power-coercive strategy, conceives of OD as a process of the imposition of legitimate authority. That is, change is imposed from above by those with sufficient hierarchical power and authority to be able to demand coercion and compliance. Here, a 'planned change' perspective may still be adopted, but the relevance of any need to readjust change tactics in the face of resistance, or any other type of feedback for that matter, may be denied. Examples of all three strategies abound in the management literature but we would particularly note Cummings and Worley (1993) for several examples of rational–empirical change and a few containing overtures of the normative–reeducative stance, and Glendon (1992) for a balanced but critical account of power-coercive strategies in action.

This discussion of the OD process and OD strategies leads us neatly onto the vexed issue of what it is exactly that OD consultants aim to change. Leavitt, Dill and Eyring (1973) propose a four-dimensional systems model of change illustrated and adapted in Figure 7.3 to include OD as a central component of this model. They assert that whilst OD efforts may focus upon one of four subsystems – *structure, technology, people, or task* – intervention effects will be mutually dependent across all four subsystems in organizations. Thus, for instance, an OD intervention to update an organization's structure from being a traditionally orthodox hierarchy of functionally specialized departments towards a matrix structure of semipermanent and over-lapping project teams will clearly have implications for the technology subsystem, the personnel employed or selected into the organization (i.e. the people subsystem), and methods of task allocation and job design (the task subsystem). As with most systems-type models, the overarching system is seen as comprising multiple and interacting subsystems. Of course, this once again highlights the issue raised earlier of the complexity of OD processes – change in one subsystem will almost inevitably result in knock-on effects of intended, and unintended, reactive changes in other dependent subsystems (see also Cummings and Worley 1993). Conceiving of organization change and development

Figure 7.3 **A systems model of OD**

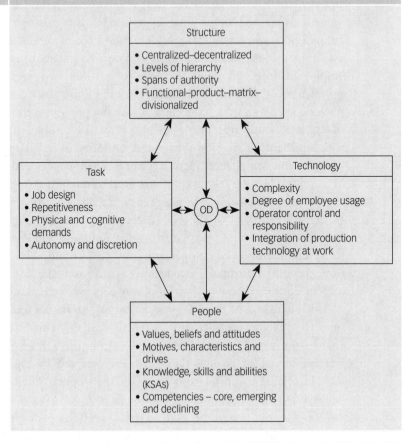

Source: Developed, adapted and extended from Leavitt, H. G. *et al.* (1973) *The Organizational World*, New York: Harcourt, Brace, Jovanovich.

in a rather different way, Golembiewski and co-workers (1976) identify three types of change.

1 *Alpha change* – where change has occurred along a stable, or set of stable, dimensions. For instance, where individuals report increased levels of participation and organization commitment, assuming that these dimensions were measured with exactly the same scale before and after the change intervention.

2 *Beta change* – where individuals recalibrate the intervals between points on a particular scale measure as a result of the change. For

instance, this could occur in our above example, where staff redefine their ratings of high versus low participation as a direct result of the OD intervention.

3 *Gamma change* – gamma change occurs where individuals do not merely recalibrate their ratings but the whole meaning of the rating concept is fundamentally altered. Thus, 'participation' prior to the change may simply have meant giving task-related information at the team meeting when asked; after the change the meaning of this construct developed to include offering ideas and creative solutions, requesting information from the team leader, and so forth. More recently, Porras and Silvers (1991) have subdivided gamma change into Gamma (A) and Gamma (B) types, Gamma (A) change being a reconfiguration of existing evaluation dimensions but without the addition of new dimension, and Gamma (B) change being the replacement of the old evaluation paradigm with completely new dimensions and configurations.

Golembiewski *et al.*'s (1976) three-dimensional typology is clearly intended to relate to employee attitude scale ratings of change, but it has applicability more widely within OD. Most OD interventions will contain elements of alpha, beta and gamma change but, perhaps conversely, a potential criticism of this typology is that it provides a 'catch-all' net into which all types of intervention will fall at one stage or another.

Summarizing this section on the OD process, it should now be apparent that any OD intervention involves a complex, multidimensional 'collection' of interrelated processes, activities and intentions. The achievement of largely intended rather than unintended outcomes will be subject to a multitude of influences and factors, but critical to planned change are the skills, knowledge and abilities (KSAs) of the change agent. Before we come on to consider this issue, the following section describes in greater detail the range of intervention techniques commonly used by OD consultants.

OD interventions

What techniques and methods are used by OD consultants? Schein (1990) describes receiving a questionnaire sent to active OD practitioners in the USA listing over fifty separate methods and techniques! Our

| Box 7.1 | **The Engineering Quality Improvement Programme (EQUIP)** |

Fiona Patterson (University of Sheffield) and Ed Henshall
(Ford of Europe)

Training to effect change

At this time, employees, managers and organizations are more frequently turning to training as a solution for work issues. From the organizational psychologist's perspective, training has never been so important. Cascio (1989) quoted a study by the American Society for Training and Development (ASTD, 1986) reporting that organizations were already investing $30 billion per year in training. The ASTD also predicted that current spending levels on training would rise by $15 billion in the near future. Moreover, the ASTD also estimated that US firms would need to spend a minimum of 2 per cent of annual payroll on training to regain their competitive advantage within a global market. It is therefore reasonable to suggest that a similar situation exists within Europe since, particularly in the automotive industry, Western organizations are already losing their competitive advantage.

Many researchers have previously portrayed the process of training as a discrete activity sited primarily within, and controlled by, the human resource management (HRM) function. However, despite national differences in training provisions for skills, knowledge and attitudes, it is increasingly recognized amongst large organizations that training must be used strategically within the overall company business plan. For example, Ernecq (1991) describes the introduction of training for staff in a French mail order company; although not the primary intention of these programmes, they resulted in extensive organizational culture change. Indeed, training is now being deployed as an organizational development intervention, where it is integrated with other HRM programmes, with the overall objective of affecting change within a broader organizational framework.

EQUIP as an organizational change programme

This case study presents a major training intervention programme designed to precipitate organizational change in Ford of ▶

Europe. The training intervention programme is called the 'Engineering Quality Improvement Programme (EQUIP)' and it is based on the total quality management philosophy (Deming, 1986; Peters and Waterman, 1982). EQUIP is not just a programme for quality in the traditional manufacturing sense but also a concept applicable to the whole organization. The programme is an organizational philosophy that teaches a set of techniques aimed at creating a 'constancy of purpose' towards the improvement of products and services. The basis of EQUIP is cross-functional co-operation, largely through marketing, design and production interacting closely, coupled with an overriding concern about quality service for the customer.

The engineering process in Ford of Europe

The traditional approach to manufacturing engineering has been to draw a clear distinction between the processes whereby a product is designed and subsequently manufactured. Typically the product is designed by one engineering group and the design is then handed 'over the wall' to another group of engineers who then design and implement the manufacturing process that will be used to produce the product. This engineering process has inherent limitations, one of which is the possibility of mismatch between the product design and the ability of the manufacturing process to produce the given design. Therefore the design might involve certain features which are either difficult or physically impossible to manufacture. In addition, due to this 'over the wall' engineering, when a problem with the product arises it is normal for as much effort to be expended by each side (design and manufacturing) in attempting to show that they were not to blame for the problem as is spent in solving the problem.

Working together in a 'simultaneous' manner requires design and manufacturing engineers to both acquire new skills and apply their existing skills in a different way. These skills include both the technical aspects of engineering and equally, if not more importantly, the manner in which engineers work together as people using behavioural or 'people' skills. It was in recognition of the need for enhanced technical and people skills that a new training programme, EQUIP, was developed within Ford. ▶

The content of EQUIP training

EQUIP requires engineers to update their existing technical skills in the area of product quality improvement and learn new technical and people skills. Applying the new skills to their best advantage means change in approach to engineering and in this respect EQUIP is seen as an agent for organizational change within Ford of Europe. The overall objective is given as:

> To EQUIP participants with an understanding of quality planning and development approaches, and the knowledge and skills essential for workplace support to enable participants to provide products and services which meet internal and external customer needs expectations [where the aim of the programme is] to propose a systematic change in the way engineers think.

EQUIP is a modular training course for engineers and their managers. The programme consists of a total of 37 days training, divided into seven different modules, and has been delivered to 4,000 engineers across Europe (primarily Britain and Germany).

Overview of EQUIP training modules

Technical skills

- *Foundation* – a conceptual overview of the programme;
- *Team oriented problem solving* – problem solving using an eight-stage approach;
- *Process management* – understanding, controlling and improving processes with emphasis on the manufacturing process;
- *Failure modes and effects analysis* – the identification of potential problems during the design of a product or process in order to take appropriate action to prevent problems from occurring;
- *Experimentation* – gaining knowledge of the manner in which a product or system functions in order to optimize performance through efficient experimentation;
- *Quality engineering* – engineering-in customer wants by maximizing the ideal function of a component or product and thereby minimizing error states;

- *Customer-focused engineering* – planning an engineering process which will deliver to the customer a product that will meet and exceed his or her expectations.

People skills

- *Team building* – the development of a cohesive and synergistic team. Almost all applications of the technical skills will be applied in cross-functional teams with many being cross-national;
- *Communication* – the maximization of overlap between intention and reception in the exchange of information between people (e.g. listening, questioning, feedback);
- *Implementation* – the effective use of tools and techniques to ensure that the EQUIP technical skills are implemented to their full advantage;
- *Innovation* – the expansion of the engineering process beyond the numeric and analytical skills which may have previously acted as constraints in order to seek new ideas and fresh approaches.

The expected outcome of the training is to change the organizational culture to one which will support the knowledge and skills taught. EQUIP involves two specific facets to facilitate this change. First, all participants are required to carry out job-based application projects, thereby promoting transfer of training to the workplace. Second, the training integrates psychological and behavioural skills with the engineering quality techniques, e.g. communication skills, group dynamics, creativity methodologies, self-awareness techniques. Since applying the technical skills requires cross-functional co-operation and teamwork, these behavioural skills are designed to enable engineers to put the technical skills into practice.

The future strategy for change

The term 'organizational development' refers to a specific approach of producing desired changes in the functioning of an organization (Hosking and Anderson, 1992). Organizational change is seen to exist wherever there are transformations in the methodologies, tools and norms of the organization. Change is ▶

181

thus a transitional concept, understandable only in the context of analysing organizations over time (Kimberly and Miles, 1980; Wilson, 1992). EQUIP was conceptualized as a planned programme for change over a number of years, where the objectives and the expected outcomes extend to the development of the whole organization and not just to the engineering function. One of the expected outcomes was that EQUIP served as a socialization process by providing the setting and mechanism for the development of group norms throughout the organization (Feldman, 1989). There is also empirical evidence which indicates that solutions based broadly on the more macro analyses of culture and organizational change, such as EQUIP, are more difficult to achieve, but that they are more likely to be sustained longer term (Cummings and Huse, 1989).

In order for Ford of Europe to respond to fierce competition within the external environment, it was recognized that EQUIP was a means of responding to external economic, technological and sociological change. The research literature suggests that the socioeconomic context in which organizations operate sets the strategic agenda for change (e.g. Pettigrew and Whipp, 1991). Hosking and Anderson (1992) have explored how organizations may introduce change not only as a reaction to environmental changes but also as a means by which to modify their relations with the environment. In this way, EQUIP was designed to provoke the necessary internal transformations to promote total quality as an organizational change process.

Questions

1 Ford of Europe assume that implementing this type of OD intervention will produce the desired outcomes, but it is difficult to measure precisely the benefits to the organization. Since many of the proposed benefits are intangible, how should the organization evaluate the success of the programme?

2 Large-scale change programmes can easily become all-embracing processes such that all organizational 'deficiencies' are expected to be solved. What recommendations would you make in terms of communicating the objectives and expected outcomes of the programme? ▶

3 Interventions like EQUIP require that the organization is
'ready' to accept such change. How should one assess an
organization's 'readiness' to change, and in what ways might
this affect the outcome of the intervention?

review will thus focus upon the five most popular and influential of
these, being:

- survey feedback
- quality circles
- process consultation
- team building
- 'learning organization' interventions.

Survey feedback

Survey feedback lies at the heart of the OD tradition and indeed forms
part of the historic roots of modern-day OD. To describe it as a
'technique' or 'method' is misleading; rather, it is a series of techniques
combined. Survey feedback, according to Mann (1964) involves a five-
stage process, shown in Figure 7.4. In its most basic form it involves the
design, administration, analysis and feedback of a questionnaire survey
of staff attitudes and opinions. But this is to grossly oversimplify what is
actually a complex and skilled procedure. The questionnaire must be
designed correctly to tap relevant issues of concern; it must be skillfully
administered to maximize accurate feedback and to minimize biased or
distorted responses; it must be analysed with appropriate statistical tests
which go considerably further than simple descriptive, percentages or
correlations; and, perhaps most critically, any results must be fed back
to staff with diplomacy and with the intent of facilitating attitudinal or
behavioural change. Most management consultants could ostensibly
undertake a survey feedback project but in our experience not all possess
the psychometric, statistical, analytical or occupational psychological
competencies necessary to execute a fully professional intervention.

Again referring to Figure 7.4, the early stages of designing the survey
questionnaire are of course critical to its later success. Question items

Figure 7.4 | **Survey feedback: a five-stage model**

Stage	Model activities
1 Survey design	OD consultant and the organization meet to discuss the survey design. Areas for questioning are established (e.g. communication, innovation, commitment, terms and conditions, etc.). Issues of timing, target staff groups (census versus sample) and logistics are decided upon.
2 Questionnaire administration	Questionnaire sent to all participants. It is a definite advantage to use sealed, prepaid addressed envelopes to return the questionnaires directly to the consultant. This will maximize feelings of trust and confidentiality and so improve response rates.
3 Survey analysis/results interpretation	Once an acceptable response rate has been achieved, questionnaires are analysed. The power of computer-based statistical packages allows detailed and high-level statistical analysis by the competent consultant. Results can be analysed by questionnaire area, by department (vertically) or by staff grade (horizontally), for instance.
4 Preliminary feedback data	The OD consultant meets with senior management to provide initial summary results. Further analyses may be commissioned at this stage, but the main purpose is to overview key findings.
5 Feedback meetings	A series of feedback meetings with different staff groups is arranged. Their purpose is primarily one of *attitude change* and *behaviour modification*. Skilled OD consultants will manage such feedback meetings with tact and sensitivity, knowledgeable of their likely impact upon employee behaviour.

Source: Developed and adapted from Mann, F. (1964) 'Studying and creating change' in W. Bennis *et al.* (eds) *The Planning of Change*, New York: Holt, Rinehart and Winston; and Cumming, T. G. and Worley, C. G. (1993) *Organization Development and Change*, Minneapolis: West.

must be generated to tap the attitudes and perceptions of interest to those designing the survey. This is, in practice, no easy task. Items must be unambiguous, applicable to all groups completing the survey, non-discriminatory in their impact upon certain minority groups and, of course, must be carefully designed not to demoralize respondents by targeting known areas of concern where there is little opportunity longer term of improving these issues. Simply by asking one can raise awareness of issues and can also raise the expectation that action will be taken to redress problem areas. It is relatively easy to throw together a list of questions notionally addressing areas for survey feedback; conversely, it is a complex task to design a valid, reliable and unbiased survey instrument.

This point of complexity and requisite skill also holds true for the later stages of the survey feedback model. Many organizations nowadays rely upon external agencies to analyse the results of major attitude surveys. They are well advised to check the track record of external consultancies, to ask for statistics which demonstrate the validity and reliability of the survey instrument and to ask for contacts for whom the consultancy has previously conducted surveys in order to check their credentials.

Quality circles

Quality circles (QCs) gained in popularity in British industry through-out the 1980s. A succinct definition of QCs is given by Van Fleet and Griffin (1989) as:

> small groups of employees doing similar or related work who meet regularly to identify, analyse, and solve product-quality and production problems and to improve general operations ... The ideal size is thought to be about ten. Circles will meet for an hour, on average of three to four times a month. Often workers will be asked to collect certain data by the following meeting. Although foremen commonly serve as leaders of the groups, workers may have acquired enough skill to serve as leaders and frequently will be elected by their fellow workers.
>
> *(Van Fleet and Griffin, 1989, page 219)*

The primary impetus for using QCs, then, is to improve output quality in production processes and, in so doing, to minimize costly waste and substandard output. In the USA, quality circles became increasingly popular throughout the 1970s and 1980s, spurred on by a widely held belief that American industry was losing competitiveness due to its poor record on quality (Kanter, 1983). It is therefore apposite for European organizations to look towards the American experience of some three decades of QCs and to ask the simple question 'Do they work?' At best, the evidence is unequivocal. In their recent review, Porras and Silvers (1991) found that several studies supported the positive impact of QCs on staff *attitudes*, including attitudes towards participation, communication and job satisfaction, but that these studies indicating improvements in *production* were offset by other research which failed to find any measurable improvement. Consequently, the research tends to indicate that whilst QCs may be expected to have a positive impact upon staff attitudes, this impact may not necessarily translate into higher levels of production. In their review, Porras and Silvers (1991) argued that the major barriers to QCs are cultural and managerial ones; to maximize their impact as an OD intervention requires an organization culture which constantly emphasizes quality whilst allowing sufficient devolvement of managerial decision making to permit such groups to make changes in their own production process. To implement QCs in order to improve total organizational quality in a less supportive climate is, it appears, wishful thinking.

Process consultation

The eminent work psychologist Edgar Schein is credited with an approach to OD which he termed 'Process Consultation' (PC) (Schein, 1987). It is a client-centred approach which emphasizes the aim of 'helping the client organization to help itself'. PC therefore has the underlying objective of facilitating and developing the capacity of the client organization to self-rejuvenate over the longer term. In Schein's own words:

> PC is a set of activities on the part of the consultant that help the client to perceive, understand, and act upon the process events that occur in the client's environment in order to improve the situation as defined by the client.
>
> *(Schein, 1987, page 11)*

Schein contrasts PC with two popular models of OD practice in organizations – the *purchase of expertise* model and the *doctor–patient* model. In the first, organizations looking for OD support act in a similar way to the manner in which they would buy-in any personnel expertise. They are assumed to have a clear understanding of the expertise needed, will recruit rationally from a labour market by advertising or eliciting tenders, and will then proceed to select the most suitable OD consultant for the 'job'. Unfortunately, the 'purchase of expertise' model has several flaws. Whilst organizations may possess a hazy idea of the skills, knowledge and abilities required for parts of the OD assignment, it is common to find that organizations need to buy-in this expertise precisely because they lack such specialist knowledge internally. A less kind and more cynical formulation of this relationship is the 'we don't know what we're doing – can you help us?' model.

The second approach, aptly titled by Schein the 'doctor–patient' model sees the organization as a patient self-presenting with a perceived malaise which the professionally trained and qualified OD consultant treats as 'doctor'. Regrettably, as we come on to discuss later in this chapter, there is no recognized professional society governing the practice of OD and no professional qualification which can be relied upon to indicate the acquisition of knowledge and skills to treat 'patient' organizations. Indeed, anyone can set up in business as an OD consultant. Such a situation is clearly far from ideal but at the present time the onus of responsibility lies with the organization to satisfy themselves that an OD consultant is competent.

Given these two models, Schein's notions of Process Consultation are laudable in their intent to improve the relationship between organizations and OD consultants. The thrust of PC – that the client organization should be helped to help itself – would be a positive development in dominant OD practices in the UK, but it is little used in the UK, however, and most OD practitioners remain firmly entrenched in the traditional 'purchase of expertise' or 'doctor–patient' approaches. Ironically, an excellent way for managers to gauge the expertise and professionalism of OD consultants is to question the consultant on the PC approach and its applicability to the organization's problems. Less scrupulous consultants will often wish to uphold, for various reasons, an asymmetrical power relationship between themselves as 'expert' and the client as 'patient'. It is clearly one way to keep the client as dependent and, over the longer term, fee paying!

Team building

In a major review of studies into the effectiveness of team building conducted in the United States between 1980 and 1992, Tannenbaum, Beard and Salas (1992) found only mixed outcomes in terms of the efficacy of team building. Of the 17 studies which were reviewed, 14 found positive changes in team members' attitudes and perceptions.

However, this contrasts with the reviewers' findings regarding longer-term improvements in team member behaviour and team performance. Only seven of the 17 studies found definite behavioural changes had resulted longer-term from the intervention, and of the four studies which measured performance, only one showed positive improvements with the others showing both positive and negative effects. This review consequently provides, at best, only qualified support for the effectiveness of team building. Team building may well result in attitude and perceptual change for individual team members, but when it comes to measuring demonstrable improvements in team productivity, the case in favour of potentially expensive team building interventions is not proven. The advice must surely be that each intervention must be validated with due regard to the organization's current situation, team climate and the objectives of the intervention itself.

We dealt with general team building interventions and techniques in Chapter 4 and so focus here specifically upon the T group technique which has a long and somewhat ignominious history in OD. T groups, or encounter groups as they have been known, commonly involve between 10 and 15 individuals brought together to examine intragroup processes and their own interpersonal styles and impacts upon others. In the industrial setting, T groups will often comprise individuals drawn from the same department or division or, alternatively, from the same grading point in the organization hierarchy.

T group sessions are commonly left purposely unstructured so that the group has only hazy instructions as to their task objectives. Interpersonal interactions are then observed as the group members try to clarify their objectives and process of working together. At this juncture the 'trainers' responsible for the T group intervention will usually adopt a notably non-interventive style, their purpose being to stimulate feelings of uncertainty in the group. Detailed feedback and debriefing comments should be provided by the trainers, however, to allow individuals to reflect upon their own feelings and upon their impact upon other group members.

Not surprisingly, T groups have been a contentious and increasingly less popular method in OD. The evidence supporting their efficiency is critically limited (Porras and Robertson, 1992; Sinangil & Avallone, 2001) whilst several notorious cases of the unprofessional use of T groups and their negative psychological effects upon attendees have further diminished their popularity in the UK.

Overlapping to some extent with T groups as an OD intervention is that of sensitivity training. In this type of training the emphasis is also on increasing the individual's awareness of their impact on others but this is achieved through means other than an encounter group. Sensitivity training will often involve a variety of exercises, simulations and role play scenarios with the OD consultant acting as observer to note aspects of an individual's interpersonal style. The observer then gives individual feedback or, if permitted by the person, feedback within the group to stimulate further discussion. Again such training needs to be handled with great care by the OD consultant and, of course, simply giving factual feedback to an individual is no guarantee of any lasting change in their behavioural repertoire at work.

Having now briefly reviewed each of the five major OD techniques we identified earlier in this section, we return to the issue of the skills, knowledge and abilities (KSAs) that an organization change consultant needs to possess to be able to intervene effectively and professionally. As we shall see, not all OD practitioners or change agents could be described as paragons of virtue and the OD industry in the UK has some way to go before it could reasonably claim the exalted status of 'a profession'.

The 'learning organization'

In more recent years, specifically from around the late 1980s to the present day, an explosive growth in the popularity of so-called 'organizational learning' has occurred. This, no doubt, has been fuelled by an industry of OD consultancies who have a strong vested interest in 'talking-up' this concept as the latest panacea for organizations to enable them to cope with their changing business environments. But can an organization learn? Can it possess knowledge? And, if so, how can this capacity be enhanced and exploited for the future good of the organization?

Levinthal (1997) takes a somewhat more supportive stance towards organizational learning. He asserts three characteristics of organizational learning; that:

- organizations develop a tendency to become more proficient at core activities;

- learning processes facilitate a flexible and adaptive capacity to a changing business environment;
- the tension between stability and change itself produces beneficial learning outcomes for the organization.

Counter to this view, Weick and Westley (1996) pose real challenges to the eulogistic organization learning literature. They question both parts of the term itself on the grounds of 'imprecise referents for the word "organization", misinterpretations of the verb "learning" and debate about whether learning is an individual or organizational phenomenon' (Weick and Westley, 1996, page 441). In their view, the combination of two imprecisely defined terms, together with an interaction effect between the two which is far from verified in work settings, produces a nonsensical construct.

Sinangil and Avallone (2001), in their recent review of the OD literature pointedly fail to cite any validation studies in favour of organizational learning. It is likely that some positive studies do exist, but there is clearly a lack of robust research to support the mass of recent consultancy offerings to enhance organizational learning. Future research may perhaps offer more hope in this direction, but for the present caution is warranted over the claims of huge improvements in organizational performance that might be gained from such interventions.

Change agents

Some readers may be surprised to learn that anyone can set up in business and call themselves a 'change agent' with their consultancy firm offering any or all of the services and expertise of an 'OD consultancy'. Moreover, although there exists a number of associations and networks for OD practitioners, there is no single, universally recognized professional training scheme or final qualification in OD as in other professions such as medicine, accountancy, law or psychology. The OD industry in the UK is a hotchpotch of different types of consultants, some possessing MBA degrees with specializations in human resource management (HRM), others possessing personal experience of change processes in a particular industrial sector to which they now offer external consultancy, and others having only general managerial experience coupled with a desire to earn a living as an independent consultant. Some postgraduate courses in organizational psychology offer modules in OD, but by no means all. It is, however, worth noting that all chartered psychologists operating as OD consultants will be governed by regulations covering ethical and professional practice upheld by the British Psychological Society. Organizations employing the services of a chartered psychologist as a change agent will at least have the powerful redress of being able to report any unprofessional practice back to the BPS. Outside of this professional structure, the situation for managers looking to buy-in consultancy expertise is very much one of *caveat emptor* – literally, let the buyer beware, at law.

Reminding ourselves of the question posed at the beginning of this section, 'what skills, knowledge and abilities (KSAs) are required for a change agent to act effectively and professionally?', we would list the following as a base-line range of competencies:

- *knowledge* of the application of OD techniques in a variety of settings, their advantages and disadvantages and the research evidence to support their efficacy;
- *commitment* to the highest standards of professional and ethical integrity, including verifiable evidence of turning down project opportunities which might have compromised professional standards;
- *networking* abilities to make constructive contacts and the inter-personal abilities to develop co-operative and productive relationships with a wide variety of individuals in the client organization;
- *elicitation skills* to be able to collect valid and reliable information on the apparent organizational problems or need for change as perceived by different individuals or groups;
- *evaluation and integration skills* to be capable of correctly weighing data from many different sources and to integrate these data points into a coherent 'picture' of the issues warranting intervention for change. As we noted earlier in this chapter there can be an inordinate volume of information to evaluate and integrate in a typical OD intervention and these skills are therefore of crucial importance;
- *diagnostic and prognosis skills* to translate this mass of information into intervention strategies and a proposed plan of action. Often, what senior managers report they want from an OD intervention bears little resemblance to the diagnosis of what is actually needed by

a competent OD practitioner. In this circumstance the practitioner's skill of being able to 'sell' the intervention to the organization becomes the deciding factor as to whether the intervention eventually goes ahead.

These competencies, we would emphasize, should be regarded as just some of the more essential KSAs to be an effective change agent. Some authors have, in the past, drawn the comparison between the skills of an OD practitioner and those of medical consultant or hospital doctor (Cummings and Worley, 1993). As we have seen, Schein (1987) specifically notes the doctor–patient model of OD as one of the more traditional models of practice standing at odds with his Process Consultation (PC) approach. Whilst there certainly are some superficial similarities between the activities of diagnosing the illness of a patient from the manifest symptoms of their condition, the OD diagnostic process encompasses many other potentially confounding factors. The OD consultant, for instance, has to elicit reports of the organization's malaise from numerous individuals – senior managers, section supervisors, trade union representatives, shop-floor workers, and so forth – all of whom are likely to have quite different views of the problem. In addition, vested interests can begin to cloud the clarity of reported problem areas and the OD consultant needs to be both politically astute and aware of when he or she is being used for political ends. So, although the analogy of the medical diagnosis is not such an accurate one after all, the point to stress is once again the sheer complexity of the task facing the OD consultant and the concomitant demands this complexity therefore places upon their skills, knowledge and abilities. It is perhaps apt to conclude this section with the title of a discussion tutorial given to postgraduate students in organization psychology by one of the authors: 'Organizations get the OD consultants they deserve' – Discuss.

Does OD work?

Given the lack of regulations or professional body to govern standards in OD, and that anyone can establish themselves in business as a 'change agent', a natural question for sceptical readers to ask is 'Does OD work?' That is, is there irrefutable evidence to support the efficacy of OD techniques and interventions in work organizations? Our experience over more recent years is that this 'bottom-line' ultimatum is being held against OD more and more, we suspect as a natural and indeed quite justified reaction by many people who have been on the receiving end of consultancy-driven change management, attitude realignment, total quality, learning organization, or whatever, programmes. Those who have experienced poorly designed and validated OD interventions have become increasingly cynical, particularly where an organization has imposed a rapid series of ill-conceived change initiatives upon staff it can begin to feel as if each successive programme is just the latest in a long line of faddish interventions.

What evidence is there that OD interventions have positive effects? The answer, according to the most recent comprehensive review by Sinangil and Avallone (2001), is that there *is* supportive evidence but that research in this area is far from conclusive or unequivocal. Sinangil and Avallone review validity evidence which gives qualified support for OD interventions which are theory driven, competently implemented, and validated post-hoc. But they also note that OD itself now faces the challenge of having to change in response to new forms of work organization, leaner organization structures, information technology, and flexible working practices requiring far greater amounts of individual and team innovation. Katz and Marshak (1996) summarizes this point very aptly: 'How do Organisation Development (OD) assumptions about change, diagnosis and intervention developed in the 1940s, 1950s, and 1960s fit in today's Information Age?' (page 40–41). It remains to be seen how OD will itself develop and whether it remains applicable to changing forms of work organization in the future.

Conclusion

In this chapter we have argued that OD as a field remains dominated by professional practice rather than applied research or theory building. In the UK, although it is a small market for OD consultancy relative to the USA, countless management consultancies now offer OD advice and techniques to potential client organizations. Whilst it is difficult to estimate with any accuracy the size of the OD market in the UK it probably runs to tens of millions of pounds of consultancy per annum. And of course the field is being increasingly influenced by global consultancy firms who have offices in many countries (e.g. McKinsey,

KPMG, Accenture, etc.). It is a veritable minefield for the naïve and unwary. Few consultancies even today attempt any form of validation or cost–benefit analysis of their practices, although in fairness there are pragmatic and methodological difficulties associated with this type of validation study (Muchinsky, 1993). Nevertheless, given the pace of ongoing change in many sectors of the economy, organizations are likely to look towards OD increasingly as a conglomeration of methods and techniques to effect change in the organization. In this chapter we have reviewed the OD process, models of organization change, prevalent methods using in OD, and the skills, knowledge and abilities of effective change agents. Throughout we have emphasized that OD is never a simple, single-track process; more likely, it is a highly complex, multi-track, multi-method process which demands the highest levels of skills and knowledge to manœuvre the subsystems of an organization towards a desired rather than an undesired end state. OD as a field holds out immense potential to support organizations and to facilitate very necessary changes in their structures, methods, and technologies. It is disappointing that the research into the efficacy of OD, and of OD techniques in particular, contains so few examples of measured OD interventions resulting in demonstrable improvements in organizational functioning.

Suggested reading

Argyris, C. and Schon, D. (1978) *Organisational Learning*, Reading, MA: Addison-Wesley.

Beckhard, R. and Harris, R. (1987) *Organisational Transitions: Managing Complex Change*, 2nd edition, Reading, Mass: Addison-Wesley.

Cummings, T. G. and Worley, C. G. (1993) *Organisation Development and Change*, 5th edition, St Paul, MN: West Publishing Co.

Kanter, R. M. (1983) *The Change Masters*, New York: Simon & Schuster.

Porras, J. I. and Silvers, R. C. (1991) 'Organisational development and transformation', *Annual Review of Psychology*, 42: 51–78.

Schein, E. (1987) *Process Consultation Volume II: Lessons For Managers and Consultants*, 2nd edition, Reading, MA: Addison-Wesley.

Sinangil H. K. and Avallone F. (2001) *Organizational Development and Change*, in N. Anderson, D. Ones, H. K. Sinangil and C. Viswesvaran (eds) *Handbook of Industrial, Work and Organizational Psychology*, Volumes I and II, London: Sage.

8   Resistance to change

After reading this chapter you should be able to

- describe classical approaches in this field to 'overcoming resistance'
- discuss possible causes of resistance to change at three levels of analysis
  (a) individual
  (b) group
  (c) organization
- describe possible manifestations of resistance, both covert and overt
- critically appraise in overview different perspectives and approaches to resistance to change.

Resistance to planned organizational change has long been an issue of concern for organization development practitioners and management scientists. Resistance has been seen at best as disruptive and troublesome and at worst as a co-ordinated process of radical militancy designed to undermine the very fabric of managerial control. But such views are revealing of the dominant perspective in resistance to change research and OD practice. Resistance has almost always been characterized as irrational, counter-productive behaviour engaged in by a minority of workers to the inevitable detriment of the organization and, in the long term, to the disbenefit of those employees themselves. But is this characterization fair and just? What of health service doctors who oppose change to hospital practices on the grounds that patient care will suffer? Or of nuclear power plant operators who resist reductions in staffing levels as they feel these may jeopardize safety? And what of teachers and lecturers who refuse to administer newly imposed testing regimes on the grounds of inept pedagogic design?

The point is that 'resistance' is wholly in the eye of the beholder. It is entirely possible that the actions of an individual within an organization may be perceived by some, as harmful resistance warranting summary dismissal and simultaneously by others as morally justified and heroic behaviour worthy of the highest praise. Given these fundamentally divergent views and attitudes, it is perhaps surprising that W/O psychologists have not been more involved in resistance to change research. Instead, much of the academic thought in this area has originated from management scientists and OD specialists. Perhaps as a function of the source of much of this literature, the predominant perspective has been that of a highly pragmatic search for managerial tools and techniques to 'overcome resistance to change' (e.g. Coch and French, 1948; Lawrence, 1969; reviewed below). It is to these classical writings on resistance that we turn first in this chapter.

Overcoming resistance: classical views

From the late 1940s to the present day there has been a steady flow of published literature advising managers on how to overcome resistance to change in their organization. To review all of this work would be a gargantuan task and so we will focus upon only the most influential papers and books published over the last five decades. These we identify as:

- Coch and French (1948)
- Lewin (1951)
- Lawrence (1969)
- Shephard (1967)
- DuBrin (1974)
- Kotter and Schlesinger (1979).

Coch and French (1948)

Lester Coch and John French Jr published their account of change in the Harwood Manufacturing Corporation pyjama factory in 1948.

Operators employed in the machine sewing shop were all on piece rate wages determined by Taylorian time and motion studies. Their job function was a monotonous but skilled one – to machine the various sections of the pyjamas into a finished product. Over the preceding years the Harwood Corp. had undergone considerable change in attempting to update its production methods and techniques with the aim of retaining competitiveness within the industry. This process had met with concerted resistance from the operators as described by Coch and French:

> One of the most serious production problems faced … has been the resistance of production workers to the necessary changes in methods and jobs. This resistance expressed itself in several ways, such as grievances about piece rates that went with the new methods, high turnover, very low efficiency, restriction of output, and marked aggression against management.
>
> *(Coch and French, 1948, page 512)*

Today, over fifty years later, many managers would be able to identify strongly with these sentiments. But the Coch and French study was exceptional for its time in the eloquence of the research design employed by the authors to evaluate experimental changes in the operator job role. They hypothesized, amongst other things, that group norms and dynamics were as much an obstacle to change as the attitudes of individual operators. Thus, the authors instituted a planned series of group meetings (which would today fall under the fashionable title of 'team briefings') to inform some groups of operators of the need for change and stimulate group participation in the change process. Other groups of workers were purposely excluded from this briefing and consultation process and the impact of both styles of change management was evaluated by Coch and French. They found that those groups to whom the change process was explained exhibited significantly less resistance following the group meetings. The authors thus concluded that explanation of the changes and participation by workers in the change process were of critical importance to minimize disruptive resistance.

This seminal study was one of the first papers to call for group-level interventions to overcome resistance and has been widely influential ever since in encouraging managers to use methods of group participation in change processes to overcome resistance caused by group norms in the workplace.

Lewin (1951)

The 'field theory' developed by Kurt Lewin, more commonly referred to as 'force field analysis', was described in detail in Chapter 7. As the model relates to resistance, Lewin conceives of *resisting forces* as a direct counter-balance to forces for change, or driving forces (Lewin, 1951). In essence, his argument is that in order to overcome inertia, resisting forces have first to be investigated and minimized before the existing driving forces can then be increased to the level required to effect the desired change. Any premature or authoritarian attempt to increase driving forces unilaterally will be met by an equal and opposite increase in resisting forces. As we have previously dealt with force field analysis in Chapter 7, suffice it to say here that Lewin's model provides an easy-to-understand method of visualizing the likely resisting and driving forces within a scenario of managed change. It provides a general model of how to conceive of possible opposing forces and may therefore assist managers to identify and explicate these forces. It does not, however, offer an explanation for the reasons underlying the resistance of particular stakeholder groups, nor does it provide much more than a general taxonomy to approaching change processes. And in this very generality lie many pitfalls for those attempting to initiate organizational change to which we will return later in this chapter.

Lawrence (1969)

Paul Lawrence's paper published in the *Harvard Business Review* in 1969 again highlighted the importance of employee participation and involvement as a means of reducing resistance to change. But additionally, drawing from the views of the human relations group which was highly influential at that time (e.g. Katz and Kahn, 1966) Lawrence argued that resistance could stem either from the *technical* aspect of proposed changes or, more probably, from the impact of change upon *social* relationships at work. He describes two near-identical examples of technical changes introduced in different organizations. In the first, the change resulted in no real modification to the social interaction between manual operatives and was met with little resistance. In the second, on the other hand, the technical change necessitated a reduction in social contact between the assembly workers, which Lawrence argues was the main cause of the resistance experienced in this company.

His article stimulated much greater attention to the social implications of organizational change. It was Lawrence's belief that resistance could be minimized as long as sufficient measures were imposed to maintain the perceived quality of social relationships at work. His article thus highlighted the importance, to employees at least, of one aspect of working life to which managers characteristically pay little attention – social interactions and interpersonal relationships. Particular difficulties arise, of course, in change processes where modifications in social relations are unavoidable owing to the technical requirements of new systems or procedures, or where it is the express intention of management to rein back the extent of social contact when this is perceived as having a detrimental effect upon productivity. Again, we should be wary of stereotyping such effects as limited to manual and clerical 'shop-floor' workers alone – regular meetings between even senior directors can take on the status of ritualistic social interaction to be guarded and preserved even if there is little functional justification for such meetings (Pettigrew, 1985).

Shephard (1967)

Herbert A. Shephard's paper entitled 'Innovation-resisting and innovation-producing organizations' argued for a dichotomy between organizational types which characteristically resist innovation and those which habitually promote and incorporate innovative ideas in products and processes. We described at some length the research into organization-level innovativeness in Chapter 5, but it is worth noting here that many of Shephard's ideas appear to be the direct forerunners of prescriptions made by internationally popular writings in the 'innovation boom' of the 1980s (e.g. Peters and Waterman, 1982; Kanter, 1983). Innovation-resisting organizations, he asserts, characteristically act as follows.

> Innovative ideas are most likely to occur to persons who have some familiarity with the situation to which the ideas would apply. Hence most novel ideas are likely to be generated at some distance from the power

center of the organization. Since new ideas are disturbances, they are effectively screened out of the stream of upward communication. But because power is centralized at the top, top support for an idea is almost a necessity if it is to move toward becoming an innovation.

(*Shephard, 1967*)

Shephard's notion of the innovation-resisting organization was founded upon the interaction of bureaucratic and hierarchical organizational structures, the restricted distribution of power and authority in such organizations, and vested interests of the established power elite. Interestingly, it was senior management whom Shephard saw as the major source of resistance to innovation and change from within and below in any organization. We could thus counter-pose this view against most other classical writings of the genre which advised management on how to overcome resistance to change processes imposed from the top down. Resistance, we should note, can occur at any level in the organization hierarchy.

DuBrin (1974)

Perhaps typical of the writings on 'how to overcome resistance to change' is Andrew DuBrin's book *Fundamentals of Organizational Behavior* published in 1974. He argues that change can occur in three areas: *Technology or business* (e.g. the installation of computerized information systems, the automation of production methods), *structure or policy* (e.g. organization structure, payment systems, work design) and *people* (i.e. personnel changes, leadership changes). Resistance levels, DuBrin holds, will be a function of whether the change is felt to have high or low impact in terms of the numbers of staff affected, the range of activities altered and the amount of resources needed to implement the change. He advises that resistance can be minimized by several interrelated strategies, all of which clearly draw on the earlier writings of the 1940s, 1950s and 1960s:

- *Select positive staff* – recruit only individuals who are flexible and open to changing circumstances.
- *Avoid coercive tactics* – use non-confrontational methods of persuasion to neutralize resistance as it emerges.

- *Minimize social changes* – reduce the perceived impact of change by minimizing the disruption to interpersonal relationships at work (see also Paul Lawrence's (1969) arguments described earlier in this section).
- *Introduce change tentatively* – sell changes to affected groups by emphasizing that the proposed change is tentative and can always be modified with the consent of management. More manipulative use of this tactic can still be witnessed in organizations where the change is introduced initially as a catastrophic upheaval only to be curtailed to a more reasonable change scenario later on. Cynical use of this tactic occurs where the modified position was in fact the real agenda for the initiators.
- *Use shared decision making* – allow participation in decision making. Whether participation is allowed in decisions concerning the core strategy of the change or the peripheral details and minutiae is open to debate and discussion.
- *Use economic incentives* – 'buy off' resistance using the whole gamut of tactics from increasing payment rates to improving fringe benefits and job perks.

Kotter and Schlesinger (1979)

The final article on resistance to which we would confer 'classical' status is Kotter and Schlesinger's 'Choosing strategies for change' which appeared in the *Harvard Business Review* in early 1979. It represents perhaps the culmination of the 'how to overcome resistance' theme, describing both the range of strategies available to managers for overcoming resistance and how to use each technique in particular circumstances. Their 'contingency theory' continuum is represented in Figure 8.1.

It shows the six strategies identified by Kotter and Schlesinger – *communication, participation, facilitation, negotiation, manipulation* and *coercion* – placed along a continuum representing the increasing salience or potency of each strategy. The techniques further to the right on the continuum are argued to be more powerful interventions, although the authors stress the role of managerial choice in deciding upon an appropriate strategy, or mix of strategies, contingent upon predominant circumstances and the power reserves of those initiating the change.

Figure 8.1   **Kotter and Schlesinger's contingency approach for overcoming resistance to change**

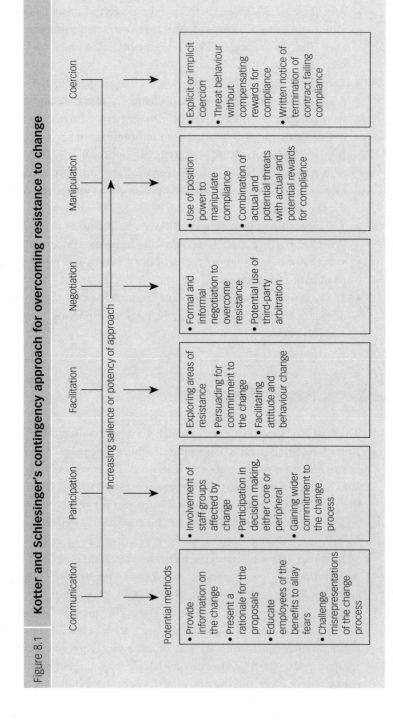

Source: Adapted and extended from Kotter, J. P. and Schlesinger, L. A. (1979) 'Choosing strategies for change', *Harvard Business Review*, March–April: 106–14.

If change can be accomplished by utilizing only less intrusive techniques to the left of the continuum, communication and participation for instance, the authors argue this should be the preferred approach. Where resistance is likely to be more deeply rooted and tenacious, and where the initiators possess the necessary power and authority, more potent techniques such as negotiation, manipulation, or even coercion, should be resorted to. Their model is useful to the extent that it emphasizes that managerial strategy should be *contingent* upon levels of resistance and the reserves of power at the behest of those initiating change.

From these classic writings on resistance, it is clear that early concerns in this area were dominated by pragmatic, managerial concerns to *overcome* resistance to change. There is a *psychological* component to some of these writings, if only that of using psychological research findings for the benefit of those initiating change. Beyond these rather rudimentary applications, however, there was little concern with the psychological impacts of change, the reasons why resistance emerges and processes through which it may be consolidated into a shared goal within the organization, or with intergroup differences in the social psychological implications of resistance to change. More recently, these concerns have become more prevalent and a number of issues specifically related to psychological aspects of resistance to change have emerged. It is to these contemporary issues that we now turn.

Contemporary issues in resistance to change

Having reviewed some of the seminal writings on resistance, we now come to discuss current debates and issues in the area. By necessity, our choice of issues is both eclectic and idiosyncratic; our intention is to alert the reader to current controversies in management and organization psychology and to provide a commentary on our interpretation of these issues, rather than to give an exhaustive review of the existing research in this area. There is also an intention on our part to highlight issues which are fundamentally *psychological* rather than *organizational* in nature. Given the predominance of studies which have adopted, either explicitly or implicitly, a managerialist or pragmatic perspective as exemplified by the work on overcoming resistance to change, our focus upon the psychological aspects of resistance to change is intended to redress this imbalance to some extent.

Amongst a plethora of possible issues for discussion, we would note three as being particularly salient and important from our perspective as organizational psychologists working in this area:

1 the *causes* of resistance at the individual, group and organizational levels of analysis;
2 the *manifestations* of resistance in organizations;
3 *perspectives on resistance* as these theoretical viewpoints relate to the psychological component of resistance.

The causes of resistance

Why do individuals and groups in organizations resist change, especially change designed to improve efficiency and profitability? A number of explanations has been put forward over the years, most of which seem commonsensical and to have some reasonable basis in organizational experience. Before we move on to these arguments, however, it is useful again to impose the levels-of-analysis framework to examine potential factors contributing to resistance at the organization, group and individual levels of analysis. Table 8.1 suggests some hypothesized relations between these factors and resulting levels of resistance. We should note that this table is exploratory and that the hypothesized relations are tentative rather than the undisputed findings of applied studies in work settings. None the less, the table suggests likely levels of resistance (high versus low) upon factors at our three levels of analysis – individual, group and organizational – as moderated by the degree of centralization or decentralization of power in the organization concerned.

Individual level

At the individual level of analysis, for instance, it is likely that under conditions of a highly centralized distribution of power, all other things being equal, individuals high on need for control (Winter, 1973) will exhibit higher levels of resistance to change since they will perceive a lack of personal control over unfolding events. Other personality factors which could account for resistance at the individual level include locus of control (Rotter, 1966), need for achievement (McLelland *et al.*,

Table 8.1 Hypothesized relations between organizational factors, centralization of power and resistance to change

Organizational factors	Power centralization versus resistance levels		
	Highly decentralized	Distributed → Resistance	Highly centralized
Individual-level factors[a]			
Personalities:			
High need for control	Low	→	High
Internal locus of control (Rotter, 1966)	Low	→	High
High need for achievement (McClelland et al., 1953)	Low	→	High
High rule of dependence	High	→	Low
High authoritarianism	Low	→	High
Prior change experience:			
Predominantly negative and/or distressful experiences	High	→	High[d]
High degree of residual resentment	High	→	High[d]
Group-level factors[b]			
High cohesiveness	High	→	High[d]
High social maintenance ('groupthink', Janis, 1982)	High	→	High[d]
High participation in decision making (Wall and Lischeron, 1977)	Low	→	High
High autonomy and self-determination	High	→	High[d]

Power centralization versus resistance levels

Organizational factors	Highly decentralized	Distributed →	Highly centralized
Organizational-level factors[c]			
Structure:			
Formal bureaucratic	High	↑	Low
Wide span of control	High	↑	High[d]
Decentralized and/or divisionalized	High	↑	Low
Climate and culture:			
High trust and openness	Low	↑	High
High participation in decision making (Wall and Lischeron, 1977)	Low	↑	High
High organization commitment (Cook and Wall, 1980)	High	↑	High[d]
Strategy:			
Product diversification	Low	↑	Low[e]
High defender strategic type (Miles and Snow, 1978)	High	↑	High[d]
Distinct core–peripheral workforce division	Low	↑	Low[e]

(a) Individual-level factors include the *personalities* of those involved in the change process, and their *attitudes* towards further change based upon past *experiences* of organizational change. Levels of resistance (high or low) assume that the change process is initiated and directed from above and that such individuals will have only limited power to influence the process.

(b) Group-level factors relate to work groups functioning on a day-to-day basis (as opposed to ad hoc project groups or groups which only meet periodically). Clearly, individual-level and group-level factors overlap. For instance, the *composition* of the group in terms of its membership is likely to relate to its cohesiveness, norms and decision-making structures.

(c) Organizational-level factors are perhaps the most numerous and diffuse of all three levels. This list is certainly not exhaustive but illustrates the hypothesized impact of organization structure, climate and culture, and strategy upon resistance levels. Other factors include technology, work organization, resources, leadership style, and so forth.

(d) Denotes scale where resistance is likely to be high on this factor regardless of whether power is centralized or decentralized (i.e. that centralization is likely not to be a *moderator*).

(e) Denotes scale where resistance is likely to be low on this factor regardless of whether power is centralized or decentralized.

1953), and rule independence and authoritarianism (Winter, 1973). But, the personalities of those involved with the change process alone cannot explain fully the reasons for resistance. Their *attitudes* based upon previous *experiences* of organizational change will have a significant impact. Kotter and Schlesinger (1979) argue, for instance, that such attitudes can be a function of a combination of four causes – a lack of trust and misunderstanding the intentions of change (again, largely determined by past experience of change), low tolerance of change, parochial self-interest, and contradictory assessments of the same process dependent upon one's vantage position within the organization. Thus, actual levels of resistance at an individual level are likely to be due to the combination of personality factors and prior experiences of similar change scenarios.

Group level

At the group level of analysis, resistance can be caused by a number of factors inherent in the structure, composition and working relationships of a group which underscore the status quo. These include group cohesiveness, social norms, participation in decision making, and autonomy for self-determination of actions. Again, the distribution of organizational power and authority will mediate levels of resistance experienced under different circumstances. A particularly embedded and tenacious form of resistance is to be expected where the group suffers from the 'groupthink' phenomenon (Janis, 1972, 1982), and where organizational power is centralized away from the group. Under such circumstances, *any* change emanating from outside the group is likely to be perceived as a consummate threat to the status quo because the group will value highly its social interactions but will possess little power to influence the change process. On the other hand, organization structures wherein autonomous work groups (AWGs) comprise the primary method of work organization are also particularly prone to this effect, and especially so where AWGs are afforded extensive degrees of autonomy (Scarborough and Corbett, 1992).

Organizational level

Finally, at the organizational level of analysis, the picture becomes something of a complex kaleidoscope of interrelated factors contributing to resistance, the view being one which is constantly changing and one which appears to be quite different depending upon one's vantage position. Amongst other factors, organization structure, climate, culture and strategy could be argued to contribute to levels of resistance (e.g. Miles and Snow, 1978; Child, 1984).

So, there is clearly a multitude of factors impinging upon levels of resistance in change scenarios. Even classifying these factors at the organizational, group and individual levels of analysis only partially simplifies the complex interplay between factors to be found in real-life cases of organizational change. Given this complexity and the wide differences between individual change scenarios, proffering highly general models and advice on how to overcome resistance is clearly fraught with danger. It is helpful, therefore, to consider some of the psychological processes which might underlie resistance.

First, *change is unknown* and therefore presents a threat to those affected by it (Hosking and Anderson, 1992). Thus, under this explanation, change is resisted simply because it *is* change. Gray and Starke (1984) have argued that such resistance can arise from either 'rational' or 'emotional' sources. Rational resistance occurs where individuals decide, on the information available to them at the time, to resist since the change is perceived as detrimental in some way to their working conditions. Emotional resistance, on the other hand, occurs as the result of negative psychological processes including anxiety, frustration and loss of self-esteem sometimes found in change processes. It is clear that the boundary between 'rational' and 'emotional' resistance could be hard to discern in reality and, moreover, that what is rational to some actors in an organizational change situation will be seen as highly emotive to others. Subsumed within this explanation is the view that individuals and groups are pre-eminently creatures of habit driven by the desire to maintain existing routines and ways of doing things. Faced with any type of external change, individuals and groups viewed in this way will display resistance as an *automatic* reaction regardless of whether the change is threatening or not. Such a paranoid reaction to change, even where the outcomes of the change process can be demonstrated to be highly beneficial, is perhaps a rather extreme one in organizational settings. The possibility, however, that change *inevitably* results in resistance should be noted as one possible explanation for why resistance occurs.

Second, *change challenges the status quo* and may be resisted because of powerful vested interests in maintaining the current equilibrium position. Those who stand to lose most, whether in terms of positional power, organizational resources, social contact at work or rewards, are likely to resist most vociferously. But, of course, such perceptions are relative and bounded by restricted knowledge and information within any organization (Simon, 1977). Thus, an autonomous work group may resist because it feels a change might compromise its freedom (e.g. Scarborough and Corbett, 1992); a senior management team may resist an OD intervention to decentralize decision making on the grounds that this would undermine its executive powers; a team of hospital nurses may resist imposed changes to bed occupancy quotas by arguing that the new system will result in a decline in standards of patient care. Crucially, vested-interest groups, sometimes referred to as 'stakeholder groups' (Burgoyne, 1994), are likely to resist more if the change is *perceived* as affecting factors *important to them* at work, be these factors social, financial, professional or whatever. It follows that attempting to persuade others using arguments which are perceived by them as less consequential will probably be an ineffective negotiation strategy. For instance, where senior managers cite increased productivity as the reason for implementing new technology, operators may be more concerned with how the machinery will affect their work routines rather than with company profitability. The empathic skills of negotiation including perceiving factors important to the other party, framing arguments within their logic and terminology, and offering concessions on factors important to them but less so to oneself, seem to be important aspects of successfully negotiating change outcomes by minimizing emergent resistance caused by perceptions of threat to established vested interests.

Third, *change often means extra workload* for those affected by it. Of course, resistance here could be argued to be 'rational' rather than 'emotive'. Recent studies of change in the British National Health Service (NHS) illustrate convincingly that resistance may be a reaction against the burden of additional work placed upon those concerned (West and Anderson, 1992). This is undoubtedly true where the new and old systems are continued in parallel for some period following the change implementation, as is often the case where new technology is introduced in information support systems (Wilson, 1992). There is consequently an impact in such situations of an increase in workload directly attributable to the change itself. Moreover, this workload can be seen as replicating other work where two systems are continued in parallel, and may thus be resented and resisted for reasons which are understandable and entirely rational for those affected in this manner. Again, this argument points up the implication that resistance often represents a wholly logical and justifiable course of action from the viewpoint of those involved, rather than being irrational and counter-productive behaviour designed only to disrupt others in the organization.

Manifestations of resistance

It is nonsensical to talk of 'resistance' as a single, unitary behaviour. Rather, it is a general class of actions carrying the intention of achieving some objective or aim; that is, resistance is 'goal-directed behaviour' (Ajzen, 1988). And, in most cases, the goal is to maintain, to as great an extent as possible, the status quo within an organization or organizational sub-unit. Figure 8.2 illustrates some of the ways in which resistance may be manifest at the individual group and organizational levels.

By codifying innovation along two continua, *covert–overt* and *individual–organization* level, we can conceive of a range of 'types' of resistance. These span from the most hidden, covert forms of resistance at an individual level including demotivation, intentional under-performance, and purposeful lack of realization of potential, through to, at the other extreme, the most outwardly visible resistance which has formalized into concerted industrial action involving large numbers of employees possibly from more than one organization or site. Between these two extremes, resistance could take on any combination of the following forms:

- reduced organization commitment;
- increased hostility to those initiating the change;
- increased absenteeism, lateness, or even sabotage of production systems;
- a reinforcement of group norms and in-group pressures resulting in reduced performance and intergroup conflict;
- increased propensity to unionization and trade union activity;

Figure 8.2 **Manifestations of resistance to change at the individual, group and organizational levels of analysis**

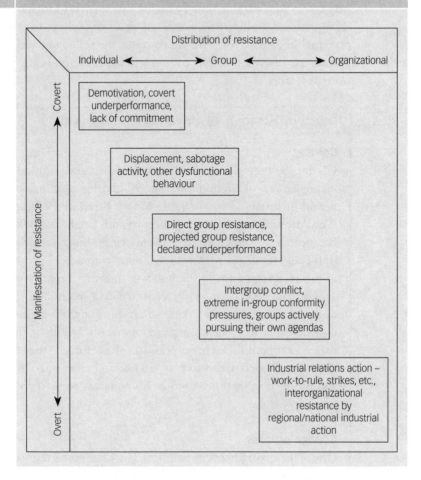

- spillover conflicts resulting from the 'projection' of resentment into other areas of negotiation (e.g. the imposition of fixed-term contracts on previously permanent contract staff resulting in demands for substantial salary increases to compensate for loss of job security).

It is clear by now that resistance can take many forms and that appropriate strategies to cope with such a diversity of action will themselves be wide ranging in scope and style. Perhaps, though, the most difficult type of resistance to deal with in many senses is highly covert resistance simply because it is hidden from public observation. As illustrated in the case study of Glazing Systems Design Ltd (Box 8.1), it may take a considerable time to identify such covert forms of resistance as intentional underperformance of staff or failure to achieve full potential in a work role. We move on in the following section of this chapter to discuss possible coping mechanisms for both covert and overt resistance.

Box 8.1 | **Covert resistance in Glazing Systems Design Ltd**

Context

Glazing Systems Design Ltd, a well-known and long-established manufacturer of aluminium framed glazing systems, was in a period of sustained commercial change. Based in the heartland of West Midlands manufacturing industry, this family-owned company had been in existence for over twenty years. But none of its senior staff could recall a period of such intense commercial pressure even in previous recessions in the building industry. Profits were down substantially, competition for contracts had intensified to such a degree that firms were working to extremely tight margins, and so cost controls were being applied rigorously by all of the firm's major competitors. These pressures had forced the company chairman, Robert Chadwick, to update and reorganize the design and production methods used by his company some three months previously.[1]

Change process

One of the departments most affected by Chadwick's reorganization was the drawing office. This department employed eight highly skilled technical designers who were responsible for producing blueprint drawings for all industrial glazing projects handled by the company. It was a time-consuming and labour-intensive job. A single blueprint could take up to thirty hours to complete and could involve as many as 100 different calculations for sizes, wind-loading factors and project costings. Seeing these labour costs ▶

---

[1] The actual names of the organization and the individuals involved in this case have been altered to preserve anonymity. The case is based, however, upon a real-life instance of covert resistance to change.

as excessive, Chadwick bought in a computer-aided design (CAD) system with the intention of transferring all such design tasks onto a networked minicomputer system purchased at the same time. The new system was installed over a single weekend and the first the technical designers saw or heard of it was when they returned to work the following Monday morning. They were told that they would be expected to complete all projects using the new system and that detailed training would be provided over the coming weeks. Several designers were unhappy with this situation, however, and slowly they began to share with each other their resentment over how the change had been imposed upon them. After a few days, Bill Graham, a senior designer and a well-respected member of staff, approached the departmental manager, George Dexter, to voice the concerns of his fellow technical designers. He was given short shrift by Dexter who replied that 'if anyone doesn't like the new system or can't be bothered to retrain to learn its capacities, I have a file full of local unemployed designers willing to take over their job'. Greeted with this response and faced with frequent breakdowns of the new system, Bill Graham decided that a different strategy of response was called for.

After careful discussion with his fellow designers, Graham, a highly intelligent and shrewd-minded individual, persuaded the group to agree to a secret 'work-to-rule'. He had calculated that the new system could, if operating as a fully functional CAD package, raise productivity by around 20 per cent. That is, he reckoned that an additional 12 drawings per week could be completed by the drawing office. Yet, the employment terms and conditions for designers remained unaltered, which in Graham's view represented a 'loss' of an average £40 per week (or 20 per cent of weekly wages). The work-to-rule therefore involved all technical designers keeping a daily record of effort applied to their tasks. If efforts were judged to be above the agreed 80 per cent maximum allowed on any single day, the designer was required to reduce effort the following day so as to maintain an 80 per cent average throughout the week. Records kept by the designers were detailed and immaculate, and it had already become the custom and practice to spend the final 15 minutes of each day to update and agree the effort graphs kept by fellow designers. Ironically, this ▶

same quarter-of-an-hour period was used each day by George Dexter and Robert Chadwick to meet to discuss how the changes were proceeding in the drawing office! Neither had any idea that the drawing office staff were consciously subverting the change process in this manner.

Questions

1 For what reasons might Bill Graham and his fellow designers be resisting this change in working practices?
2 Could particular theories of employee motivation be applied to this case to explain their work-to-rule?
3 Are Graham and his colleagues justified in their undeclared work-to-rule? What social psychological theories may explain these actions?
4 How would you advise Robert Chadwick and George Dexter
    (a) to have managed the change process differently in the first place?
    (b) to respond to this covert resistance, assuming that it becomes visible to them sooner or later?

To summarize, resistance is *goal-directed behaviour*, the manifestation of which will vary substantively between situations. In some cases resistance will focus primarily at the intra- or inter-individual level and may be more *covert* in nature than in other circumstances where resistance may be group based or even organization wide, involving *overt* conflict mediated by a formal procedure of industrial action. Resistance can be grounded upon either *rational* or *emotive* responses, or perhaps more often a combination of the two. And finally, resistance will be *perceived* by others as being more or less *justified* dependent upon the value judgements and position in the organizational system of the perceiver.

Perspectives on resistance

Several authors have noted that resistance to organizational change is so common as to be a ubiquitous facet of planned change processes. Fewer have asserted that resistance is a rational and justifiable human behaviour in the face of change (Hosking and Anderson, 1992). This is probably due to the managerialist orientation of most of the influential writings reviewed earlier in this chapter, whose explicit purpose was to advise on how to overcome resistance to change. Even today, relatively few studies have been conducted in the psychological impact of change as this influences resistance, although we have noted the main research findings and offered some tentative hypotheses in earlier sections of this chapter.

In this section of the chapter, we explore briefly a number of different perspectives on resistance. Rather than conclude by replicating well-publicized points of advice on how to overcome resistance, it is our view that a more constructive stance is to question fundamentally the range of perspectives on resistance evident in the research literature. Again, by necessity, our choice of perspectives, and our interpretation of the views, attitudes and beliefs subsumed within each perspective, is essentially a personal one. Our comments are meant, once more, to reflect the *psychological* component of each perspective. We characterize and identify four main perspectives on resistance:

- resistance as an unavoidable and natural behavioural response to the perceived threat of change;
- resistance as a politically motivated and co-ordinated campaign of insurrection and class struggle;
- resistance as a constructive counter-balance to ill-founded organization change;
- resistance as the manifestation of difficulties in restructuring cognitive schemas, codes of action or organization culture in the midst of change.

Resistance as unavoidable behavioural response

In an earlier section of this chapter, we argued that individuals may resist change simply because it represents a move into the unknown. In this perspective, individual employees are assumed to 'resist first and ask questions later'. As such, although resistance may be portrayed as a 'natural' behavioural response, it has implicitly been assumed to be an irrational and counter-productive behaviour by many of the writers on resistance.

The question which then arises is 'are some individuals more likely to be resistant than others?' That is, do individual differences exist between individuals in their propensity to resist as determined by particular personality characteristics? This is an important and challenging question to which, regrettably, little research effort has been devoted by work psychologists. As DuBrin (1974) argued, one means to minimize the likelihood of resistance arising in the first place is to select 'positive' people into an organization. But we need to unpack the constellation of personality traits inferred by this general term 'positive'. Certainly, a cursory review of two of the most popular tests of personality currently available in the UK – the 16PF and Saville and Holdsworth's Occupational Personality Questionnaire (OPQ) – reveals a number of dimensions which we would expect to be predictive of resistance, but we would stress that further research is called for in this area.

Resistance as politically motivated insurrection and class struggle

In some ways this perspective on resistance is the most intriguing of the four perspectives discussed in this section. Conceiving of any form of resistance as radical insurrection motivated by political considerations and carried out for planned political ends, necessarily implies that the perceiver takes a radical view of such actions, whether in favour of, or in opposition to, resistance. It is not so surprising, then, to find that this perspective has been advocated from two diametrically opposed political and managerial viewpoints.

- Radical Marxist and labour process theorists concerned with worker alienation and the oppression of the working classes by the owners of the means of production (e.g. Braverman, 1974; Salaman, 1979; Thompson and McHugh, 1990).
- Management gurus preaching the gospel of the unitary organization striving for a common goal but hindered by a minority of troublemakers supported by militant trade unions (e.g. Peters and Waterman, 1982; Iacocca, 1984).

From the first of these polemic viewpoints, resistance stems from the fundamentally inequitable employment relationships between workers and organization in association with the unavoidable alienation felt by employees as a result of bureaucratic organization structures and control mechanisms (Braverman, 1974). A real resurgence of interest in this perspective, widely termed 'labour process theory', has been evident over the last twenty years or so (see Thompson and McHugh, 1990, for an accessible review of this perspective), but in principle, the core arguments in this perspective have remained constant.

- The power of an employer over an employee is substantial, this relationship being founded upon the only means of sustenance open to most employees – payment for labour.
- Counterpoised against this asymmetrical employment relationship is the alienation felt by employees and caused by bureaucratic work methods and excessive managerial control over behaviour at work (e.g. Salaman, 1979).
- Work relations are thus characterized as the domination and exploitation of one class (the working class) by another (the owners of the means of production).
- Resistance to change arises from this fundamentally antagonistic employment relationship, the power of individual workers being utterly dependent upon their capacity to mobilize collective action (e.g. strikes, works-to-rule, etc.) to disrupt the production process.

Diametrically opposed to these views are those popularized with some vigour by authors such as Peters, Waterman, Kanter and Iacocca largely in the 1980s deluge of 'excellence' writings on organizations (e.g. Peters and Waterman, 1982; Kanter, 1983). It is revealing that in none of these texts is the topic of 'resistance to change' even included in the index but that phrases such as 'empowerment', 'energizing the grass roots', 'entrepreneurship' and 'commitment to excellence' head sections which make central arguments. Resistance appears repressed, denied and consigned to a bygone era of 1960s/1970s industrial relations characterized by militancy and disruption by strikes which has been long since swept away by the socioeconomic reforms of the Reagan and Thatcher administrations.

Resistance as constructive counter-balance

We began this chapter by noting that resistance to change may not necessarily be a bad thing; resistance can thus act as a counter-balance to change which is ill-conceived, poorly enacted, or simply detrimental to the productive efficiency of the organization. The imposition of league tables ranking primary and secondary school performance despite flaws in the original statistical returns; the introduction of Japanese-style management control and obligatory participation mechanisms without any concession to cultural differences in employee expectations (Oliver and Wilkinson, 1992); and the use of interventive team-building training to force cohesion and solidarity in teams where a degree of heterogeneity is actually called for (see also Chapter 4), are all possible scenarios where resistance from individuals lower down the organization hierarchy is both beneficial and well intentioned. Returning to our earlier discussion of the causes of resistance, the distinction drawn between 'rational' and 'emotive' sources of resistance made by Gray and Starke (1984) can be applied here to argue that such resistance is once again highly rational. Only the unerring perseverance of management down the track of an irrational change process might invoke more desperate forms of emotional resistance – demotivation, underperformance or even sabotage, for instance.

Finally, we would draw the reader's attention to Shephard's (1967) notion that the task-specific knowledge needed to generate workable innovations is likely to be held by those intimately involved with the job itself. That individuals are also likely to lack the reserves of power and authority at the disposal of senior management may render such rational resistance relatively impotent. Senior management may, in many change scenarios, possess the necessary power to impose the change agenda from above, but the important messages transmitted by junior staff regarding the impracticalities of some aspects of the proposed agenda may be lost within the 'noise' of a complexity of signals of resistance. For managers to assume the mantle of superior knowledge and rationality, and to dismiss *all* such messages and signs of disruptive resistance, is clearly a grave mistake.

Resistance as cognitive and cultural restructuring

The fourth and final perspective on resistance we offer is to conceive of resistance as a by-product of the restructuring of cognitive schemas at the individual level and as the recasting of corporate culture and climate at the organizational level. There is mounting evidence that processes of organization change are often experienced by individuals as difficult and disruptive personal transitions demanding a significant restructuring of their cognitive schemas and knowledge maps, and updating of their skills, abilities and attitudes to work (Bouwen and Fry, 1991; Bouwen et al., 1992; Anderson and King, 1993). Bouwen et al. (1992) describe four cases of major change projects in organizations in the fast-food, banking, building materials and consumer electronics sectors of Belgian industry. In all four cases the change provoked tension between what they termed the 'dominant logic' (the existing mind-set of ways of doing tasks in the organization) and the 'emergent logic' (the new cognitive schemas demanded by the changed situation which will govern future action). None of the cases witnessed a smooth transition from dominant to emergent logic and individuals involved reported personal difficulties in transforming their ways of thinking and ways of acting to accommodate the new scenario. So, resistance, we would argue, may well accompany such upheavals for individuals struggling to restructure their frames of reference both cognitively and socially.

At the organizational level of analysis, an equivalent process of restructuring of culture and climate may underlie observable resistance to organizational change. In any organization, mechanisms are present to maintain stability and inertia, including its formal structure, work organization, culture and climate (Child, 1984; Wilson, 1992). In periods of relative stability such mechanisms are essential to keep the organization in 'steady state', but during times of change they become obstacles in-built to the very fabric of the organization. As such, these mechanisms resemble the cognitive schemas of individuals except that they guide actions at the collective level of the team, department or organization overall.

To summarize, four perspectives on resistance are discernible from the literature – resistance as natural response, resistance as class struggle, resistance as constructive counter-balance and resistance as individual and organizational restructuring. Different change processes can be perceived by different individuals as provoking any one, or any combination, of these four views of resistance. Such perceptions will clearly depend upon a whole host of factors, but the important point to note is that differences in perspective are almost inevitable in change processes affecting large numbers of individuals and work groups.

Conclusion

To conclude, resistance to change remains a fascinating but surprisingly under-researched topic in organizational psychology. At first glance resistance behaviour appears to be a rather simple, unidimensional action, but the more deeply one looks into this topic, the more complex, multidimensional and value laden one's perceptions seem to become. Early management research in this area was dominated by the desire to identify and overcome resisting forces, and this theme has remained prevalent to the present day in the managerial literature. We have argued at several points in this chapter that such a perspective has unjustifiably oversimplified resistance to change by portraying any form of resistance as harmful, illogical and counter-productive to the mutual benefit of managers and employees alike. But a careful examination of the reasons why resistance occurs in the first instance and a review of its many possible forms of manifestation on organizations reveal that resistance can often be wholly justifiable behaviour under the circumstances. Moreover we have argued that resistance can, on specific occasions, be a highly productive counter-balance against poorly planned organization change imposed from above.

Given these arguments, our penultimate section in this chapter considered resistance from four distinctly different perspectives – resistance as natural response, as class struggle, as constructive counter-balance, and as individual and organizational restructuring. More research is needed under all of these four perspectives to redress the imbalance of the existing literature with its preponderance of managerialist research in the 'how to overcome resistance' vein. We must move away from seeing organizational members who resist change only as bad patients who refuse to take their medicine; resistance may equally well be seen as a defence mechanism against the pathogens of change.

Suggested reading

Coch, L. and French, J. R. P., Jr (1948) 'Overcoming resistance to change', *Human Relations*, 11: 512–32.

Hosking, D. M. and Anderson, R. R. (eds) (1992) *Organizational Change and Innovation: Perspectives and Practices in Europe*, London: Routledge.

Kotter, J. and Schlesinger, L. (1979) 'Choosing strategies for change', *Harvard Business Review*, 57: 106–14.

Wilson, D. C. (1992) *A Strategy of Change: Concepts and Controversies in the Management of Change*, London: Routledge.

9 Future directions for practice and research

Innovation and change have remained high on the agenda for researchers and practitioners since the explosion of interest in these topics at the start of the 1980s. Given the social, economic and technological developments impacting on contemporary organizations, this seems likely to be the case for the foreseeable future. Few would disagree that the topics covered in this book, ranging from individual creativity, through group and organizational innovation, to OD and resistance to change, are key issues for managers today. We hope we have shown that psychology can make a distinctive contribution to understanding these areas, and that it can play a valuable role in informing good managerial practice. We would encourage the reader to follow up some of the suggestions for further reading at the end of each chapter, and also to draw upon work from neighbouring disciplines such as organizational behaviour (OB) and the sociology of organizations.

This concluding chapter will bring together under four broad headings a number of themes which have run through the book and focus on their implications for present and future managers in organizations:

1 Levels of analysis: monitoring and integrating multiple perspectives;
2 The importance of relationships;
3 The limits of managerial control;
4 The application of psychological knowledge.

Finally we will outline the research agenda in the psychology of innovation and change, which will hopefully inform good practice in years to come.

Levels of analysis: monitoring and integrating multiple perspectives

The distinction between individual, group and organizational levels of analysis is, as we made clear in the first chapter of this book, a convenient one for reviewing the literature on innovation and change. Most research focuses on one level to try to explain the causes, development and/or effects of change processes. However, it is clear from the material we have presented that no one level of analysis can be fully understood in isolation from the others: individual creative performance is partly determined by group and organizational structure and climate; organizational innovativeness relies upon effective group functioning (including decision making) and the skills, knowledge and abilities of individual change agents and idea champions; the success of work group innovation is contingent upon the characteristics of and interaction between a group's members, as well as its relationship with its wider organizational environment. (Of course, change in organizations will be influenced at all levels by the prevailing economic, social and political conditions, though this is going beyond the current text's psychological perspective.)

For the manager, the major implication of the above is that any innovation/change he or she is responsible for will require attention at multiple levels within the organization. The manager will need to maintain vigilance in monitoring the effects of change well beyond its immediate intended area of impact, in order to react to the almost inevitable 'setbacks and surprises' (Schroeder *et al.*, 1989) that will occur. Given this, it is advisable in all but the smallest of organizations to share or delegate responsibility for change management rather than allowing one senior manager to oversee the implementation process on his or her own. This does not mean that the only acceptable strategy is that of the equal-status project management team, taking joint decisions on an innovation's progress. For some organizations – and some innovations – it might be more effective to nominate a single authoritative figure to head an innovation initiative, but he or she should seek the regular and close involvement of other managers and technical experts.

The importance of relationships

At all levels of analysis, we would argue that an understanding of innovation and change processes requires a strong focus on relationships and interactions between people in organizations. In the creativity literature, we have seen, for example, the often crucial role of a mentor figure (or figures) in creative achievement. Beyond such special relationships, social psychological research has shown how creative performance is embedded in and shaped by the wider social world of the creator. Freeman's (1993) study demonstrates this even in an occupational setting as apparently individualistic as American visual arts in the late twentieth century, where careers developed not simply as the unfolding of some 'natural' talent, but through relationships with family, fellow artists and members of the 'art world'. At the group level, innovation can be influenced by intergroup relationships and intragroup dynamics. At the organizational level, recent research has highlighted the importance of networking and relationship building within and between organizations.

Given the above, it is rather surprising that relationships are not commonly identified as a pervasive theme in the literature. At least in part, this probably reflects opposing biases in research which tend to draw attention away from a relational perspective. On the one hand, there is a tendency to seek explanations *within* people in terms of thinking skills, personality traits and so on. On the other hand, there is an opposite tendency to look at groups and organizations as if they were entities in themselves that can be treated as if independent of the people they are composed of. A relational perspective emphasizes that innovation is about people, without taking a reductionist approach that seeks to explain the phenomenon in terms of traits, skills, knowledge and so on *within* the individual. We are not suggesting that psychological research into innovation should only be about relationships and interactions, but we do argue that these areas should become much more central to theory and empirical investigation.

The limits of managerial control

At numerous points in this book we have stressed the complex and unpredictable character of organizational innovation and change. This

223

can be seen, for instance, in the multifaceted nature of individual creativity, exemplified by Mumford and Gustafson's (1988) notion of creativity as a 'syndrome' embracing thinking styles, personality, life history and the social situation (see Chapter 3). It is also evident in our criticisms of overly simple OD models (see Chapter 7) and of narrow and judgemental explanations of resistance to change (Chapter 8). We addressed the issue most directly in Chapter 6, where we suggested that there has been a tendency to overestimate the extent to which managers can control change processes. This 'illusion of manageability' broke down into three components:

- the *illusion of linearity* – that change processes move through a linear sequence of discrete stages;
- the *illusion of predictability* – that managers can accurately predict what is going to happen next in a change process;
- the *illusion of control* – that, as change processes are linear and predictable, managers can exert a high degree of control over them.

For practising managers, the main implication of the above is that they need to acknowledge the limits of their ability to shape the progress and outcomes of innovation and change initiatives. Good planning and careful monitoring can certainly stack the odds in their favour, but in any one case, there will almost always be influences which are unanticipated and beyond the manager's direct control. This reinforces our comments at the end of the previous section regarding the advisability of not investing sole responsibility for innovation/change management in one individual. We would also repeat our assertion made in Chapter 6 that the characteristics of vigilance and flexibility are likely to be of great value to managers involved in innovation and change processes.

Applying psychological knowledge

A key aim of this book, indeed of the whole series, is to provide managers and others in organizations with a sound understanding of the psychological dimension of contemporary organizational life, in a way which makes it possible to improve their practice. We have not taken a prescriptive approach, telling them precisely what to do in particular circumstances. It is our belief that there are very few aspects of organizational change and innovation which are simple and predictable enough to be managed by following step-by-step guidelines. Rather, our objective has been to provide a degree of knowledge about the phenomena which will help equip managers with the analytical skills necessary to enhance their performance.

We will not reiterate here the implications for practice we highlighted at the end of previous chapters. We would, however, like to draw attention to one area where a heightened understanding of the psychology of innovation may bring real benefit to an organization – namely, the effective use of change agents. An understanding of innovation and change informed by research evidence should equip organizations to make good decisions about the kind of change agent they need in a particular case. This includes the personal qualities required by the agent and whether the change agent should be external or internal. Similarly, the availability of senior staff with a good grasp of the kind of material we have covered in this book should increase the likelihood of the organization finding a suitable person to act as an internal change agent (where such a role is deemed important). Whilst we would entirely agree that in some circumstances an external change agent is more appropriate, we feel that there are many occasions when organizations turn to an external source simply because they do not have the requisite skills available amongst their own members. At worst, this can result in an expensive failure that demotivates senior staff who feel their own knowledge and experience have been ignored by highly paid 'outsiders' with a hot line to top management.

The research agenda

Just as we see innovation and change as topics which will be of great and growing significance for organizations for the foreseeable future, so we feel confident that these areas will assume an increasingly dominant place in occupational psychological research. Organizations will need to find ways to keep their managers abreast of academic developments which have major practical implications for them. Thankfully, it seems that researchers are becoming more conscious of their responsibility to convey their expertise to practising managers, encouraged by the widening market for accessible but not oversimplified texts on innovation and change. We list below some of the topics and issues which we believe will be high on the innovation/change research agenda over the next couple of decades.

Evaluation of innovation and change interventions

We have seen that at all levels of analysis, a major shortcoming is the relative scarcity of evaluation studies of various types of intervention to facilitate innovation and change in organizations. As managers become better educated in occupational psychological principles (for instance, through the inclusion of psychology-based modules on management and business studies courses at undergraduate and postgraduate levels), they will demand evidence of rigorous evaluation of different intervention strategies before deciding which (if any) to use. For academics, this practitioner demand will encourage research to evaluate the effectiveness of interventions such as:

- creativity training programmes
- idea generation techniques
- team building for innovation
- various approaches to organization development.

Longitudinal research design

Focus on process

We have stressed the importance of understanding innovation and change as processes, not one-off events. This has implications for the kind of research needed in the field in future, since much of the existing literature is based on 'input–output' models of innovation that treat what happens between the two as a 'black box'. We would argue that there should be:

- more longitudinal studies, tracing innovations as they develop;
- greater attention given to temporal issues in innovation and change, at all levels of analysis;
- greater emphasis on understanding innovation and change processes in organizational contexts.

We would also hope to see a growth in non-positivist research, attempting to understand innovation and change processes in terms of the construction of meaning in the course of interaction. It is rather ironic that a research area centrally concerned with 'the new' has been tardy in engaging fully with wider debates about theory and methodology in applied psychology.

Cross-disciplinary research

The distinctive contribution of occupational psychology is perhaps of greatest worth when integrated with perspectives from other disciplines, both other branches of psychology and outside disciplines. Cross-disciplinary research is already common and in future will, we maintain, provide opportunities for important insights into many aspects of organizational innovation and change. These include:

- collaboration with cognitive, lifespan developmental and social psychology to examine the nature of individual creative performance at work;
- integration of social psychological and occupational psychological perspectives on group functioning and its impact on innovation (as discussed in Chapter 4);
- collaboration with economists to understand better the business environment within which innovation occurs;
- joint projects with organizational sociologists and social anthropologists to deepen our understanding of resistance to change in organizations.

A final word

We have sought in this book to provide a thorough overview of a broad range of psychological research into innovation and change in organizations. We hope that you will have discovered some specific topics which you will want to investigate in greater depth, perhaps starting with the further reading we have suggested. If there is one message which we would like you to take with you from this book it is that organizational change is a complex, unpredictable phenomenon, very rarely responsive to simple 'quick fix' strategies. It is all the more important because of this to gain an understanding of its underlying psychological principles. We would like to think that reading this book has left you better prepared to face the challenges of involvement in innovation and change in organizations.

References

Abernathy, W. J. and Utterback, J. M. (1978) 'Patterns of industrial innovation', *Technology Review*, June/July: 40–7.

Abrams, Dominic and Hogg, Michael A. (1990) 'The context of discourse: Let's not throw the baby out with the bathwater', *Philosophical Psychology* (3): 219–25.

Ajzen, I. (1988) *Attitudes, Personality and Behaviour*, Buckingham: Open University Press.

Allen, V. L. (1975) 'Social support for nonconformity', in L. Berkowitz (ed.) *Advances in Experimental Social Psychology Volume II*, New York: Academic Press.

Amabile, T. M. (1983) *The Social Psychology of Creativity*, New York: Springer-Verlag.

Amabile, Teresa M. (1987) 'The motivation to be creative', in Scott G. Isaksen (ed.), *Frontiers in Creativity: Beyond the Basics*. Buffalo, NY: Bearly Ltd.

American Society for Training and Development (1988) *Gaining the Competitive Edge*, Alexandria, VA: American Society for Training and Development.

Ancona, Deborah G. (1990) 'Outward bound: Strategies for team survival in the organization', *Academy of Management Journal*, 33: 334–65.

Ancona, Deborah G. and Chong, Chee-Leong (1999) 'Cycles and synchrony: The temporal role of context in team behavior', in Ruth Wageman (ed.), *Research on Managing Groups and Teams: Volume 2, Groups in Context*, Stamford, CT: JAI Press.

Andeasen, Nancy C. (1987) 'Creativity and mental illness: Prevalence rates in writers and their first-degree relatives', *American Journal of Psychiatry*, 144: 1288–92.

Anderson, N. R. and King, N. (1991) 'Managing innovation in organizations', *Leadership and Organizational Development Journal*, 12: 17–21.

Anderson, N. R. and King, N. (1993) 'Innovation in organizations', in C. L. Cooper and I. T. Robertson (eds) *International Review of Industrial and Organizational Psychology, Volume 8*, Chichester: Wiley.

Anderson, N. R. and Shackleton, V. (1993) *Successful Selection Interviewing*, Oxford: Blackwell.

Anderson, N. R. and St John Birch (2001) *Team Selection Inventory*, Windsor, Berks: ASE/NFER-Nelson.

Anderson, N. R. and West, M. A. (1994) *The Team Climate Inventory*, Windsor, Berks ASE.

Anderson, N. R. and West, M. A. (1999) *Team Climate Inventory*, second edition, Windsor, Berks: ASE/NFER-Nelson.

Asch, S. E. (1956) 'Studies of independence and conformity: A minority of one against a unanimous majority', *Psychological Monographs: General and Applied*, 70: 1–70 (whole No. 416).

Axtell, Carolyn M., Holman, D. J., Unsworth, Kerrie L., Wall, Toby D., Waterson, Patrick E. and Harrington, E. (2000) 'Shopfloor innovation: Facilitating the suggestion and implementation of ideas', *Journal of Occupational and Organizational Psychology*, 73: 265–85.

Aydin, C. E. and Rice, R. E. (1991) 'Social worlds, individual differences and implementation: Predicting attitudes toward a medical information system', *Information and Management*, 20: 119–36.

Baer, John (1994) 'Why you shouldn't trust creativity tests', *Educational Leadership*, 51: 80–3.

Barras, R. (1986) 'Towards a theory of innovation in services', *Research Policy*, 15: 161–73.

Barron, R. (1955) 'The disposition toward originality', *Journal of Abnormal and Social Psychology*, 51: 478–85.

Barron, F. and Harrington, D. W. (1981) 'Creativity, intelligence and personality', *Annual Review of Psychology*, 32: 439–76.

Bartlett, F. C. (1932) *Remembering*, Cambridge: Cambridge University Press.

Bartram, D., Anderson, N. R., Kellet, D., Lindley, P. and Robertson, I. T. (1995) *Review of Level B Personality Inventories*, Leicester: BPS Books.

Basadur, M., Graen, G. B. and Green, G. (1982) 'Training in creative problem solving: Effects on ideation and problem finding and solving in an industrial research organization', *Organizational Behaviour and Human Performance*, 30: 41–70.

Basadur, M., Graen, G. B. and Scandura, T. A. (1986) 'Training effects on attitudes toward divergent thinking amongst manufacturing engineers', *Journal of Applied Psychology*, 71: 612–17.

Basadur, Min (1995) *The Power of Innovation*, London: Pitman Professional Publishing.

Basadur, Min (1997) 'Organizational development interventions for enhancing creativity in the workplace', *Journal of Creative Behavior*, 31: 59–72.

Basadur, Min, Runco, Mark A. and Vega, Luis. A. (2000) 'Understanding how creative thinking skills, attitudes and behaviors work together: A causal process model', *Journal of Creative Behavior*, 34(2): 77–100.

Bass, Bernard M. (1985) *Leadership and Performance Beyond Expectations*, New York: Free Press.

Belbin (1981) *Management Teams: Why they Succeed or Fail*, London: Heinemann.

Belbin, R. Meredith (1993) *Team Roles at Work*, Oxford: Butterworth-Heinemann.

Berry, L. M. and Houston, J. P. (1993) *Psychology at Work: An Introduction to Industrial and Organizational Psychology*, Madison, WI: Brown and Benchmark.

Bouchard, T. J. (1972), 'A comparison of two group brainstorming procedures', *Journal of Applied Psychology*, 56: 418–21.

Bouwen, R. and Fry, R. (1991) 'Organizational innovation and learning. Four patterns of dialogue between the dominant logic and the new logic', *International Studies in Management and Organization*, 21(4): 37–51.

Bouwen, R., Steyaert, C. and De Visch, J. (1992) 'Organizational innovation', in D. M. Hosking and N. R. Anderson (eds) *Organizational Change and Innovation: Psychological Perspectives and Practices in Europe*, London: Routledge.

Bouwen, René and Fry, Ron (1996) 'Facilitating group development: Interventions for a relational and contextual construction', in Michael A. West (ed.), *Handbook of Work Group Psychology*, Chichester: Wiley.

Bouwen, René, De Visch, Jan and Steyaert, Chris (1992) 'Innovation projects in organizations: Complementing the dominant logic by organizational learning', in Dian Marie Hosking and Neil Anderson (eds), *Organizational Change and Innovation: Psychological Perspectives and Practices in Europe*, London: Routledge.

Brahm, Carolyn and Kleiner, Brian H. (1996) 'Advantages and disadvantages of group decision-making approaches', *Team Performance Management*, 2(1): 30–5.

Braverman, M. (1974) *Labor and Monopoly Capital: The Degradation of Work in the Twentieth Century*, New York: Monthly Review Press.

Brewer, Marilynn B. (1996) 'Managing diversity: The role of social identities', in Susan E. Jackson and Marian N. Ruderman (eds), *Diversity in Work Teams: Research Paradigms for a Changing Workplace*, Washington DC: American Psychological Association.

Brilharte, J. K. and Jochem, L. M. (1964) 'Effects of different patterns on outcomes of problem-solving discussions', *Journal of Applied Psychology*, 48, 175–9.

Brown, L. A. (1981) *Innovation Diffusion: A New Perspective*, London: Methuen.

Brown, Vincent and Paulus, Paul B. (1996) 'A simple dynamic model of social factors in group brainstorming', *Small Group Research*, 27(1): 91–114.

Bruner, J. (1962) 'The conditions of creativity', in H. Gruber *et al.* (eds) *Contemporary Approaches to Creative Thinking*, New York: Atherton Press.

Burgoyne, J. (1994) 'Stakeholder analysis', in C. Cassell and G. Symon (eds) *Qualitative Methods in Organizational Research*, London: Sage.

Burman, Erica and Parker, Ian (1993) *Discourse Analytic Research*, London: Routledge.

Burns, T. and Stalker, G. M. (1961) *The Management of Innovation*, London: Tavistock.

Burr, Viv (1995) *An Introduction to Social Constructionism*, London: Routledge.

Butt, Trevor (2001) 'Social action and personal constructs', *Theory and Psychology*, 11(1): 75–95.

Butt, Trevor, Burr, Viv, and Epting, Franz (1997) 'Core construing: discovery or invention?', in Greg J. Neimeyer and Robert A. Neimeyer (eds), *Advances in Personal Construct Theory, vol. 4*, New York: Springer.

Carletta, Jean, Garrod, Simon, and Fraser-Krauss, Heidi (1998) 'Placement of authority and communication patterns in workplace groups: The consequences for innovation', *Small Group Research*, 29(5): 531–59.

Carrero, Virginia, Peiró, José and Salanova, Marisa (2000) 'Studying radical organizational innovation through grounded theory', *European Journal of Work and Organizational Psychology*, 9(4): 489–514.

Cascio, W. F. (1989) 'Using utility analysis to assess training outcomes', in Goldstein and Associates (eds) *Training and Development in Organisations*, London: Jossey-Bass.

Chauncey, H. and Hilton, T. L. (1983) 'Aptitude tests for the highly gifted', in R. S. Albert (ed.) *Genius and Eminence: The social psychology of creativity and exceptional achievement*, Elmsford, NY: Pergamon Press.

Child, J. (1977) *Organisations: A Guide to Problems and Practice*, 1st edition, London: Harper & Row.

Child, J. (1984) *Organisations: A Guide to Problems and Practice*, 2nd edition, London: Harper & Row.

Chin, R. and Benne, K. D. (1976) 'General strategies for effecting changes in human systems', in W. G. Bennis *et al.* (eds) *The Planning of Change*, 3rd edition, Holt-Saunders.

Clapham, Maria M. (1997) 'Ideational skills training: A key element in creativity training programs', *Creativity Research Journal*, 10(1): 33–44.

Coch, L. and French, J. R. P. Jr (1948) 'Overcoming resistance to change', *Human Relations*, 2, 512–32.

Cohen, Gillian (1996) *Memory in the Real World*, 2nd edition, Hove: Psychology Press.

Cook, John, and Wall, Toby D. (1980) 'New work attitude measures of trust, organizational commitment and personal need non-fulfilment'. *Journal of Occupational Psychology*, 53(1): 39–52.

Cooper, Juett R. (1998) 'A multidimensional approach to the adoption of innovation', *Management Decision*, 36(8): 493–502.

Cooper, William H., Gallupe, Brent R., Pollard, Sandra and Cadsby, Jana (1998) 'Some liberating effects of anonymous electronic brainstorming', *Small Group Research*, 29(2): 147–78.

Cox, C. (1926) *Genetic Studies of Genius, Volume 2: The early mental traits of 300 geniuses*, Stanford, CA: Stanford University Press.

Cramond, Bonnie, Matthews-Morgan, Juanita, Torrance, E. Paul and Zuo, Li (1999) 'Why should the Torrance tests of creative thinking be used to access creativity?', *Korean Journal of Thinking and Problem-Solving*, 9(2): 77–101.

Crossley, Michele L. (2000) *Introducing Narrative Psychology: Self, Trauma and the Construction of Meaning*, Buckingham: Open University Press.

Csikszentmihalyi, M. (1988) 'Society, culture and person: A systems view of creativity', in R. Sternberg (ed.) *The Nature of Creativity*, Cambridge: Cambridge University Press.

Csikszentmihalyi, Mihaly (1996) *Creativity: Flow and the Psychology of Discovery and Invention*, New York: HarperCollins.

Csikszentmihalyi, Mihaly, Getzels, Jacob W. and Kahn, S. P. (1984) *Talent and Achievement*, Report to the Spencer and MacArthur Foundations, Chicago, IL.

Cummings, T. G. and Huse, E. F. (1989) *Organizational Development and Change*, 4th edition, New York: West.

Cummings, T. G. and Worley, C. G. (1993) *Organizational Development and Change*, 5th edition, Minneapolis/St Paul: West.

Curral, L. A., Forrester, R. H., Dawson, J. F. and West, M. A. (2001) 'It's what you do *and* the way that you do it: Team task, team size and innovation-related group processes', *European Journal of Work and Organizational Psychology*, 10(2): 187–204.

Daft, R. L. (1978) 'A dual-core model of organizational innovation', *Academy of Management Journal*, 21: 193–210.

Damanpour, F. (1990) 'Innovation effectiveness, adoption and organizational performance', in M. A. West and J. L. Farr (eds) *Innovation and Creativity at Work: Psychological and Organizational Strategies*, Chichester: Wiley.

Damanpour, F. and Evan, W. M. (1984) 'Organizational innovation and performance: The problem of "Organizational lag"', *Administrative Science Quarterly*, 29: 392–409.

Damanpour, Fariborz and Gopalakrishnan, Shanthi (2001) 'The dynamics of the adoption of product and process innovation in organizations', *Journal of Management Studies*, 38(1): 45–65.

de Bono, E. (1971) *Lateral Thinking for Management*, New York: McGraw-Hill.

Deming, W. E. (1986) *Out of the Crisis*, Cambridge, MA: MIT Center for Advanced Engineering Study.

Diehl, M. (1992) 'Production loss in brainstorming groups: The effects of group composition on fluency and flexibility of ideas', paper presented at the Joint Meeting of the European Association of Experimental Social Psychology and the Society for Experimental Social Psychology, Leuven, Belgium.

Diehl, M. and Stroebe, W. (1987) 'Productivity loss in idea-generating groups: Tracking down the blocking effect', *Journal of Personality and Social Psychology*, 53: 497–509.

Dougherty, Deborah and Hardy, Cynthia (1996) 'Sustained product innovation in large, mature organizations: Overcoming innovation-to-organization problems', *Academy of Management Journal*, 39(5): 1120–53.

DuBrin, A. J. (1974) *Fundamentals of Organizational Behavior: An Applied Perspective*, New York: Pergamon Press.

Dunphy, D. C. and Stace, D. A. (1988) 'Transformational and coercive strategies for planned organizational change: Beyond the OD model', *Organizational Studies*, 9: 317–34.

Eiduson, B. T. (1974) '10-year longitudinal Rorschachs on research scientists', *Journal of Personality Assessment*, 38: 405–10.

Ekvall, Göran (1996) 'Organizational climate for creativity and innovation', *European Journal of Work and Organizational Psychology*, 5(1): 105–23.

Ernecq, J. M. (1991) 'Planned and unplanned organizational change: Consequences and implications', in D. M. Hosking and N. R. Anderson (eds) *Organizational Change and Innovation: Psychological Perspectives and Practices in Europe*, London: Routledge.

Ettlie, J. E. (1995) 'Product-process development integration in manufacturing', *Management Science*, 41: 1224–37.

Evans, J. R. (1991) *Creative Thinking in the Decision and Management Sciences*, Cincinnati, OH: South-Western.

Fadiman, James and Frager, Robert (1994) *Personality and Personal Growth, 3rd edition*, New York: HarperCollins.

Farris, G. F. (1973) 'The technical supervisor: Beyond the Peter principle', *Technical Review*, 75, April.

Fay, D. and Frese, M. (2001) 'The concept of personal initiative: An overview of validity studies', *Human Performance*, 14(1): 97–124.

Fay, D., Sonnentag, S. and and Frese, M. (1998) 'Stressors, innovation, and personal initiative: Are stressors always detrimental?', in C. L. Cooper (ed.), *Theories of Organizational Stress*, Blackwell: Oxford.

Feldman, S. P. (1989) 'The broken wheel: The inseparability of autonomy and control in innovation within the organisation', *Journal of Management Studies*, 26: 83–102.

Ferracuti, Stefano, Cannoni, Eleonora, Burla, Franco and Lazzari, Renato (2000) 'Correlations for the Rorschach with the Torrance tests of creative thinking', *Perceptual and Motor Skills*, 89(3, pt 1): 863–70.

Fiedler, F. and House, R. J. (1988) 'Leadership theory and research', in C. L. Cooper and I. T. Robertson (eds) *International Review of Industrial and Organizational Psychology, Volume 3*, Chichester: Wiley.

Finke, Ronald A. (1996) 'Imagery, creativity and emergent structure', *Consciousness and Cognition*, 5: 381–93.

Finke, Ronald A., Ward, T. M., and Smith, S. M. (1992) *Creative Cognition: Theory, Research and Applications*, Cambridge MA: MIT Press.

Fontana, David (1997) 'The challenge of creativity', *Transpersonal Psychology Review*, 1(4): 35–7.

Ford, Cameron M. (1995) 'Striking inspirational sparks and fanning creative flames: a multi-domain model of creative action taking', in Cameron M. Ford and Dennis A. Gioia (eds), *Creative Action in Organizations: Ivory Tower Visions and Real World Voices*, Thousand Oaks CA: Sage.

Frager, Robert (1989) 'Transpersonal psychology: Promise and prospects', in R. Valle and S. Halling (eds), *Existential-phenomenological Perspectives in Psychology*, New York: Plenum.

Freeman, Mark (1993) *Finding the Muse: A Sociopsychological Inquiry into the Conditions of Artistic Creativity*, Cambridge: Cambridge University Press.

Frese, M. (2001) 'Dynamic self-reliance: An important concept for work in the twenty-first century', in C. L. Cooper and S. E. Jackson (eds), *Creating Tomorrow's Organizations: A handbook for future research in organizational behaviour*, Chichester: Wiley.

Frese, M., Fay, D., Hilburger, T., Leng, K. and Tag, A. (1997) 'The concept of personal initiative: Operationalization, reliability and validity in two Germany samples', *Journal of Occupational and Organizational Psychology*, 70: 139–61.

Frese, M., Kring, W., Soose, A. and Zempel, J. (1996) 'PI at work: Differences between East and West Germany', *Academy of Management Journal*, 39: 37–63.

Freud, Sigmund (1963) 'The paths to the formation of symptoms', Lecture XXIII in *Introductory Lectures on Psycho-Analysis*, London: The Hogarth Press and The Institute of Psycho-Analysis.

Frost, Peter J. and Egri, Carolyn P. (1990a) 'Influence of political action on innovation: Part 1', *Leadership and Organization Development Journal*, 11(1): 17–25.

Frost, Peter J. and Egri, Carolyn P. (1990b) 'Influence of political action on innovation: Part 2', *Leadership and Organization Development Journal*, 11(2): 4–12.

Gallupe, R. B., Bastianutti, L. M. and Cooper, W. H. (1991) 'Unblocking brainstorms', *Journal of Applied Psychology*, 76: 137–42.

Gallupe, R. Brent, DeSanctis, Gerardine and Dickson, Gary W. (1988) 'Computer-based support for group problem-finding: An experimental investigation', *MIS Quarterly*, 12(2): 277–96.

Galton, F. (1869) *Hereditary Genius*, London: Macmillan, London and Appleton.

Garcha, M. (1969) '"Synectics" analogies spark creative ideas', *Employee Relations Bulletin*, Report no. 1140, Waterford: National Foreman's Institute.

Gedo, Mary M. (1980) *Picasso: Art as Autobiography*, Chicago: University of Chicago Press.

Gendrop, Sylvia C. (1996) 'Effect of an Intervention in Synectics on the Creative Thinking of Nurses', *Creativity Research Journal*, 9(1): 11–19.

Gergen, K. J. (1978) 'Experimentation in social psychology: A reappraisal', *European Journal of Social Psychology*, 8: 507–27.

Gersick, C. J. G. (1989) 'Marking time: Predictable transitions in work groups', *Academy of Management Journal*, 32: 274–309.

Gersick, Connie J. C. (1994) 'Pacing strategic change: The case of a new venture', *Academy of Management Journal*, 37: 9–45.

Getzels, J. W. and Csikszentmihalyi, M. (1976) *The Creative Vision: A Longitudinal Study of Problem-Finding in Art*, New York: Wiley-Interscience.

Ghiselin, B. (1963) 'Ultimate criteria for two levels of creativity', in C. W. Taylor and F. Barron (eds) *Scientific Creativity: its recognition and development*, New York: Wiley.

Ghiselin, B., Rompel, R. and Taylor, C. W. (1964) 'A creative process checklist: Its development and validation', in C. W. Taylor, *Widening Horizons in Creativity*, New York: Wiley.

Glendon, I. (1992) 'Radical change within a British university', in D. M. Hosking and N. R. Anderson (eds) *Organizational Change and Innovation: Psychological Perspectives and Practices in Europe*, London: Routledge.

Glover, J. A. (1979) 'Levels of questions asked in interview and reading sessions by creative and relatively non-creative college students', *Journal of Genetic Psychology*, 135: 103–8.

Golembiewski, R. T., Billingsley, K. and Yeager, S. (1976) 'Measuring change and persistence in human affairs: Types of generated designs', *Journal of Applied Behavioural Science*, 12: 133–57.

Gonzalez, Maria A., Campos, Alfredo and Pérez, Maria José (1997) 'Mental imagery and creative thinking', *Journal of Psychology*, 131(4): 357–64.

Gopal, Abhijit and Prasad, Pushkala (2000) 'Understanding GDSS in symbolic context: Shifting the focus from technology to interaction', *MIS Quarterly*, 24(3): 509–46.

Gordon, W. J. J. (1961) *Synectics*, New York: Collier.

Gough, H. G. (1979) 'A creative personality scale for the adjective check list', *Journal of Personality and Social Psychology*, 37: 1398–405.

Gowan, John C. (1978) 'The facilitation of creativity through meditational procedures', *Journal of Creative Behavior*, 12(3): 156–60.

Gray, J. L. and Starke, F. A. (1984) *Managing Change in Organizational Behaviour: Concepts and Applications*, 3rd edition, New York: Bell & Howell.

Gruber, H. E. and Davis, S. N. (1988) 'Inching our way up Mount Olympus: The evolving systems approach to creativity', in R. Sternberg (ed.) *The Nature of Creativity*, Cambridge: Cambridge University Press.

Guastello, Stephen J. (1995) 'Facilitative style, individual innovation, and emergent leadership in problem solving groups', *Journal of Creative Behavior*, 29(4): 225–39.

Guilford, J. P. (1956) 'The structure of intellect', *Psychological Bulletin*, 53: 267–93.

Guilford, J. P. (1959) 'Traits of creativity', in H. H. Anderson (ed.) *Creativity and its Cultivation*, New York: Harper.

Guzzo, R. A. and Dickson, M. W. (1996) 'Teams in organizations: Recent research on performance and effectiveness', *Annual Review of Psychology*, 47: 307–38.

Hage, J. and Dewar, R. (1973) 'Elite values versus organizational structure in predicting innovation', *Administrative Science Quarterly*, 18: 279–90.

Hampden-Turner, Charles (1999) 'Control, chaos, control: a cybernetic view of creativity', in Ronald E. Purser and Alfonso Montuori (eds), *Social Creativity: Volume II*, Cresskill NJ: Hampton Press.

Handy, C. (1985) *Understanding Organizations*, Harmondsworth: Penguin.

Handy, Charles (1996) 'Rethinking organizations', in T. Clark (ed.) *Advancement in Organizational Behaviour: Essays in Honour of Derek S. Pugh*, Aldershot: Ashgate.

Harmon, L. R. (1955) 'Social and technological determiners of creativity', in C. W. Taylor (ed.) *The 1955 University of Utah research conference on the identification of creative talent*, Salt Lake City: University of Utah Press.

Harrington, D. M. (1975) 'Effects of explicit instructions to "be creative" on the psychological meaning of divergent thinking test scores', *Journal of Personality*, 43: 434–54.

Hartley, Jean F. (1996) 'Intergroup relations in organizations', in Michael A. West (ed.), *Handbook of Work Group Psychology*, Chichester: Wiley.

Hill, Karl G. and Amabile, Teresa M. (1993) 'A social psychological perspective on creativity: Intrinsic motivation and creativity in the classroom and workplace', in Scott G. Isaksen, Mary C. Murdock, Roger L. Firestein and Donald J. Treffinger (eds), *Understanding and Recognizing Creativity: The Emergence of a Discipline* Norwood NJ: Ablex.

Hocevar, D. and Bachelor, P. (1989) 'A taxonomy and critique of measurements used in the study of creativity', in J. A. Glover *et al.* (eds) *Handbook of Creativity*, New York: Plenum Press.

Hogg, Michael A. and Abrams, Dominic (1988) *Social Identifications: A Social Psychology of Intergroup Relations and Group Processes*, London: Routledge.

Hollway, W. (1991) *Work Psychology and Organizational Behaviour: Managing the Individual at Work*, London: Sage.

Hosking, D. M. and Anderson, N. R. (eds) (1992) *Organizational Change and Innovation: Psychological Perspectives and Practices in Europe*, London: Routledge.

Howard, N. (1987) 'Business probe: The creative spark', in A. D. Timpe (ed.) *Creativity: The Art and Science of Business Management*, New York: KEND Publishing.

Howell, Jane M. and Higgins, Christopher A. (1990) 'Champions of technological innovation', *Administrative Science Quarterly*, 35(2): 317–41.

Hudson, L. (1966) *Contrary Imaginations*, London: Methuen.

Huse, E. (1980) *Organizational Development and Change*, Minneapolis/St Paul: West.

Iacocca, L. (1984) *An Autobiography*, New York: Bantam.

Isaksen, Scott G. and Dorval, K. Brian (1993) 'Toward an improved understanding of creativity within people: the level-style distinction', in Scott G. Isaksen, Mary C. Murdock, Roger L. Firestein and Donald J. Treffinger (eds), *Understanding and Recognizing Creativity: The Emergence of a Discipline*, Norwood NJ: Ablex.

Isaksen, Scott G., Murdock, Mary C., Firestein, Roger L. and Treffinger, Donald J. (eds) (1993) *Understanding and Recognizing Creativity: The Emergence of a Discipline*, Norwood NJ: Ablex.

Jamison, Kay R. (1989) 'Mood disorders and patterns of creativity in British writers and artists', *Psychiatry*, 52: 125–34.

Jamison, Kay R. (1993) *Touched with Fire: Manic Depressive Illness and the Artistic Temperament*, New York: The Free Press.

Janis, I. L. (1972) *Victims of Groupthink: A Psychological Study of Foreign Policy Decisions and Fiascos*, Boston: Houghton Mifflin.

Janis, I. L. (1982) *Groupthink*, 2nd edition, Boston: Houghton Mifflin.

Jarvenpaa, Sirkka L., Rao, V. Srinivasan and Huber, George P. (1988) 'Computer support for meetings of groups working on unstructured problems: A field experiment', *MIS Quarterly*, 12(4): 645–66.

Jessup, Leonard M., Connolly, Terry and Galegher, Jolene (1990) 'The effects of anonymity on GDSS group process with an idea generating task', *MIS Quarterly*, 14(3): 313–20.

Johnson-Laird, P. N. (1988) 'Freedom and constraint in creativity', in R. Sternberg (ed.) *The Nature of Creativity*, Cambridge: Cambridge University Press.

Jung, Carl G. (1966) *The Spirit in Man, Art and Literature*, London: Routledge and Kegan Paul.

Kabanoff, B. and Rossiter, J. (1994) 'Recent developments in applied creativity', in C. L. Cooper and I. T. Robertson (eds) *International Review of Industrial and Organizational Psychology, Volume 9*, Chichester: Wiley.

Kanter, R. M. (1983) *The Change Masters*, New York: Simon & Schuster.

Katz, R. (1982) 'The effects of group longevity on project communication and performance', *Administrative Science Quarterly*, 27: 81–104.

Katz, D. and Kahn, R. (1966) *The Social Psychology of Organizations*, New York: Wiley.

Katz, J. H. and Marshak, R. (1996) 'Reinventing organization development theory and practice', *Organizational Development Journal*, 14(1), Spring.

Kay, Gail (1995) 'Effective meetings through electronic brainstorming', *Journal of Management Development*, 14(6): 4–25.

Kelly, George A. (1955) *The Psychology of Personal Constructs* (2 vols), New York: W. W. Norton & Co.

Kelly, J. R., Futoran, G. C., and McGrath, J. E. (1990) 'Capacity and capability: Seven studies of entrainment of task performance rates', *Small Group Research*, 21(3): 283–314.

Khasky, Amy D. and Smith, Jonathan C. (1999) 'Stress, relaxation states and creativity', *Perceptual and Motor Skills*, 88: 409–16.

Kilbourne, Lynda M. and Woodman, Richard W. (1999) 'Barriers to organizational creativity', in Ronald E. Purser and Alfonso Montuori (eds), *Social Creativity, Volume II*, Cresskill NJ: Hampton Press.

Kimberly, J. R. (1981) 'Managerial innovation', in P. C. Nystrom and W. H. Starbuck (eds) *Handbook of Organizational Design*, Oxford: Oxford University Press.

Kimberly, J. R. and Evanisko, M. J. (1981) 'Organizational innovation: The influence of individual, organizational and contextual factors on hospital adoption of technological and administrative innovations', *Academy of Management Journal*, 24: 689–713.

Kimberly, J. R., Miles, R. H. and associates (1980) *The Organizational Life-Cycle*, San Francisco: Jossey-Bass.

King, N. (1989) 'Innovation in elderly care organizations: Process and attitudes', unpublished PhD thesis, University of Sheffield.

King, N. (1990) 'Innovation at work: The research literature', in M. A. West and J. L. Farr (eds) *Innovation and Creativity at Work: Psychological and Organizational Strategies*, Chichester: Wiley.

King, N. (1992) 'Modelling the innovation process: An empirical comparison of approaches', *Journal of Occupational and Organizational Psychology*, 65: 89–100.

King, N. (2000) 'Making ourselves heard: The challenges facing advocates of qualitative research in work and organisational psychology', *European Journal of Work and Organizational Psychology*, 9(4): 589–96.

King, N. and Anderson, N. R. (1990) 'Innovation in working groups', in M. A. West and J. L. Farr (eds) *Innovation and Creativity at Work: Psychological and Organizational Strategies*, Chichester: Wiley.

King, N. and Anderson, N. R. (1995) *Innovation and Change in Organizations*, 1st edition, London: Routledge.

King, N., Anderson, N. R. and West, M. A. (1991) 'Organizational innovation in the UK: A case study of perceptions and processes', *Work and Stress*, 5: 331–9.

King, N. and West, M. A. (1987) 'Experiences of innovation at work', *Journal of Managerial Psychology*, 2: 6–10.

Kirton, M. J. (1976) 'Adaptors and innovators: A description and measure', *Journal of Applied Psychology*, 61: 622–9.

Kirton, M. J. (1989) *Adaptors and Innovators: Styles of Creativity and Problem-Solving*, London; Routledge.

Klein, Katherine J. and Sorra, Joann Speer (1996) 'The challenge of innovation Implementation', *Academy of Management Review*, 21(4): 1055–80.

Kotter, J. P. and Schlesinger, L. A. (1979) 'Choosing strategies for change', *Harvard Business Review*, March–April, 106–14.

Kramer, Michael W., Kuo, Chao Lan and Dailey, John C. (1997) 'The impact of brainstorming techniques on subsequent group processes: Beyond generating ideas', *Small Group Research*, 28(2): 218–42.

Lapp, William M., Collins, Lorraine and Izzo, Charles V. (1994) 'On the enhancement of creativity by alcohol: Pharmacology or expectation?' *American Journal of Psychology*, 107(2): 173–206.

Lawrence, P. R. (1969) 'How to deal with resistance to change', *Harvard Business Review*, January–February, 115–22.

Lawrence, P. R. and Lorsch, J. R. (1967) *Organization and Environment*, Cambridge MA: Harvard University Press.

Leavitt, H. G., Dill, W. R. and Eyring, H. B. (1973) *The Organizational World: A Systematic View of Managers and Management*, New York: Harcourt, Brace, Jovanovich.

Lehman, H. (1953) *Age and Achievement*, Princeton, NJ: Princeton University Press.

Lehman, H. (1965) 'The production of master's work prior to age 30', *Gerontologist*, 5: 24–30.

Levinthal, D. (1997) 'Three facets of organizational learning: Wisdom, inertia, and discovery', in R. Garud, P. R. Naygar and Z. B. Shapira (eds), *Technical Innovation: Oversights and Foresights*, Cambridge: Cambridge University Press.

Lewin, K. (1951) *Field Theory in Social Science*, New York: Harper & Row.

Lewis, Laurie K. and Seibold, David R. (1993) 'Innovation modification during intraorganizational adoption', *Academy of Management Review*, 18(2): 322–54.

Loftus, E. F. (1979) *Eyewitness Testimony*, Cambridge, MA: Harvard University Press.

Lovelace, R. F. (1986) 'Stimulating creativity through managerial intervention', *R&D Management*: 16: 161–74.

Lubart, Todd I. and Getz, Isaac (1997) 'Emotion, metaphor and the creative process', *Creativity Research Journal*, 10(4): 285–301.

Mackie, D. (1987) 'Systematic and nonsystematic processing of majority and minority persuasive communications', *Journal of Personality and Social Psychology*, 53: 41–52.

MacKinnon, D. W. (1962) 'The personality correlates of creativity: A study of American architects', in *Proceedings of the Fourteenth Congress on Applied Psychology*, Volume 2, Copenhagen: Munksgaard.

Mancuso, James (1996) 'Constructionism, personal construct psychology and narrative psychology', *Theory and Psychology*, 6: 47–70.

Mann, F. (1964) 'Studying and creating change', in W. G. Bennis *et al.* (eds) *The Planning of Change*, New York: Holt, Rinehart & Winston.

Manz, C. C., Bastien, D. T., Hostager, T. J. and Shapiro, G. L. (1989) 'Leadership and innovation: A longitudinal process view', in A. Van de Ven *et al.* (eds) *Research on the Management of Innovation: The Minnesota Studies*, New York: Harper & Row.

Margerison, C. and McCann, D. (1990) *Team Management*, London: Mercury.

Maslow, Abraham (1971) *The Farther Reaches of Human Nature*, New York: Viking Press.

Mayer, R. J. (1990) 'Personal empowerment in organizational development', in F. Massarik (ed.) *Advances in Organization Development*, vol. 1, Norwood, NJ: Ablex Publishing Corporation.

McGrath, J. E. (1985) 'Groups and the innovation process', in R. L. Merritt and A. J. Merritt (eds) *Innovation in the Public Sector*, Beverly Hills, CA: Sage.

McGrath, J. E. (1991) 'Time, interaction and performance (TIP): A theory of groups', *Small Group Research*, 22(2): 147–74.

McGrath, J. E. and O'Connor, Kathleen M. (1996) 'Temporal issues in work groups', in Michael A. West (ed.), *Handbook of Work Group Psychology*, Chichester: Wiley.

McLelland, D. C., Atkinson, J. W., Clark, R. A. and Lowell, E. I. (1953) *The Achievement Motive*, New York: Appleton-Century-Crofts.

McLeod, Poppy L., Lobel, Sharon A. and Cox, Taylor H. (1996) 'Ethnic diversity and creativity in small groups', *Small Group Research*, 27(2): 248–64.

Meadows, I. S. G. (1980) 'Organic structure and innovation in small work groups', *Human Relations*, 33: 369–82.

Meston, Carolyn M. and King, Nigel (1996) 'Making sense of "resistance": Responses to organizational change in a private nursing home for the elderly', *European Journal of Work and Organizational Psychology*, 5(1): 91–102.

Meyer, A. D. (1982) 'Adapting to environmental jolts', *Administrative Science Quarterly*, 27: 515–82.

Michael, W. B. and Colson, K. R. (1979) 'The development and validation of a life experience inventory for the identification of creative electrical engineers', *Educational and Psychological Measurement*, 39: 463–70.

Miles, R. E. and Snow, C. C. (1978) *Organizational Strategy, Structure and Process*, New York: McGraw-Hill.

Miller, D. (1986) 'Configurations of strategy and structure: Towards a synthesis', *Strategic Management Journal*, 7: 233–49.

Miller, D. and Friesen, P. H. (1978) 'Archetypes of strategy formulation', *Management Science*, 24: 921–33.

Mohr, L. B. (1969) 'Determinants of innovation in organizations', *American Political Science Review*, 63: 111–26.

Monroe, Russell R. (1991) 'Creative brainstorms: A story of madness and genius', *Journal of the American Academy of Psychoanalysis*, 19(3): 462–70.

Montuori, Alfonso and Purser, Ronald E. (1995) 'Deconstructing the lone genius myth: Toward a contextual view of creativity', *Journal of Humanistic Psychology*, 35(3): 69–112.

Montuori, Alfonso and Purser, Ronald E. (1999) *Social Creativity, Volume I*, Cresskill NJ: Hampton Press.

Morgan, G. (1986) *Images of Organization*, Beverly Hills, CA: Sage.

Morrison, Ann M. (1992) *The New Leaders: Guidelines on Leadership Diversity in America*, San Fransisco: Jossey-Bass.

Moscovici, S. (1976) *Social Influence and Social Change*, London: Academic Press.

Muchinsky, P. M. (1993) *Psychology Applied to Work*, 4th edition, Pacific Grove, CA: Brooks/Cole.

Mumford, M. D. and Gustafson, S. B. (1988) 'Creativity syndrome: Integration, application and innovation', *Psychological Bulletin*, 103: 27–43.

Myers, I. B. and McCaully, M. H. (1985) *A Guide to the Development and Use of the Myers-Briggs Type Indicator*, Palo Alto, CA: Consulting Psychologists Press.

Neisser, Ulric (1982) *Memory Observed: Remembering in Natural Contexts*, San Francisco: Freeman.

Nelkin, D. (1973) *Methodone Maintenance: A Technological Fix*, New York: Braziller.

Nemeth, C. J. and Wachtler, J. (1983) 'Creative problem-solving as a result of majority vs minority influence', *European Journal of Social Psychology*, 13: 45–55.

Nicholls, J. G. (1972) 'Creativity in the person who will never produce anything original and useful: The concept of creativity as a normally distributed trait', *American Psychologist*, 27: 717–27.

Nicholson, N. (1990) 'Organizational innovation in context: culture, interpretation and application', in M. A. West and J. L. Farr (eds) *Innovation and Creativity at Work: Psychological and Organizational Strategies*, Chichester: Wiley.

Nicholson, N. and West, M. A. (1988) *Managerial Job Change: Men and Women in Transition*, Cambridge: Cambridge University Press.

Nkomo, Stella (1996) 'Identities and the complexity of diversity', in Susan E. Jackson and Marian N. Ruderman (eds), *Diversity in Work Teams: Research Paradigms for a Changing Workplace*, Washington DC: American Psychological Association.

Normann, R. (1971) 'Organizational innovativeness: Product variation and reorientation', *Administrative Science Quarterly*, 16: 203–15.

Nystrom, H. (1990) 'Organizational innovation', in M. A. West and J. L. Farr (eds) *Innovation and Creativity at Work: Psychological and Organizational Strategies*, Chichester: Wiley.

O'Reilly III, Charles A., Williams, Katherine Y. and Barsade, Sigal (1998) 'Group demography and innovation: Does diversity help?' in Deborah H. Gruenfeld (ed.), *Research on Managing Groups and Teams: Volume 1, Composition*, Stamford, Connecticut: JAI Press.

Offner, Anne K., Kramer, Thomas J., and Winter, Joel P. (1996) 'The effects of facilitation, recording, and pauses on group brainstorming', *Small Group Research*, 27(2): 283–98.

Oliver, N. and Wilkinson, B. (1992) *The Japanization of British Industry*, 2nd edition, Oxford: Blackwell.

Osborn, A. (1953) *Applied Imagination*, New York: Scribner.

Oxley, Nicole L., Dzindolet, Mary T., and Paulus, Paul B. (1997) 'The effects of facilitators on the performance of brainstorming groups', *Journal of Social Behavior and Personality*, 11(4): 633–46.

Parkhurst, Howard B. (1999) 'Confusion, lack of consensus, and the definition of creativity as a construct', *Journal of Creative Behavior*, 33(1): 1–21.

Parnes, S. J. (1967) *Creative Behavior Guidebook*, New York: Scribner.

Parnes, S. J. (1967) *Creative Behavior Workbook*, New York: Scribner.

Parnes, S. J., Noller, R. B. and Biondi, A. M. (eds) (1977) *Guide to Creative Action*, New York: Scribner.

Patterson, F. (1999) *Innovation Potential Indicator*, Oxford: Oxford Psychologist's Press.

Payne, R. L. (1987) 'Individual differences and performance amongst R&D personnel: Some implications for management development', *R&D Management*, 17: 153–61.

Pelz, D. C. (1983) 'Quantitative case histories of urban innovations: Are there innovation stages?', *IEEE Transactions on Engineering Management*, 30: 60–7.

Peters, T. J. and Waterman, R. H. (1982) *In Search of Excellence: Lessons from America's Best Run Companies*, New York: Harper & Row.

Pettigrew, A. M. (1985) *The Awakening Giant: Continuity and Change in Imperial Chemical Industries*, Oxford: Blackwell.

Pettigrew, A. M. and Whipp, R. (1991) *Managing Change for Competitive Success*, Oxford: Blackwell.

Pettigrew, Andrew M. and Fenton, Evelyn M. (2000) *The Innovating Organization*, London: Sage.

Pierce, J. L. and Delbecq, A. (1977) 'Organizational structure, individual attitude and innovation', *Academy of Management Review*, 2: 27–33.

Pisano, G. P. and Wheelwright, S. C. (1995) 'The new logic of high-tech R&D', *Harvard Business Review*, 73(5): 93–105.

Porras, J. I. and Robertson, P. J. (1992) 'Organization development: Theory, practice and research', in M. D. Dunnette and L. M. Hough (eds) *Handbook of Industrial and Organizational Psychology*, 2nd edition, Volume III, Palo Alto, CA: Consulting Psychologists Press.

Porras, J. I. and Silvers, R. C. (1991) 'Organizational development and transformation', *Annual Review of Psychology*, 42: 51–78.

Puhakka, Kaisa (1994) 'Cognitive psychology and the personal constructs theory of George Kelly', in James Fadiman and Robert Frager (eds), *Personality and Personal Growth* (3rd edition), New York: HarperCollins.

Purser, Ronald E. and Montuori, Alfonso (1999) *Social Creativity, Volume II*, Cresskill NJ: Hampton Press.

Ramirez, I. L. and Bartunek, J. M. (1989) 'The multiple realities and experiences of internal organisation development consultation in health care', *Journal of Organizational Change Management*, 2: 40–57.

Raskin, E. A. (1936) 'Comparison of scientific and literary ability: A biographical study of eminent scientists and men of letters of the nineteenth century', *Journal of Abnormal and Social Psychology*, 31: 20–35.

Reber, A. S. (1985) *Penguin Dictionary of Psychology*, Harmondsworth: Penguin.

Reicher, S. D. (1984) 'The St. Paul's riot: An explanation of the limits of crowd action in terms of a social identity model', *European Journal of Social Psychology*, 14: 1–21.

Reichers, A. E. and Schneider, B. (1990) 'Climate and culture: An evolution of constructs', in B. Schneider (ed.) *Organizational Climate and Culture*, San Francisco: Jossey-Bass.

Richards, Ruth (1994) 'Creativity and bipolar mood swings: Why the association?' in Melvin P. Shaw and Mark A. Runco (eds), *Creativity and Affect*, Norwood NJ: Ablex.

Richards, Ruth (1999a) 'Affective disorders', in Mark A. Runco and Steven R. Pritzker (eds), *Encyclopedia of Creativity, Vol. 1*, San Diego: Academic Press.

Richards, Ruth (1999b) 'Everyday creativity', in Mark A. Runco and Steven R. Pritzker (eds), *Encyclopedia of Creativity, Vol. 1*, San Diego: Academic Press.

Roe, A. (1952) 'A psychologist examines sixty-four eminent scientists', *Scientific American*, 187: 21–5.

Rogers, C. R. (1954) 'Toward a theory of creativity', *ETC, A Review of General Semantics*, 11: 249–60.

Rogers, E. M. (1983) *Diffusion of Innovations*, 3rd edition, New York: Free Press.

Roman, Mel and Stastny, Peter (1987) 'An inquiry into art and madness: The career of Jochen Seidel', *Annual of Psychoanalysis*, 15: 269–91.

Rotter, J. B. (1966) 'Generalised expectancies for internal versus external control of reinforcement', *Psychological Monographs*, 80 (1, whole No. 609).

Roukes, Nicholas (1988) *Design Synectics*, Worcester MA: Davis Publications.

Ruigrok, Winfried, Achtenhagen, Leona, Rüegg-Stürm, Johannes and Wagner, Mathias (2000) 'Hilti AG: Shared leadership and the rise of the communicating organization', in Andrew Pettigrew and Evelyn Fenton (eds), *The Innovating Organization*, London: Sage.

Runco, Mark A. (1993) 'Divergent thinking, creativity and giftedness', *Gifted Child Quarterly,* 37(1): 16–22.

Runco, Mark A. and Pritzker, Steven R. (eds) (1999) *Encyclopedia of Creativity (Volumes I and II),* San Diego CA: Academic Press.

Salaman, G. (1979) *Work Organizations: Resistance and Control,* London: Longman.

Sauer, J. and Anderson, N. R. (1992) 'Have we misread the psychology of innovation? A case study from two NHS hospitals', *Leadership and Organizational Development Journal,* 13: 17–21.

Scarborough, H. and Corbett, J. M. (1992) *Technology and Organization: Power, Meaning and Design,* London: Routledge.

Schaeffer, C. E. (1969) 'The prediction of creative achievement from a biographical inventory', *Educational and Psychological Measurement,* 29: 431–7.

Schaeffer, C. E. (1970) *Manual for the Biographical Inventory: Creativity (BIC),* San Diego: Educational and Industrial Testing Service.

Schein, E. H. (1987) *Process Consultation,* Volumes I and II, Reading MA: Addison-Wesley.

Schein, E. H. (1990) 'Back to the future: Recapturing the OD vision', in F. Massarik (ed.) *Advances in Organization Development, Volume I,* Norwood, NJ: Ablex.

Schneider, B. (1975) 'Organizational climates: An essay', *Personnel Psychology,* 28: 447–79.

Schroeder, R. G., Van de Ven, A., Scudder, G. D. and Polley, D. (1989) 'The development of innovation ideas', in A. Van de Ven *et al.* (eds) *Research on the Management of Innovation: The Minnesota Studies,* New York: Harper & Row.

Scott, Susanne G. and Bruce, Reginald A. (1994) 'Determinants of innovative behavior: A path model of individual innovation in the workplace', *Academy of Management Journal,* 37(3): 580–607.

Shephard, H. A. (1967) 'Innovation-resisting and innovation-producing organizations', *Journal of Business,* 40: 470–7.

Shin, Junseob (1997) 'The effects of executive leadership on organizational innovation in nonprofit, human service organizations', unpublished PhD thesis, University of Pittsburgh, US.

Simon, H. A. (1977) *The New Science of Management Decisions,* Englewood Cliffs, NJ: Prentice-Hall.

Simon, H. A. (1985) 'Psychology of scientific discovery', paper presented at 93rd Annual APA Meeting, Los Angeles.

Simonton, D. K. (1980) 'Thematic frame and melodic originality in classical music: A multivariate computer-content analysis', *Journal of Personality,* 48: 206–19.

Simonton, D. K. (1991) 'Emergence and realization of genius: The lives and works of 120 classical composers', *Journal of Personality and Social Psychology,* 61, 829–40.

Sinangil, H. K. and Avallone, F. (2001) 'Organizational development and change', in H. K. Sinangil and C. Viswesvaran (eds), *Handbook of Industrial, Work and Organizational Psychology*, Vols. I and II, London/New York: Sage.

Skevington, S. (1981) 'Intergroup relations and nursing', *European Journal of Social Psychology*, 11: 43–59.

Sosik, John J., Avolio, Bruce J. and Kahai, Surinder S. (1997) 'Inspiring creativity: Coparing anonymous and identified electronic brainstorming', *Small Group Research*, 29(1): 3–31.

Sosik, John. J., Kahai, Surinder S. and Avolio, Bruce J. (1998) 'Transformational leadership and dimensions of creativity: Motivating idea generation in computer-mediated groups', *Creativity Research Journal*, 11(2): 111–21.

Staw, B. M. (1984) 'Organizational behaviour: A review and reformulation of the field's outcome variables', *Annual Review of Psychology*, 35: 627–66.

Stein, M. I. (1974) *Stimulating Creativity Volume 1: Individual Procedures*, New York: Academic Press.

Stein, M. I. (1975) *Stimulating Creativity Volume 2: Group Procedures*, New York: Academic Press.

Sternberg, R. J. (ed.) (1988) *The Nature of Creativity*, Cambridge: Cambridge University Press.

Sternberg, R. J. and Davidson, J. E. (1983) 'Insight in the gifted', *Educational Psychologist*: 18, 51–7.

Steyaert, Chris, Bouwen, René and van Looy, B. (1996) 'Conversational construction of new meaning configurations in organizational innovation: A generative approach', *European Journal of Work and Organizational Psychology*, 5(1): 67–89.

Stocking, N. (1985) *Initiative and Inertia: Case Studies in the NHS*, London: Nuffield Provincial Hospitals Trust.

Stoner, J. A. F. (1961) 'A comparison of individual and group decisions involving risk', unpublished Master's thesis, Massachusetts Institute of Technology.

Storr, Anthony (1972) *The Dynamics of Creation*, Harmondsworth: Penguin Books.

Stroebe, W. (1994) 'Why groups are less effective than their members', *Social Psychology Section Newsletter* No. 31, Leicester: British Psychological Society.

Swafford, J. (1992) *The New Guide to Classical Music*, London: Papermac.

Symon, Gillian (2000) 'Everyday rhetoric: Argument and persuasion in everyday life', *European Journal of Work and Organizational Psychology*, 9(4): 477–88.

Tajfel, H. (ed.) (1978) *Differentiation between Social Groups: Studies in the Social Psychology of Intergroup Relations*, London: Academic Press.

Tajfel, H. (1982) *Social Identity and Intergroup Relations*, London: Cambridge University Press.

Tannenbaum, S. I., Beard, R. L. and Salas, E. (1992) 'Team building and its influence on team effectiveness: An examination of conceptual and empirical developments', in K. Kelley (ed.) *Issues, Theory and Research in Industrial/Organizational Psychology*, London: North-Holland.

Taylor, C. W. (1988) 'Various approaches to and definitions of creativity', in R. Sternberg (ed.) *The Nature of Creativity*, Cambridge: Cambridge University Press.

Taylor, W. G. K. (1989) 'The Kirton adaption–innovation inventory: A re-examination of the factor structure', *Journal of Organizational Behaviour*, 10: 297–307.

Teft, M. (1990) 'A factor analysis of the TTCT, MBTI and KAI: The creative level-style issue re-examined', unpublished master's thesis, State University College at Buffalo, Center for Studies in Creativity, Buffalo, NY.

Ten Berge, Jos (1999) 'Breakdown or breakthrough? A history of European research into drugs and creativity', *Journal of Creative Behavior*, 33(4): 257–76.

Terman, L. M. (1947) 'Psychological approaches to the biography of genius', in P. E. Vernon (ed.) *Creativity*, Harmondsworth: Penguin.

Thompson, P. and McHugh, D. (1990) *Work Organisations: A Critical Introduction*, London: Macmillan.

Torrance, E. P. (1974) *The Torrance Tests of Creative Thinking: Technical-norms Manual*, Bensenville, IL: Scholastic Testing Services.

Torrance, E. P. (1988) 'The nature of creativity as manifest in its testing', in R. Sternberg (ed.) *The Nature of Creativity*, Cambridge: Cambridge University Press.

Torrance, E. P. and Khatena, J. (1970) 'What kind of person are you?', *The Gifted Child Quarterly*, 14: 71–5.

Travis, Frederick (1979) 'The transcendental meditation technique and creativity: A longitudinal study of Cornell University undergraduates', *Journal of Creative Behavior*, 13(3): 169–80.

Triandis, Harry C. (1996) 'The importance of contexts in studies of diversity', in Susan E. Jackson and Marian N. Ruderman (eds), *Diversity in Work Teams: Research Paradigms for a Changing Workplace*, Washington DC: American Psychological Association.

Turner, J. C. (1991) 'Some considerations in generalizing experimental social psychology', in G. M. Stephenson and J. Davis (eds) *Progress in Applied Social Psychology, Volume 1*, Chichester: Wiley.

Turner, J. C. (1981) *Social Influence*, Buckingham: Open University Press.

Tushman, M. L. (1977) 'Special boundary roles in the innovation process', *Administrative Science Quarterly*, 22: 587–605.

UK Government White Paper on Competitiveness (1994) London: HMSO.

Unsworth, Kerrie L. (2001) 'Unpacking innovation', unpublished Ph.D. thesis, Institute of Work Psychology, University of Sheffield.

Unsworth, Kerrie L., Brown, Hilary and McGuire, Lauren (2000) 'Employee innovation: the roles of idea generation and idea implementation', paper presented at SIOP Conference, New Orleans, Louisiana, 14–16 April.

Valacich, Joseph S., Dennis, Alan R., and Nunamaker, J. F. Jr. (1992) 'Groupsize and anonymity effects on computer-mediated idea generation', *Small Group Research*, 23(1): 49–73.

Van de Ven, A., Angle, H. L. and Poole, M. S. (eds) (1989) *Research on the Management of Innovation: The Minnesota Studies*, New York: Harper & Row.

Van de Ven, Andrew H., Polley, Douglas E., Garud, Raghu and Venkataraman, Sankaran (1999) *The Innovation Journey*, New York: Oxford University Press.

Van Fleet, D. D. and Griffin, R. W. (1989) 'Quality circles: A review and suggested future directions', in C. L. Cooper and I. T. Robertson (eds) *International Review of Industrial and Organizational Psychology, Volume 4*, Chichester: Wiley.

Vernon, P. E. (ed.) (1970) *Creativity*, Harmondsworth: Penguin.

Walberg, H. J., Rasher, S. P. and Parkerson, J. (1980) 'Childhood and eminence', *Journal of Creative Behavior*, 13: 225–31.

Wall, Toby D, and Lischeron, Joseph A. (1977) *Worker participation: A critique of the literature and some fresh evidence*, New York: McGraw-Hill.

Wallach, M. A. (1985) 'Creativity testing and giftedness', in F. D. Horowitz and M. O'Brien (eds) *The Gifted and Talented: Developmental Perspectives*, Washington, DC: American Psychological Association.

Wallas, G. (1926) *The Art of Thought*, London: Jonathon Cape.

Weenig, Mieneke W. H. (1999) 'Communication networks in the diffusion of an innovation in an organization', *Journal of Applied Social Psychology*, 29(5): 1072–92.

Weick K. E. and Westley, F. (1996) 'Organizational learning: Affirming an oxymoron', in S. R. Clegg, C. Hardy and W. R. Nord (eds), *Handbook of Organization Studies*, London: Sage.

Weisberg, R. W. (1986) *Creativity: Genius and Other Myths*, New York: Freeman.

Weisberg, R. W. (1993) *Creativity: Beyond the Myth of Genius*, New York: Freeman.

West, M. A. (1987) 'Role innovation in the world of work', *British Journal of Social Psychology*, 26: 305–15.

West, M. A. (1990) 'The social psychology of innovation in groups', in M. A. West and J. L. Farr (eds) *Innovation and Creativity at Work: Psychological and Organizational Strategies*, Chichester: Wiley.

West, M. A. (1997) *Developing Creativity in Organizations*, Leicester: BPS Books.

West, M. A. (2001) 'The human team: Basic motivations and innovations', in N. Anderson, D. S. Ones, H. K. Sinangil and C. Viswesvaran (eds), *Handbook of Industrial, Work and Organizational Psychology*, Vols. I and II, London/New York: Sage.

West, M. A. and Anderson, N. R. (1992) 'Innovation, cultural values, and the management of change in British hospitals', *Work and Stress*, 6: 293–310.

West, M. A. and Farr, J. L. (1990) 'Innovation at work', in M. A. West and J. L. Farr (eds) *Innovation and Creativity at Work: Psychological and Organizational Strategies*, Chichester: Wiley.

West, M. A. and Farr, J. L. (eds) (1990) *Innovation and Creativity at Work: Psychological and Organizational Strategies*, Chichester: Wiley.

West, M. A. and Wallace, M. (1991) 'Innovation in health care teams', *European Journal of Social Psychology*, 21: 303–15.

Williams, Malcolm and May, Tim (1996) *An Introduction to the Philosophy of Social Research*, London: UCL Press.

Wilson, D. C. (1992) *A Strategy of Change: Concepts and Controversies in the Management of Change*, London: Routledge.

Wilson, J. W. (1966) 'Innovations in organizations: Notes toward a theory', in J. D. Thompson (ed.) *Approaches to Organizational Design*, Pittsburgh: Pittsburgh University Press.

Winter, D. G. (1973) *The Power Motive*, New York: Free Press.

Witte, E. (1972) 'Field research on complex decision-making processes – the phase theorem', *International Studies of Management and Organisation*, Vol. 2, 156–82.

Woodman, R. W. (1981) 'Creativity as a construct in personality theory', *Journal of Creative Behaviour*, 15: 43–66.

Worth, Piers J. (2001) 'Everyday creativity: A life span perspective', unpublished Ph.D. thesis, Institute of Educational Technology, The Open University, Milton Keynes, UK.

Yamada, Hiroyuki and Tam, Alice Yu Wen (1996) 'Prediction Study of Adult Creative Achievement: Torrance's Longitudinal Study of Creativity Revisited', *Journal of Creative Behavior*, 30(20): 144–9.

Zaltman, G., Duncan, R. and Holbek, J. (1973) *Innovations and Organizations*, New York: Wiley.

Index

If you have enjoyed reading this book, why not read other titles in the same series.

Managing Employee Performance
Design and Implementation in Organizations

Richard S Williams, *Principal Psychology, Assessment and Consultancy Unit, The Home Office*

- Clearly describes the key approaches to designing, implementing and managing an effective performance management system, and sets these approaches within the broader context of the organization.
- Covers the importance of mission and strategy, reviewing and rewarding performance, and the controversies surrounding performance-related pay.
- Relevant to all those who have a responsibility for designing, introducing or managing a performance management system.

Thomson Learning 2002, 296pp, 1-86152-780-2, Paperback

Impression Management
Building and Enhancing Reputations at Work

Paul Rosenfeld, *US Navy Personnel, Research, Studies & Technology Department*, **Robert A Giacalone**, *Surtman Professor of Business Ethics, University of North Carolina at Charlotte* and **Catherine A Riordan**, *Professor of Psychology, Central Michigan University*

- Describes the ways that individuals in work settings use enhancing impression management tactics to look good and protective impression management techniques to minimize deficiencies and avoid looking bad.
- Covers theory, measurement and current business practice.
- Illustrates the practical effects of impression management on organizations.

Thomson Learning 2002, 256pp, 1-86152-970-8, Paperback

Creating the Healthy Organization

Well-being, Diversity and Ethics at Work

Sue Newell, *Professor of Management, Royal Holloway College, University of London*

- Explores the impact of work organizations on individual employees, groups and the wider community.
- Argues that the creation of working environments which promote positive well-being and eliminate unfair discrimination is the key to long term sustainability.
- Relevant to all those who are involved in maintaining a policy of good human relations while achieving competitive success.

Thomson Learning 2002, 264pp, 1-86152-784-5, Paperback

Managing Teams

A Strategy for Success

Nicky Hayes, *University of Bradford*

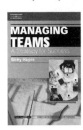

- Explores our knowledge about how teams work, how and why they become effective and how they influence an organization.
- Uses practical examples, organizational experience and the psychological mechanisms underlying teams and team management.
- Describes how managers at all levels can improve teamworking.

Thomson Learning 2002, 240pp, 1-86152-782-9, Paperback

Recruitment and Selection

A Framework for Success

Dominic Cooper, *B-Safe Ltd*, **Ivan T Robertson**, *Professor of Occupational Psychology, Manchester School of Management, UMIST* and **Gordon Tinline**, *Managing Consultant, Robertson Cooper Ltd*

- Offers a framework for action to assist selectors in accurately predicting employees' future behaviour at work.
- Identifies customer needs, establishes the necessary evaluative and decision-making standards and optimizes the return on investment.
- Describes and discusses selection methods.

Thomson Learning 2002, 288pp, 1-86152-781-0, Paperback

To order any of these titles:

UK	International
Tel: +44 (0)1264 342 932	Tel: +44 (0)1264 343 022
Fax: +44 (0)1264 342 761	Fax: +44 (0)1264 342 761
E-mail: thomsonlearning.orders@itps.co.uk	E-mail: thomsonlearning.orders@itps.co.uk